Guns of the
Special Forces
2001–2015

Guns of the Special Forces 2001–2015

Leigh Neville

Pen & Sword
MILITARY

First published in Great Britain in 2015 by
PEN & SWORD MILITARY
An imprint of
Pen & Sword Books Ltd
47 Church Street
Barnsley
South Yorkshire
S70 2AS

Copyright © Leigh Neville, 2015

ISBN 978-1-47382-106-4

Typeset by Concept, Huddersfield, West Yorkshire, HD4 5JL.
Printed and bound in India by Replika Press Pvt. Ltd.

Pen & Sword Books Ltd incorporates the imprints of Pen & Sword Archaeology, Atlas, Aviation, Battleground, Discovery, Family History, History, Maritime, Military, Naval, Politics, Railways, Select, Social History, Transport, True Crime, and Claymore Press, Frontline Books, Leo Cooper, Praetorian Press, Remember When, Seaforth Publishing and Wharncliffe.

For a complete list of Pen & Sword titles please contact
PEN & SWORD BOOKS LIMITED
47 Church Street, Barnsley, South Yorkshire, S70 2AS, England
E-mail: enquiries@pen-and-sword.co.uk
Website: www.pen-and-sword.co.uk

Contents

Introduction

As a teenager, the author of *Guns of the Special Forces* discovered a book that would literally change his life. That book was *Guns of the Elite* by George Markham. Subtitled *Special Forces Firearms: 1940 to the Present*, it documented the use of specialist small arms by special operations forces (SOF) across the globe. From the earliest days of legendary units like the British Special Air Service (SAS) in the Western Desert during the Second World War – all shemaghs, beards and Tommy Guns – right up to the rise in specialist counter terrorist intervention units in their archetypal black Nomex flight suits and balaclavas, the book had it all. First published in 1987, it was responsible for lighting the fire of what has become for the author a lifelong fascination with military small arms and in particular those employed by special operations units. That fascination has led ultimately to the book you hold in your hands.

Guns of the Special Forces is intended as an update or continuation of that wonderful work by George Markham. It takes its starting point from the beginning of what has become known as the Global War on Terror and focuses largely on this post-2001 era. To provide necessary context, some historical background is provided in each chapter, largely to explain how and why certain weapons systems, types and calibres have come to dominate the modern battlespace. The spotlight is, however, firmly on those small arms deployed during operations in Afghanistan, Iraq and other far-flung battle-fields like Mali and Somalia.

Rather than a bland sales catalogue of who uses what, this book aims to examine each broad category of small arms employed by military SOF units in these counter insurgency and counter terrorism actions. Within each chapter we will investigate the specific operational needs that drive the procurement or development of a weapon or weapon type, how those weapons are then employed on the battlefield and by whom. We will also look in detail at what are the current and future trends in terms of SOF small arms development and the impact of the lessons learnt from Afghanistan and Iraq.

SOF is a broad term and some definition may be worthwhile, particularly as to how it differs from the more common term Special Forces. The United Kingdom for instance refers to all of their special operations units generically as Special Forces (indeed it is often shortened simply to UKSF), as do the Australians. The Americans and the Canadians, and increasingly most European nations, now use the term SOF to cover all manner of special operations units from Navy SEALs to Air Force Para Rescue Jumpers. In the United

States, Special Forces also has a very distinct meaning, referring of course to the Army Special Forces who wear the famous Green Beret. For our purposes, SOF is the more inclusive and the term that will be used throughout the text.

Now that we have an agreed term to describe these soldiers, Marines, sailors and airmen, what exactly do they do and how does one define a special operation or indeed a special operator? Delta Force founder Colonel Charlie Beckwith once famously described a special operation as one that resulted in '*a medal, a body bag, or both*'. Admiral Bill McRaven, top Navy SEAL and former head of the Joint Special Operations Command (JSOC) and later the US military's entire Special Operations Command (SOCOM) gave his version several years ago: '[*it is*] *conducted by forces specifically trained, equipped, and supported for a specific target whose destruction, elimination, or in the case of hostages, the rescue of, is a political or military imperative.*'

His former command SOCOM lists a number of core operations that it considers special operations:

- Direct Action (DA)
- Special Reconnaissance (SR)
- Countering Weapons of Mass Destruction (C-WMD)
- Counter Terrorism (CT)
- Unconventional Warfare (UW)
- Foreign Internal Defence (FID)
- Security Force Assistance (SFA)
- Hostage Rescue and Recovery (HR)
- Counter Insurgency (COIN)
- Foreign Humanitarian Assistance (FHA)
- Military Information Support Operations (MISO)
- Civil Affairs Operations (CA)

A brief perusal of these mission types illustrates the breadth of tasks that fall under the SOF banner. Almost all of these missions have been undertaken by the United States and Coalition SOF since 2001 in Iraq, Afghanistan, Somalia, Libya, Syria, Mali and elsewhere. Perhaps three of the most common mission types in the past decade have been Direct Action, Special Reconnaissance and Foreign Internal Defence and these can be used to provide some context for the operations that special operators have been called upon to conduct during the War on Terror.

Direct Action (DA) relates to short-term strike missions that are commonly designed to capture or kill a designated terrorist or insurgent high value target (HVT), such as a bomb maker or logistician (these operations are commonly referred to as Night Raids in Afghanistan). This perhaps exemplifies in the minds of the public the role of SOF and is often seen as the sexy end of the special operations continuum. It's not the purpose of this book to comment on the success or otherwise of the counter insurgencies in Afghanistan and Iraq, but many informed commentators have observed that in the wake of the September 11 attacks, DA quickly became the focus of SOF, sometimes to the exclusion of other, perhaps more longer term and impactful efforts, like Civil Affairs or Information Operations. The Abbottabad raid in pursuit of Usama bin Laden was the classic example of a Direct Action mission.

Special Reconnaissance (SR) often actively supports DA operations. As the title suggests, SR is the current terminology for what would have been known in Vietnam as long-range reconnaissance patrols. SR is the other bread and butter activity of most SOF units. It entails infiltrating into a hazardous location and establishing a covert observation post to monitor enemy activity. This may be done to track an enemy commander such as the fateful Operation Red Wings in Afghanistan (the subject of the book and Hollywood film *Lone Survivor*) or the famous mission conducted by Special Force ODA 551 (Operational Detachment Alpha) in the Karbala Gap in the opening days of the invasion of Iraq. ODA 551 established themselves in a quarry littered with unexploded Iraqi artillery munitions to watch for tank movements in support of a planned advance by the 3rd Infantry Division. Both missions were classic examples of Special Reconnaissance.

Finally we turn to Foreign Internal Defence (FID). This is the process of training and mentoring a foreign army or security force to repulse a domestic insurgency. It has traditionally been amongst the core missions of the US Army's Special Forces who have long experience in working alongside foreign militaries in embedded training teams teaching basic small unit and counter insurgency skills. FID became the eventual focus in both Iraq and Afghanistan as it became apparent the Coalition could not '*kill their way to success*'. A classic example of FID has been the Village Stability Operations (VSO) in Afghanistan that saw even Navy SEALs become mentors to the Afghan National Army.

In any case, it has primarily been Direct Action missions that have fuelled the growth in small arms development for SOF. Combat optics that superimpose a holographic red dot over the target, short barrelled carbines no bigger than a traditional submachine gun, suppressed pistols with infra-red laser sights, and all manner of developments in calibres and ammunition have been the result of this focus on raiding and commando type operations.

Admiral McRaven went on to further define what made a successful special operation. He argued that a successful mission generally has six important characteristics: purpose, simplicity, speed, security, repetition and surprise. In other words and addressing each of McRaven's points: a simple plan with a clear and well understood purpose, rehearsed as many times as possible and carried out with good adherence to operational security (no leaks) will likely succeed if carried out with speed and surprise on the ground. One could perhaps add one other characteristic to his assessment, that of being equipped with the right weapons and equipment for the task at hand.

Like the missions themselves, there are a number of factors that contribute to a successful SOF small arm. SOF units are obsessive about their weapons and for good reason. The small arms they carry need to operate reliably in some of the harshest environments on earth. From the snow peaked mountains of the Hindu Kush to the backstreets of Mogadishu, to the middle of the Atlantic Ocean, reliability is of prime importance. A weapon prone to stoppages (jams) is reduced to an expensive club in combat operations. Along with reliability, the special operator is looking for a number of other factors in his or her choice of weapon.

Next comes weight and overall length. If not parachuting or walking into a target location, SOF operate in and around ground vehicles, boats or helicopters and the targets themselves are often within buildings, aircraft or ships. These confined environments necessitate compact weapons systems to reduce the chance of a weapon getting hung up on a door or a window as an assaulter breaches a target location. Additionally any reduction in weight is greatly appreciated by the operator. During many of the Special Reconnaissance missions conducted during the early years of Operation Enduring Freedom (OEF) in Afghanistan, small SOF patrols would insert on foot and remain in place surveilling a target for many weeks on end before exfiltrating out again, most commonly on foot. In such circumstances, any reduction in weapon, and ammunition, weight can be a lifesaver.

Along with reliability, weight and compactness, SOF weapons need to be surgically accurate. Operators may find themselves shooting at Close Quarter Battle (CQB) ranges inside a building one moment and at the next shooting at targets interspersed among civilian non-combatants on a busy street. The operators need the confidence that if the shooter does his part, his weapon will also do its part. The weapon needs to be robust enough to maintain this accuracy after being dragged through the dust and mud of an operational environment. The chosen weapon also needs to produce reliable terminal effects downrange on the target. This doesn't necessarily mean selecting the biggest calibre. As more than one operator has told the author, neutralising a threat is all about shot placement, not calibre.

With such an exhaustive list of requirements, it's easy to see why only a relatively small number of small arms make the grade with elite special operations units. When a particular weapon works well for one of these units, those experiences are passed on to sister units and further adoption of that weapon often follows. Look at the worldwide success of the Heckler and Koch MP5 submachine gun in the wake of the famous Iranian Embassy siege in London in May 1980. The SAS themselves had only procured the MP5 after witnessing its employment in 1978 by the German GSG9 counter terrorist unit in Mogadishu, Somalia during an operation to rescue hostages held on a hijacked Lufthansa airliner.

That mission, Operation Feuerzauber or Fire Magic, also saw the first operational deployment of a device the SAS had been working on for some time, the stun or flashbang grenade. A similar process occurs today with the US Army's Delta Force special mission unit for instance. Delta's selection of weapons and equipment goes on to inform other SOF units within both its parent commands, JSOC and SOCOM, and even into the wider conventional Army and allied Coalition SOF units.

Special operations and the weapons carried by special operators also attract perhaps the most comment in the pages of firearms magazines and on internet forums. This content ranges from the informed to the frankly delusional. It has also led to a number of myths that have developed and are repeated ad nauseam until it is difficult for the reader to sort the wheat from the chaff. Indeed it's worth shooting down a few of these before we go any further.

One common myth is that special operators can choose their own weapons, or indeed take personally owned firearms into a theatre of war. This has happened on the rare occasion but it is far from commonplace. The exception that proves the rule is of course the late Chris Kyle of *American Sniper* fame. The former Navy SEAL sniper mentioned several times in media interviews before his untimely death in 2013 that he carried not one but two personally owned pistols during operations in Iraq. These were apparently a .45ACP SIG Sauer P220 and a .45ACP Springfield Armoury TRP Operator. In an interview with *Shooting Times* in February 2013 he stated, *'We were issued the SIG P226, but I'm not a fan of 9mm. On one deployment, I brought my own SIG P220 in .45 ACP.'* One can only assume that his command were not aware of this or that SEALs enjoy unique leeway.

In some top-tier special operations units such as the British SAS, Delta and the Naval Special Warfare Development Group (DEVGRU or SEAL Team 6), each operator is assigned a small number of weapons from which he can choose for each mission. DEVGRU operators for example are equipped with two 5.56 × 45mm Heckler and Koch HK416 carbines of different barrel lengths (one being set up for longer range shooting with a magnified optic and the other optimised for closer range shooting), a suppressed (silenced) submachine gun for specific CQB tasks, a cut-down 40mm grenade launcher capable of engaging area targets out to several hundred metres, and at least two pistols.

Even the pistols are for different circumstances, one being optimised for overt assaults with a light mount and extended magazine, and the other designed from the ground up for suppressed use. The operator can largely choose the weapon that best suits the requirements of each individual mission. The same is true of the elite within an elite: Delta Force recce/sniper operators have a number of rifles on hand for different ranges, environments and operational circumstances. Within reason the veteran recce/sniper operators can carry whatever weapon they feel will give them the edge.

In most SOF units, such as the US Army's Special Forces or Ranger Regiment, or Britain's Special Forces Support Group (SFSG), the majority of operators will carry a common weapon system such as the 5.56×45mm M4A1 carbine. Ammunition and magazine interchangeability, ease of resupply and training considerations are the key reasons that one common weapons platform is selected. Specially trained personnel such as the Weapons Sergeants in an ODA may carry Mk11 or Mk12 Special Purpose Rifles to provide a surgical strike capability at extended ranges but the majority of operators will be carrying the same basic weapon.

This is also true with pistols; all operators who are assigned a sidearm will likely be carrying the same model. Apart from specific operational requirements where a suppressed or concealable pistol may be beneficial, everyone gets that same Beretta, Glock or SIG. Even in the Tier One special mission units, operators will be carrying the same pistol, again purely for reasons of commonality of ammunition and magazines. Anyone who has seen the Ridley Scott film *Black Hawk Down* will remember the scene where one of the Delta snipers resupplies his partner with a 1911 pistol magazine, a great illustration of why it makes sense in the real world for everyone to carry the same weapons.

In fact, the widespread SOF use of pistols is another of the biggest myths. The likes of *24*, *Homeland* and similar Hollywood thrillers have much to answer for in this regard. Most service members, indeed the overwhelming majority including many in SOF, will complete their military careers without having handled let alone fired a pistol. Those that are issued a sidearm will fire it infrequently on the qualification range and even less in contact with the enemy. Stories of modern soldiers using their pistols in combat are rare because the occurrence itself is rare. Pistols are a last ditch personal defence weapon, not a weapon of choice. To paraphrase a common cliché, only an idiot would bring a pistol to a gunfight.

Apart from those rare situations where even an ultra-compact carbine is too long and unwieldy such as in passenger aircraft cabins or when deploying a ballistic shield, or during covert operations where concealed pistols are the only realistic option, special operators will simply not use the pistol as a primary weapon. Even the exotic suppressed pistols carried by some units are catering to a specific identified need, and even then these are mostly used for shooting out lights rather than silently taking out terrorists. The SOF pistol remains a defensive rather than an offensive weapon. We will discuss this at some further length later in the book and cover how the SOF pistol is actually employed in combat.

Perhaps the biggest myths relating to SOF small arms are the internet horror stories relating to the supposed ineffectiveness of the 5.56×45mm rifle round common to the M4A1 carbine (although the 9×19mm versus .45ACP controversy must run a close second!). Many readers will have heard these stories – that the 5.56 × 45mm was developed to wound rather than kill the enemy. Or that the 5.56 × 45mm will simply go through an opponent, creating an inconsequential wound that requires the operator to fill his target with holes in the hope of incapacitating him. Or that the 5.56x45mm will be deflected from its course by something as insubstantial as a blade of grass!

All these tales have been repeated many times across the internet and in the pages of firearms magazines. Indeed much has been written about the relative effectiveness or ineffectiveness of various calibres and bullet types upon human opponents. There are often competing scientific theories about what actually happens when a person is shot and what actually causes the incapacitation effect to occur. There is at least wide agreement that when a human being is struck by a rifle bullet, two things happen.

One is that the bullet creates what is known as a permanent wound cavity. This is produced by the behaviour of the round itself and, to a degree, by the size and design of the bullet. The permanent wound cavity is what principally causes incapacitating effects upon a human target – the mythical 'stopping power'. A bullet may fragment into many pieces, it may mushroom in the manner of a hollowpoint or it may yaw. Yawing is a term for a bullet tumbling or flipping and turning around upon itself within the wound, literally making a bigger hole as it travels through the body. All of these actions will cause a larger and more serious permanent wound cavity. If the bullet or a part of the bullet strikes a major organ or artery as it travels through the body then incapacitation will be quicker and more likely than bullets that pass through the body without significantly fragmenting or yawing.

The second thing to occur when a rifle round strikes a person is what is termed the temporary or secondary wound cavity. This is created by what is commonly referred to as hydrostatic shock. In simple terms this temporary wound cavity is produced by the shock effect on the tissue as the round enters and travels through the body. The effect is not unlike the ripples caused by a wave in the ocean, the passage of the bullet temporarily disrupts the tissue, pushing it out of the way of the round. This only occurs with rifle and machine-gun bullets, as pistol rounds do not exhibit the necessary velocity to disrupt the surrounding tissue to any great extent.

Again any fragmenting, tumbling or expanding will create a bigger temporary wound cavity. This can increase incapacitation and lethality if this shock effect hits a major organ or the spine for instance, but in most cases the tissue and the organs themselves are only temporarily disrupted and they will move back into place after the passage of the bullet. Rifle bullets thus need to produce the largest permanent and secondary wound cavities possible to increase the chances of incapacitating a hostile. Note we talk about causing incapacitation rather than causing death. The special operator needs to eliminate the threat and put the enemy out of the fight as quickly as possible. Once he is out of the fight he can be re-engaged and killed if the threat persists – if he is still moving and has a weapon to hand for instance – but the key is to cause him to cease any hostile acts.

Over the course of the wars in Iraq and most particularly in Afghanistan there have been repeated calls for a return to the heavier 7.62×51mm rifle calibre. Some Tier One SOF snipers with operational experience in both theatres contend that when engaging an insurgent with 5.56×45mm between two and four rounds are necessary to cause incapacitation, whereas with the larger 7.62×51mm round similar incapacitation occurs after only one to two rounds. Common sense and wound ballistics supports this assertion that the larger the bullet, the more damage it will cause as a larger permanent wound cavity will be produced. But does that necessarily mean that the 5.56×45mm is an ineffective calibre and should be replaced?

The most concerning criticism of the 5.56×45mm is in terms of lethality. These arguments boil down to one simple fact: the 5.56×45mm with full metal jacket, or ball projectiles like the US issue M855A1, begin to lose significant velocity beyond 200 metres. In short barrelled rifles (SBRs) and carbines like the M4A1 this effect is further increased thanks to the shorter length of the barrel. Ball or full metal jacket rounds that rely on their tumbling or yaw effect to produce an incapacitating permanent wound cavity – as they are not designed to expand – do not generally perform well as the velocity decreases and the range increases.

Accounts of 5.56×45mm ball rounds producing through-and-through wounds like the so-called Green Tip rounds used during the *Black Hawk Down* incident are symptomatic of this. That many of the military issue 5.56×45mm bullets are designed to penetrate helmets and body armour with integral steel penetrators only exaggerates the problem as while the armour penetration capability is increased, the chance of the round yawing is reduced because of the bullet's design. Ball rounds need to hit the target at a high velocity to reliably yaw and thus to stand a chance of reliably incapacitating a foe by creating a significant wound cavity. The loss in velocity with the 5.56×45mm can be countered however by using heavier weight bullets and by the bullet's design itself.

In comparison, the heavier 7.62×51mm maintains its velocity far more consistently over longer ranges and thus, yard for yard, strikes the target at a greater velocity than the 5.56×45mm. This will result in more reliable fragmentation or yawing of the round and when combined with the 7.62×51mm's greater physical mass, a larger permanent wound cavity is likely. Indeed if larger calibre rounds like the 7.62×51mm fail to yaw, they still tend to produce a larger wound simply because of their greater mass.

So should special operators, and their infantry colleagues for that matter, be swapping out their 5.56×45mm assault rifles and carbines for the 7.62×51mm? In short, no. Suffice it to say that most of the horror stories relating the ineffectiveness of the 5.56x45mm seem to be largely apocryphal in nature. Indeed even some of the most well-known are nearly impossible to substantiate and approach the status of an urban myth. Many question that surely after over a decade of extremely high-tempo operations in Iraq and Afghanistan we should have a significant body of hard evidence to draw from rather than seemingly isolated cases reported on the internet? Surely every combat infantryman and special operator would return from their tours with graphic evidence of the 5.56 × 45mm's poor performance?

Is the 5.56 × 45mm the best military assault rifle round? Far from it. Is it as ineffective as its detractors claim? Far from it. The answer lies somewhere in between and we will discuss all of this in much more detail later in the book as well as a number of other controversies like the great 9 × 19mm versus .45ACP debate and the much heralded death of the submachine gun.

Along with perhaps increasing their technical knowledge of small arms, the author hopes that the reader will gain a greater understanding too of the tremendous valour, dedication and sacrifice of the modern special operator. He also hopes that this book will provide the reader with just a little of the enjoyment that George Markham's *Guns of the Elite* provided him all those years ago. Enjoy!

Leigh Neville
Sydney
August 2015

Acknowledgements

The author firstly wishes to thank his wife Jodi Fraser-Neville for her support. He would also like to thank John 'Shrek' McPhee for his unique insights from a career spent in special operations and to former Master Sniper, Nathan Vinson for his extensive knowledge of the world of the sniper. A number of other serving operators have shared their experiences who must remain nameless. Nathan Wyatt at Knight's Armament Company, Kelly Stumpf at Colt Canada and Andy Falcone at Heckler and Koch all assisted admirably in the development of this book and also deserve special mention.

Acronyms

ATPIAL	Advanced Target Pointer Illuminator Aiming Laser
AWG	Asymmetric Warfare Group
BAR	Browning Automatic Rifle
CA	Civil Affairs
CAG	Combat Applications Group
CDTE	Counter Defilade Target Engagement
CNS	Central Nervous System
COIN	Counter Insurgency
CQB	Close Quarter Battle
CQBR	Close Quarter Battle Rifle
CQBW	Close Quarter Battle Weapon
CS	Confined Spaces
CSR	Clandestine Sniper Rifle
CT	Counter Terrorism
C-WMD	Counter Weapons of Mass Destruction
DA	Direct Action
DEVGRU	Naval Special Warfare Development Group
DM	Designated Marksman
DMR	Designated Marksman Rifle
DPV	Desert Patrol Vehicle
DR	Dual Role
ECOS-O	Enhanced Combat Optical Sight – Optimized
EGLM	Enhanced Grenade Launcher Module
EOD	Explosive Ordnance Disposal
FAST	Fleet Anti-terrorist Security Team
FHA	Foreign Humanitarian Assistance
FIBUA	Fighting In Built Up Areas
FID	Foreign Internal Defence
FN	Fabrique Nationale
GMV	Ground Mobility Vehicle
GSG9	Grenzschutzgruppe 9
HAMR	Heat Adaptive Modular Rifle
HR	Hostage Rescue
HRT	Hostage Rescue Team
IAR	Infantry Automatic Rifle
JSOC	Joint Special Operations Command

KAC	Knight's Armament Company
LAM	Laser Aiming Module
LB	Long Barrel
LMG	Light Machine Gun
LMT	Lewis Machine & Tool
LRDG	Long Range Desert Group
LVAW	Low Visibility Assault Weapon
LWMMG	Lightweight Medium Machine Gun
MACV/SOG	Military Assistance Command Vietnam/Studies & Observation Group
MARSOC	Marine Special Operations Command
MASS	Modular Accessory Shotgun System
MCS	Modular Combat Shotgun
MHS	Modular Handgun System
MISO	Military Information Support Operations
MOA	Minute of Angle
MOS	Military Occupational Specialty or Modular Optic Series
MOUT	Military Operations in Urban Terrain
MRE	More Real Estate
MSR	Modular Sniper Rifle
NATO	North Atlantic Treaty Organisation
ODA	Operational Detachment Alpha
OEF	Operation Enduring Freedom
OIF	Operation Iraqi Freedom
OSS	Office of Strategic Services
OTB	Over-The-Beach
OTC	Operator Training Course
PDW	Personal Defence Weapon
PM	Precision Match
QD	Quick Detachable
QRF	Quick Reaction Force
RAS	Rail Adaptor System
RAWS	Ranger Antitank Weapons System
RAZAR	Rapid Adaptive Zoom for Assault Rifles
RDS	Red Dot Sight
RRLP	Reduced Ricochet Limited Penetration
SAS	Special Air Service
SASR	Special Air Service Regiment
SASS	Semi-Automatic Sniper System
SAW	Squad Automatic Weapon
SBR	Short Barrel Rifle
SBS	Special Boat Service
SCAR	Special operations forces Combat Assault Rifle

SDM	Squad Designated Marksman
SDV	SEAL/Swimmer Delivery Vehicle
SFA	Security Force Assistance
SFIW	Special Forces Individual Weapon
SFSG	Special Forces Support Group
SFW	Special Forces Weapon
SMG	Sub Machine Gun
SOCOM	Special Operations Command
SOF	Special Operations Forces
SOST	Special Operations Science and Technology
SPC	Special Purpose Cartridge
SPR	Special Purpose Rifle
SR	Special Reconnaissance
SWS	Sniper Weapon System
TAG	Tactical Assault Group
TB	Threaded Barrel
UGL	Underslung Grenade Launcher
USMC	United States Marine Corps
UW	Unconventional Warfare
VBSS	Visit-Board-Search-Seizure
VSO	Village Stability Operations

Chapter One

Combat Pistols

Overview

Along with the MP5 submachine gun and perhaps now the M4A1 carbine, pistols have always been one of the firearms that the general public instantly associates with special operations forces. The image of the commando with a suppressed pistol emerging from the shadows to silence a patrolling sentry, or the secret agent using his Walther PPK to dispatch enemies of the state, is one that has been reinforced by countless movies and books. But what's the reality in today's gritty counter insurgency wars?

But first, a little history. During the Second World War, a large number of pistol designs were pressed into service by the Allied and Axis SOF. The most commonly encountered in Allied hands was the famous .45ACP Colt M1911 (more commonly known as the Colt .45), the 9×19mm Browning GP-35 (or High Power) and a number of .38 calibre revolvers, including the legendary

An Australian Commando from Tactical Assault Group (East) aims his 9×19mm Heckler & Koch USP Tactical during a hostage rescue exercise. (*LAC Rodney Welch, Australian SOCOMD*)

British Webley. Rather uniquely, the Browning GP-35 was also employed by the Germans as the Belgian Fabrique Nationale (FN) factories that manu-factured the Browning were captured in 1940. The GP-35 or Pistole 640(b) in German service was issued to Waffen SS and Brandenburger special opera-tions personnel. Along with the Pistole 640(b), the Brandenburgers also carried the standard 9×19mm Pistole 38 (better known as the Walther P38).

A range of specialist pistols were also developed for SOF and partisan use deep behind German lines, like the British .32ACP Welrod suppressed pistol. Officially known as the Hand Firing Device Mk1, a later version was developed in 9×19mm that appears to have remained available in SAS and Special Boat Service (SBS) armouries until the early 1990s. The Welrod was a true suppressed pistol, developed from the ground up as a sentry elimination or covert assassination tool. The suppressor was integral to the pistol and featured a unique bolt action that meant that apart from the sound of the firing pin, there was virtually no mechanical noise from the weapon what-soever. The trade-off for such suppression meant that the rate of fire was markedly slowed and the operator would have been well advised to make sure his first shot was well aimed!

The diminutive .45ACP M1942 Liberator smoothbore was also designed for extremely close range shooting, firing the heavier .45ACP round from a fixed five-round magazine. The Liberator was supplied to resistance agents as a simple to use concealable self-defence weapon. Like the Welrod, each round had to be manually chambered, although extracting the spent casing was hardly straightforward. The shooter was forced to insert a writing pen, stick or similar shaped object down the barrel to push the spent cartridge casing out of the rear of the firing mechanism before another could be loaded! One can only imagine trying to accomplish that under fire!

Intriguingly, some twenty-five years later Heckler & Koch developed a far more effective pistol for stay-behind resistance groups in Europe, the H&K VP70M. The first polymer framed pistol – the forerunner to the later Glock – the VP70M was designed to be used by West German special operations and stay-behind teams should the Soviet Shock Armies ever cross the border. The VP70M even featured an attachable shoulder stock allowing fully-automatic fire. It was never widely adopted and is today better known for featuring in the science fiction film *Aliens,* and for having one of the heaviest trigger pulls ever featured on a pistol – a whopping 8kg – than for being used in anger.

The civilian .22LR High Standard H-D Model was developed at the behest of the wartime Office of Strategic Services (OSS) as a suppressed undercover weapon. Featuring an integral suppressor permanently affixed to the weapon, it was known in OSS service as the M/S for Military/Silent. Versions of the M/S were also produced lacking serial numbers for use in sterile or deniable operations to eliminate any links to the United States. The M/S also featured a slide lock that stopped the slide actioning, a development later seen on other specially suppressed pistols including the Navy SEAL issue 9×19mm Mk22 Mod0 Hush Puppy of Vietnam fame. The Israeli Mossad secret service also used suppressed .22LR Berettas for covert assassinations during the post-Munich, Wrath of God missions. With such a small underpowered round, their tactic was to get up close to the intended target and empty the magazine into the head as the only way to reliably incapacitate a target.

Vietnam saw the previously mentioned 9×19mm Mk22 Mod0 Hush Puppy, a modified Smith & Wesson Model 39, become the next evolution in specialist SOF pistols. Along with the slide lock, the Mk22 fired heavy subsonic 158-grain bullets known as Green Tips. It was a very quiet weapon, but one not built for longevity as the suppressor on the Hush Puppy supposedly could only handle thirty or so shots before its suppressive baffles gave out. Various suppressed .22LRs such as the Colt Woodsman were also used by SOF teams in Vietnam.

Surprisingly, revolvers saw a brief return to service during the conflict in the very specific, and highly dangerous, environment of tunnel clearing. The AAI Tunnel Rat revolver was a Smith & Wesson Model 29 firing specially designed .44 Magnum shot shells and was deployed by Special Forces operators and Tunnel Rats tasked with the job of crawling into Viet Cong tunnel systems to pursue the insurgents. The Browning GP-35 High Power was another firm favourite and continued to serve alongside the classic M1911A1 in Special Forces and CIA hands during the conflict. The High Power was never officially adopted by the Special Forces despite its widespread use and their naval counterparts, the SEALs, actually adopted the first 9×19mm pistol in official US military service.

The 9×19mm Smith & Wesson Model 39 (predecessor to the later Mk22 Mod0 Hush Puppy) was adopted by the SEALs in the 1960s alongside their .38 Special Model 15 revolvers. According to noted SEAL historian Kevin Dockery, the SEALs had apparently wanted the heavier .357 Magnum Model 19 revolver but due to a budget conscious procurement officer, ended up with the .38! Both the 9×19mm and the .38 accompanied the SEAL Teams to Vietnam.

Surprisingly, this was not the only time SEALs carried revolvers over automatics. SEAL Team Six soon after their formation in the late 1970s also purchased a number of stainless steel .357 Magnum Smith & Wesson Model 66s for maritime over-the-beach (OTB) use. As they could be quickly drained of water, revolvers were an early favourite with the SEALs. Automatic pistols face a far greater chance of a stoppage or, if the barrel is full of water, a more catastrophic failure that may injure the operator (today all pistols used by the SEALs and SBS for instance are OTB rated). Due to the punishing environments the SEALs operated in and the pressures of dive training on the weapons' frames, the Model 66s had to be replaced. SEAL Team Six evaluated and purchased a new .357 Magnum revolver in 1984, this time the Model 686 in a 4-inch barrelled stainless steel model.

Post-Vietnam, the emerging threat of international terrorism caused a shift in SOF priorities. After the tragic wakeup call of the Black September hostage taking and murders at the 1972 Munich Olympic Games, combat pistols again came to the fore as an important tool in the SOF armoury. European counter terrorist teams, predictably enough, tended toward German Heckler and Koch and Swiss SIG Sauer designs. In the United States the FBI established the fledgling Hostage Rescue Team (HRT) to combat domestic terrorist incidents. Taking their cue from the British SAS they were initially equipped with customised 9 × 19mm Browning High Powers. The US Army's counter terrorist 1st Special Forces Operational Detachment – Delta – better known to the public as Delta Force, was also established in the late 1970s. Delta was equipped with their now iconic custom .45ACP M1911A1s from its earliest days.

The famed German Border Police counter terrorist unit, Grenzschutz-gruppe 9 (GSG9), was also formed in direct response to the Munich Massacre. GSG9 initially employed the 9 × 19mm Heckler and Koch P9S and the .38 Special Smith & Wesson Model 36, a 2-inch barrelled snub-nosed revolver designed principally for concealability and an odd choice, more fitting for a television detective than a GSG9 operator. Both sidearms were first used operationally during Operation Feuerzauber, the assault on the hijacked Lufthansa airliner at Mogadishu Airport, Somalia in 1977. Inside the airliner, the little .38 Special revolver (firing non-hollowpoint, ball ammunition) was used at close range against one terrorist with the GSG9 operator forced to dump all five rounds in the cylinder into the target with no immediate effect. A second GSG9 operator had to step in to finish off the terrorist with a burst from his 9 × 19mm HK54 submachine gun.

After the operation, the .38 Special was fully replaced in GSG9 service by both the P9S and the 9 × 19mm squeeze-cocking Heckler and Koch P7 or PSP pistol. The P7 was a unique design, featuring a cocking mechanism in the pistol grip that required a firm squeeze of some 7kg to chamber a round. This meant the P7 could be safely carried with a round in the chamber with no external safety applied – a requirement from German police trials in the early 1970s. It also meant that this unique design could be fired by holding back the trigger and squeezing the cocking lever. The P7M13 with a larger magazine capacity was launched in the US and, despite some police sales, it never proved popular and was unfortunately discontinued. The P7 was also eventually replaced in GSG9 service by a custom OTB verified 9 × 19mm Glock 17 known as the P9M.

The British SAS and SBS maintained their 9 × 19mm Browning High Power pistols for many years for both their black-role counter terrorism missions and green-role wartime operations. The High Power was known for its reliability and its magazine capacity – at thirteen rounds (plus one in the chamber), the Belgian pistol had a much higher capacity than any of its peers until designs like the Beretta M92 (M9) began to appear in the mid-1980s. Twenty-round extended magazines were also produced by FN for the SAS and debuted at the Prince's Gate operation. The High Power was a solid combat pistol design and, apart from replacement low-light sights, SAS High Powers were apparently left largely unmodified.

The Browning was finally replaced by the SIG Sauer 9 × 19mm P226 and P228 series in the late 1980s. Intriguingly, the SAS had also apparently used a factory modified, shortened version of the P226 prior to the development of the P228 called the P226K. This P226K was issued primarily for use on plain clothes counter terrorist duties in Northern Ireland. The Browning was also the issue weapon for the Canadian, New Zealand and Australian SOF for many years, along with the FBI's Hostage Rescue Team. The HRT used their Wayne Novak custom High Powers until they switched to Les Baer customised .45ACP Para Ordnance P14s that featured a double-stack magazine of fourteen rounds. Magazine related stoppages forced the HRT to look for a single-stack .45ACP design and they later adopted the .45ACP Springfield Custom Operator. Double-stack magazines are often the cause of reliability issues in 1911 pattern pistols, an issue Delta ran into in Iraq.

A Royal Marine from 43 Commando Fleet Protection Group deploying the venerable 9 × 19mm L9A1 Browning High Power during exercises simulating opposed boarding of pirate vessels. *(PH2 Class Kevin H. Tierney.)*

Whatever particular model selected, the combat pistol has been tradition-ally viewed as a last-ditch self-defence weapon for those military personnel who had jobs other than infantry or special operations; tank or armoured vehicle crews (although when deployed they soon acquired carbines or submachine guns to supplement their sidearms), drivers, radio operators, intelligence types and the like. Pistols have also long been a status symbol for officers within the world's militaries. It is also a distinctive badge of rank that denotes a commissioned officer. The conventional thinking regarding the issue of pistols to officers was that they did not require a rifle or carbine as they had other more important things to worry about rather than shooting at the enemy. Indeed if things had degenerated to the point an officer was using his pistol then there were bigger problems afoot! Since the Second World War, savvy infantry officers have swapped their pistols for rifles, both to improve their chances should they be involved in a surprise encounter with the enemy and to make themselves less of a target to enemy snipers who will look for the obvious signifiers such as rank slides, radio aerials or sidearms.

On today's battlefields, the issue of the pistol is very much as a secondary back-up to the principal shoulder weapon. Should the rifle or carbine suffer a catastrophic malfunction, be taken out of the fight by a stray enemy round or blast from an IED or otherwise be rendered inoperable, the pistol is the last line of defence. A well-trained SOF operator might just hold back the enemy long enough for help to arrive or to incapacitate a close range threat to allow his primary weapon to be brought back into action. A US Navy SEAL in Fallujah was forced to engage three armed insurgents at point blank range with his SIG Sauer P226 pistol whilst being shot an incredible twenty-seven times with 7.62×39mm rounds. Thankfully his body armour stopped most of the rounds and the SEAL survived the encounter – the insurgents did not.

Former SEAL Mark Owen described a typical situation when a SEAL might use his sidearm in his book *No Hero*. Whilst conducting a building assault in Baghdad with his SEAL Team Five colleagues, he suffered a stoppage with his M4A1: '*I got about four shots off and was halfway up the stairs when my M-4 (sic) jammed. There was no time to fix it, so I let it drop. My rifle hung across my chest as I slid my pistol out of the holster on my leg.*' His pistol, a 9×19mm SIG Sauer P226, kept him armed and in the fight until he could clear his carbine. Similarly, a British officer serving in southern Iraq commented: '*I heard about one of our soldiers who was caught in a contact with a stoppage he couldn't clear, he was apparently terrified. I made sure I always took two weapons out with me after that.*' A former US Army special operator explained the role of his pistol during building raids in Iraq as '*an emergency back-up*' should everything else go wrong or an operator was wounded and couldn't bring his carbine to bear.

The British Army have issued a 9×19mm SIG pistol, either the L105A2 (P226R), the L107A1 (P228R) or the L117A1 (P229R), to every service member deploying to Helmand Province, Afghanistan. They realised that a secondary weapon was essential during deadly compound clearances. Pistols also offered a far handier weapon when clearing enemy tunnels and bunkers. Pistols also have other advantages in certain parts of the world. US service-men in Iraq reported they received much greater compliance from unruly civilians when brandishing a pistol than a rifle or a carbine. The civilians feared the pistol as it was culturally known as the mark of Saddam Hussein's feared internal security police and thus commanded instant respect.

Despite these advantages, pistols still have the odds stacked against them – they are difficult to shoot well, particularly under stress and in low light conditions; they fire a very low powered round in comparison to even sub-machine guns, and they are only accurate even in very experienced hands at relatively close ranges. As mentioned in the Introduction, soldiers, including most operators assigned to SOF units, do not receive anything like the level of training and range time on the pistol as they do on the rifle and squad auto-matic weapon or light machine-gun.

Despite developments such as the American SOCOM Offensive Handgun programme that attempted to provide US SOF units with a dedicated offen-sive pistol, in the overwhelming majority of cases SOF pistols will be employed in a purely defensive scenario. No special operator ever enters into a firefight with his pistol as his primary weapon if he can help it – that type of tactic is best left to Jack Bauer and similar Hollywood creations. The Offensive Handgun programme was an attempt to design a pistol for a very specific set of circumstances – the suppressed elimination of enemy sentries and guard dogs, or for use on a curious individual when a hide site is about to be com-promised. Those who have seen the otherwise regrettable Bruce Willis film *Tears of the Sun* may remember suppressed .45ACP Mk23s being used in this manner.

Another real-world offensive use of the pistol is by an operator carrying a ballistic shield as the British SAS often did in southern Iraq during house assaults targeting insurgent leaders. In this scenario, their SIG Sauer P226 pistols were the only weapon that could be reasonably deployed by the shield-man due to the bulkiness of the device. The only other scenario requir-ing an offensive role for the pistol is one requiring deep concealment such as the British SAS conducting Operation Flavius in Gibraltar in 1988. The SAS troopers had been tasked with interdicting three terrorists intent on setting off a car bomb. As they were on foot and attired as everyday tourists, the SAS operators had to rely on their 9 × 19mm Browning High Powers rather than on MP5s or HK53s. Beyond such limited scenarios, the pistol is most definitely a defensive tool, even in SOF hands.

If the pistol must be deployed, the operator needs it to go bang every time. Reliability along with size and magazine capacity – rather than calibre or make – have become the primary criteria for modern SOF pistols. Indeed a former Delta operator mentioned to the author that if he was conducting an operation where the pistol was his only option, he was going to '*take two .45s. If I am carrying a rifle I might take a Glock 19 or a Glock 26. I want something small but that holds a lot of bullets.*' The operator will attempt to stop their adversary as quickly as possible, dumping a large number of rounds into the target to eliminate the threat. A US Army Special Forces instructor summed it up for noted military historian Dick Couch, whilst teaching pistol marksmanship to a Ranger class: '*Most of your range time has been static firing – shooting for nice groups or double-tapping a silhouette target. In a gunfight, you're going to shoot that son of a bitch until he goes down, and you're going to keep shooting him.*'

As will be covered in the next section on pistol techniques, operators are no longer firing neat double taps – they are firing multiple rounds in rapid succession and as many as are required to incapacitate the enemy. This is why magazine capacity has become such a large factor in the selection of an SOF pistol. The shooter needs to have enough rounds in the magazine to engage and re-engage a target until they are out of the fight. Consider that some insurgents and terrorists will be using pain nullifying narcotics or wearing body armour, let alone suicide bomb vests, and the reason becomes clear.

The Austrian Glock family of polymer framed pistols have gained considerable popularity with SOF units across the globe for this very reason – reliability and high capacity, all in a compact package. Stoppages are a rarity with the Glock platform. This was one of the key reasons the British Army recently adopted a fourth generation 9 × 19mm Glock 17 as their new sidearm replacing a number of SIG Sauer models and the venerable L9A1 Browning High Power. Many SOF have also adopted the Glock as it continues to function with minimum maintenance in hot, dry and dusty environments like those found in Iraq and Afghanistan.

Many special operators encountered the Glock 17 and its compact little brother the Glock 19 whilst mentoring or training local security forces. The Glock was the most common sidearm purchased for the new Afghan and Iraqi militaries, although in a surprise move the US purchased the 9 × 19mm Beretta M92FS as the new sidearm of the Afghan National Army. Other SOF units like Delta were experimenting with the Glock platform years before. Some Delta operators had even carried them into Afghanistan back in the opening days of the War on Terror in 2001.

One type of sidearm which has fallen out of favour with SOF, despite being supremely reliable, is the revolver. Apart from a bare handful of European counter terrorist units, like the French GIGN who still have the .357 Magnum Manhurin MR73 in their armoury, the revolver is all but obsolete in special operations use. The revolver has a limited six-round capacity, is slower to reload and is more difficult to conceal due to the bulkiness of the cylinder, not to mention lacking the ability to be suppressed despite what you may have seen in the movies. Revolvers cannot be suppressed as noise escapes from the gap between the cylinder and the barrel. Even the one area in the SOF world

The old and the new – the 9 × 19mm L9A1 Browning High Power on the right and the 9 × 19mm Glock 17 or L131A1 with rail system. *(Richard Watt, Ministry of Defense)*

Force Recon Marines practise transition drills with their .45ACP MEU (SOC) M1911A1s. This pistol, of which several variants existed, was replaced by the Kimber Interim CQB Pistol and finally the M45A1 CQB. *(LCpl Andrew J. Carlson, US Marine Corps)*

where revolvers held an edge, in OTB maritime operations where they could be easily drained and immediately brought into action, has seen them replaced by the likes of the HK45C, a design that can now be OTB certified and fired after immersion in water.

Some units that use pistols extensively such as Delta and DEVGRU allow some latitude in that operators have several weapons to choose from, in a similar manner to their rifles, based on the requirements of a particular operation. DEVGRU operators have both the suppressed .45ACP HK45C and the 9 × 19mm Mk25 (SIG Sauer P226R) available in their range bag, along with a number of integrally suppressed .22LR Ruger MkIIs purchased back in the early 1980s that still make an appearance. Other units such as US Army Special Forces may issue the compact 9 × 19mm Glock 19 over the issue Beretta M9 for certain situations where concealment is a key operational requirement. Similarly, within UK Special Forces the compact P228 is available for plain-clothes duties.

A sampling from one of Delta's small arms cages at Fort Bragg may give the reader an interesting insight into the incredible range of pistols such SOF units have available for specific purposes. The author could identify a vast array of Glocks of many denominations and calibre; a smaller but still substantial range of 1911 platforms of several makes, both in single and double

A US Army 10th Special Forces Group operator conducts a course of fire with the compact 9 × 19mm Glock 19, an increasingly popular choice with both Special Forces and MARSOC. (*SSgt Tyler Placie, US Air Force*)

stack designs; a small number of what appeared to be 9 × 18mm Soviet Makarov PMs (undoubtedly for sterile use in denied areas) and even a hand-ful of .357 Magnum medium-frame Smith & Wesson revolvers, most likely for maritime dive ops. Bear in mind that these were the contents of only one of their cages! A former Delta operator explained that if the operation was a uniformed one, such as an overt hostage rescue or kill/capture mission, then the operators would all be carrying the same issue Glock. If it were more covert, the choice of sidearm would come down to both personal choice and appropriateness to the mission.

Ultimately, SOF units will use whatever it takes to remove the threat and successfully complete the mission. In 2011, during a takedown by DEVGRU's Gold Squadron of a pleasure yacht hijacked by pirates, one hijacker leapt upon the first SEAL into the cabin. As they grappled on the floor, the second assaulter realised that rounds from his HK416 or pistol may strike his colleague so he drew his custom Winkler knife and cut the pirate's throat. Tragically the SEAL himself was killed only months later when the Chinook helicopter he was travelling in was shot down by insurgents in Wardak Province, Afghanistan.

Calibres and Ammunition

Two calibres have long dominated SOF pistols – the 9 × 19mm or 9mm Parabellum and the .45 Auto Colt Pistol or ACP. Historically the United States stuck with the .45ACP and the Colt M1911 platform until NATO standard-isation saw the 9 × 19mm M9 Beretta replace the M1911 in 1985. The rest of the world had been using the venerable 9 × 19mm since at least the Second World War, if not before. Much of the popularity of the 9 × 19mm centred on the widespread adoption of the classic Browning High Power in Europe, ironically designed by an American, John Browning, who also famously designed the original Colt M1911. The High Power was virtually the Glock of its day.

Some other calibres existed in SOF armouries but these were in limited use for special purposes only – principally integrally suppressed .22LR and .380ACPs. The .22LR is particularly well suited to being suppressed as it is a relatively quiet round to begin with and works well in subsonic loads that avoid the audible crack of the sonic barrier being breached. Delta operators to this day still have integrally suppressed .22LR Rugers available for when lights or guard dogs need to be quietly placed out of commission.

Operations during the War on Terror have seen the 9 × 19mm all but replace the .45ACP in SOF use. The units that still use a .45ACP based platform can be counted on one hand: US Marine Special Operations Command (MARSOC) Raiders, DEVGRU and, at least until relatively recently, Delta. The .45ACP will always have its adherents and debating the advantages and disadvantages of the 9 × 19mm versus the .45ACP could fill its own book. Much of the criticism of the 9 × 19mm, however, has more to do with bullet design than the calibre itself and more precisely its performance with standard-issue ball, sometimes known as Full Metal Jacket or FMJ ammunition.

With the high velocity of the 9 × 19mm and the non-expanding design of the ball round, it tended to over-penetrate, punching cleanly through the body rather than yawing, slowing and delivering its energy within the target. Hollowpoints and similar bullets, explicitly designed to mushroom or frag- ment to increase the permanent wound cavity, cannot be issued for use by many SOF units due to a provision in the Hague Conventions that bans the use of expanding bullets. Some SOF units avoid this restriction as military lawyers judged that troops engaged in counter terrorism missions were per- mitted to use expanding rounds as they were safer to non-combatants, reducing the risk of over-penetration.

To be clear, .45ACP ball is certainly preferable to 9 × 19mm ball in nearly all cases. It is only when modern 9 × 19mm expanding rounds are compared to .45ACP expanding rounds that the gap narrows considerably. The .45ACP can also make for a more effective suppressed pistol as many .45ACP loads are already subsonic. The mass of the .45ACP helps here in terms of pro- ducing that all important permanent wound cavity, compared to the lighter subsonic 9 × 19mm.

Before we go much further into the calibre debate, and really it should be more a bullet design debate, it's worth quoting at length from what the FBI have recently said about pistol bullets and how they actually interact with human targets, as it also complements the discussion on the effectiveness of rifle rounds discussed in the introduction to this book. From the FBI's Fire- arms Training Unit at Quantico:

> Wounding factors between rifle and handgun projectiles differ greatly due to the dramatic differences in velocity, which will be discussed in more detail herein. The wounding factors, in order of importance, are as follows:
>
> A. Penetration:
> A projectile must penetrate deeply enough into the body to reach the large vital organs, namely heart, lungs, aorta, vena cava and to a lesser extent liver and spleen, in order to cause rapid blood loss. It has long been established by expert medical professionals, experienced in evalu- ating gunshot wounds, that this equates to a range of penetration of 12–18 inches, depending on the size of the individual and the angle of the bullet path (e.g., through arm, shoulder, etc.). With modern properly designed, expanding handgun bullets, this objective is realized, albeit more consistently with some law enforcement projectiles than others.[1]

1. *Handgun Wounding Factors and Effectiveness*: Firearms Training Unit, Ballistic Research Facility, 1989.

B. Permanent Cavity:

The extent to which a projectile expands determines the diameter of the permanent cavity which, simply put, is that tissue which is in direct contact with the projectile and is therefore destroyed. Coupled with the distance of the path of the projectile (penetration), the total permanent cavity is realized. Due to the elastic nature of most human tissue and the low velocity of handgun projectiles relative to rifle projectiles, it has long been established by medical professionals, experienced in evaluating gunshot wounds, that the damage along a wound path visible at autopsy or during surgery cannot be distinguished between the common handgun calibre used in law enforcement. That is to say an operating room surgeon or Medical Examiner cannot distinguish the difference between wounds caused by .35 to .45 calibre projectiles.

C. Temporary Cavity:

The temporary cavity is caused by tissue being stretched away from the permanent cavity. If the temporary cavity is produced rapidly enough in elastic tissues, the tensile strength of the tissue can be exceeded resulting in tearing of the tissue. This effect is seen with very high velocity projectiles such as in rifle calibre, but is not seen with handgun calibre. For the temporary cavity of most handgun projectiles to have an effect on wounding, the velocity of the projectile needs to exceed roughly 2,000 fps. At the lower velocities of handgun rounds, the temporary cavity is not produced with sufficient velocity to have any wounding effect; therefore any difference in temporary cavity noted between handgun calibre is irrelevant. 'In order to cause significant injuries to a structure, a pistol bullet must strike that structure directly.'[2]

D. Fragmentation:

Fragmentation can be defined as 'projectile pieces or secondary fragments of bone which are impelled outward from the permanent cavity and may sever muscle tissues, blood vessels, etc., apart from the permanent cavity'.[3] Fragmentation does not reliably occur in soft tissue handgun wounds due to the low velocities of handgun bullets. When fragmentation does occur, fragments are usually found within one centimeter (.39 inch) of the permanent cavity.[4] Due to the fact that most modern premium law enforcement ammunition now commonly uses bonded projectiles (copper jacket bonded to lead core), the likelihood of fragmentation is very low. For these reasons, wounding effects secondary to any handgun calibre bullet fragmentation are considered inconsequential.

2. DiMaio, V.J.M.: *Gunshot Wounds*, Elsevier, New York, NY, 1987, p. 42.
3. Fackler, M.L., Malinowski, J.A.: 'The Wound Profile: A Visual Method for Quantifying Gunshot Wound Component', *Journal of Trauma* 25: 522–529, 1958.
4. *Handgun Wounding Factors and Effectiveness*: Firearms Training Unit, Ballistic Research Facility, 1989.

Effective pistol rounds thus need to be able to penetrate a minimum of 12 inches into a human target to offer the best chance of striking a major artery or organ and any fragmenting effect, which is far from reliable due to the lower velocities of pistol rounds, is beneficial. Unlike rifle rounds, there is no temporary wound cavity created by pistol bullets and there is little discernible difference in the permanent wound cavity produced by a modern 9 × 19mm or a .45ACP or indeed the permanent wound cavity produced by the newest kid on the block, the .40S&W.

This latter calibre was developed as a consequence of an incident in Miami in 1986 in which two FBI agents were shot dead and five seriously wounded in an extended gunfight with a pair of notorious armed robbers who were armed with a semi-automatic 5.56 × 45mm Ruger Mini-14 and a 12 gauge pump-action shotgun along with a brace of .357 Magnum revolvers. The agents carried a mix of various .38 Special and .357 Magnum (although only loaded with .38 Special +P loads) revolvers, several 9 × 19mm Smith and Wesson Model 459 pistols and two 12 gauge shotguns of their own. During the firefight, the FBI were out-gunned with the suspects initially dominating the fight with the Mini-14. After five minutes of intense gunplay, the two robbers were dead or dying as were two FBI agents with another five lying wounded.

The FBI investigation into the incident placed much of the blame on the .38 Special and 9 × 19mm bullets the agents were firing as both suspects survived multiple hits before expiring. In response the FBI adopted a new Smith & Wesson pistol chambered for a calibre new to the FBI, the 10mm Auto. Tests in ballistic gelatine seemed to indicate the superiority of the 10mm Auto. There was only one problem. The recoil of the 10mm Auto, even in what was a reasonably large framed pistol, was simply too much for most agents.

Qualification scores dropped to the point where a reduced power 10mm load had to be introduced which unfortunately caused reliability issues. At the same time, Smith & Wesson developed a competing calibre by trimming down the 10mm Auto casing to allow it to be chambered in pistols originally designed for the 9 × 19mm. With ballistic performance comparable to the 10mm Auto, but in a smaller and somewhat more controllable package, the newly christened .40S&W was soon available in offerings from Smith & Wesson and Glock and was consequently adopted by the FBI.

It was immediately popular with police departments across the United States looking for a heavier calibre sidearm without reducing magazine capacity. In actual shootings, the new round appeared to outperform the 9 × 19mm by most measures. Initially military SOF units were cautious, trialling the new round but with few adoptions. Iraq changed that, with Delta Force controversially replacing their custom .45ACP pistols with new .40S&W Glocks as detailed later in this chapter.

Glock 22s in .40S&Ws even began to appear in some Army Ranger holsters on deployments to Afghanistan with a newly designed load – the 165-grain

US Army Special Forces in Afghanistan in 2013 armed with an Mk17 and an unusual sidearm – a .40S&W Glock 22 complete with weapon light. (*SSG Kaily J. Brown, US Army*)

Expanding Full Metal Jacket that expanded like a hollowpoint but was fully jacketed, thus helping to increase expansion prospects as it lacks the plug of an exposed hollowpoint that can get filled by clothing as it strikes its target. The .40S&W was criticised by some operators as offering little more than the 9 × 19mm beyond increased recoil. Some also complained their pistol frames suffered from the increased pressure to the extent that blown out frames were not uncommon. As will be detailed later, many users are now moving away from the .40S&W and back toward the 9 × 19mm and the .45ACP.

Bullet design, particularly in pistol calibre, has come a long way in the last decade. To paraphrase an old military saying: amateurs talk calibre, professionals talk bullets. Where the .40S&W and the .45ACP could be verified in the 1990s as more effective in terms of incapacitation potential than similar 9 × 19mm designs of the time, bullet development has not stood still. As mentioned in the latest FBI findings above, today's 9 × 19mm designs are now the equal to the best .40S&W and .45ACP offerings, at least in hollowpoint and similar expanding rounds. Along with this increase in incapacitation performance, the 9 × 19mm is both easier to shoot well (and remember the maxim that incapacitation is all about shot placement), and holds more rounds than comparable designs in .45ACP or .40S&W. It is also far less harsh on the pistols themselves.

No discussion of SOF pistol calibre can be complete without mention of the legendary Glaser Safety Slug and its ilk. Many counter terrorist units once used a range of specialist frangible loads such as the Glaser Safety Slug and the formidably titled Blitz Action Trauma round, although their use outside a very limited set of operational circumstances is rare today. These rounds typically suspended number 6 or number 12 shotgun birdshot in the tip of the bullet's hollowpoint. As the round struck the target, the hollowpoint opened up sending the birdshot into the target.

Shooting results on human targets were often impressive, although they were far from the panacea that some of their supporters claimed. Unfortunately, their very unique design severely curtailed their applicability for SOF operations. The challenge was that such rounds would be stopped by almost any solid barrier, meaning that if an operator had to shoot through cover, for instance a car door or windscreen, the round would strike the barrier and stop prematurely. For the same reason they were of no use against hostiles wearing body armour. Even the scenario most suited for such loads – shooting within a hijacked airliner – soon brings up the barrier defeat problem, indeed just as soon as a terrorist ducks down behind a seat!

Tactics and Techniques

Modern combat pistol shooting has come a long way from the Sykes-Fairbairn methods instructed to commandos in the Second World War and outlined in their famous book *Shooting to Live*. The fundamentals, of course, remain largely the same – shooting accurately, often in low light conditions, at close range against multiple determined opponents. Most SOF units now train in what is variously known as instinctive or point shooting, again a direct descendant from Sykes and Fairbairn, and indeed Colonel Rex Applegate, and their pioneering work in the field of CQB pistol shooting. This type of shooting is well suited to achieving the objective: to get the enemy out of the fight as quickly as possible. Instinctive or point shooting works well at close range, however at ranges beyond 10 to 15 metres, operators will need to use at least the front sights for any accuracy.

In the 1980s, most SOF trained in a technique known as the Mozambique Drill that would see two pistol rounds fired into the centre mass of the target with a third and final round delivered subsequently to the head. A consideration with the Mozambique Drill had always been hitting a human head under extreme stress in low light or night time conditions. Add in the complication of wearing a respirator (gas mask) and/or night vision goggles and it becomes that much more difficult.

The human head is both a small target in comparison to the central body mass and is a constantly moving target making it very easy to miss in a gunfight in even the best of conditions. With the evolving nature of the threat encountered in counter terrorism and counter insurgency operations since

An Australian operator from 2 Commando Regiment steadies his suppressed 9 × 19mm Heckler & Koch USP Tactical whilst conducting a night vision shoot. Note the visible laser marker, normally an infra-red version is used that can only be seen through night vision goggles. (*CPL Chris Moore, Australian SOCOMD*)

11 September, and the not inconsiderable chance that the enemy may be wearing a suicide bomb vest, this drill has been largely eclipsed within military SOF units. Special operators today will fire as many rounds as needed to incapacitate their target and neutralise the threat as quickly as possible.

Consider the 1988 Operation Flavius shooting of three IRA terrorists in Gibraltar mentioned earlier as an example. It is a good but rare example of SOF using only pistols on an operation, and against targets who may have been carrying a remote control detonator for a car bomb. One terrorist was shot a total of fifteen times by two operators, another six times, whilst the third was hit twice in the head and three or four times in the body (sources differ). Whilst not the most cheery topic of discussion, this demonstrates the sort of shooting which is essential when forced to use pistols against terrorists who may be carrying detonators or who may themselves be human bombs.

One recent US Army SOF technique involves firing a number of rounds across the target's pelvic girdle (typically at least two pairs), effectively taking the target's feet out from under him and bypassing any body armour or suicide bomb vest. This is immediately followed by a number of rounds across the upper chest as the target is falling to ensure the target is not getting back up in a hurry. Or, in the case of a confirmed suicide bomber, multiple shots into the head until the target ceases movement.

Once the target is down, operators are trained to shoot into any hostile on the ground as a security measure against insurgents 'playing possum' – this is particularly true when operating against opponents who regularly booby trap themselves and their wounded. This tactic is rather euphemistically termed 'insurance' or 'security' rounds. Compare this to standard police pistol training that emphasises firing one round, or perhaps at best a double-tap, and then pausing to re-evaluate the threat before deciding to fire again. Even most military pistol training still centres on the double-tap of an aimed 'pair'.

The US Army Rangers instil in their training that if the Ranger has to use his pistol, he is already in a bad place and must put accurate and fast rounds into the enemy to allow him to extricate himself back to his buddies or to his rifle. The Rangers currently train to fire fast aimed pairs to the centre body mass followed by two rounds to the head, repeating as necessary until the hostile drops.

As we have seen earlier, with pistol rounds being so unreliable in their ability to incapacitate an adversary, firing into the centre body mass offers the best chance of striking a major organ or artery. Firing multiple rounds into the area exponentially increases that chance. Otherwise the severing of the central nervous system is the guaranteed way to put an enemy immediately out of the fight.

The FBI have stated that:

> Shots to the Central Nervous System (CNS) at the level of the cervical spine (neck) or above, are the only means to reliably cause immediate incapacitation. In this case, any of the calibre commonly used in law enforcement, regardless of expansion, would suffice for obvious reasons. Other than shots to the CNS, the most reliable means for affecting rapid incapacitation is by placing shots to large vital organs thus causing rapid blood loss. Simply stated, shot placement is the most critical component to achieving either method of incapacitation.

Many firearms instructors work from the maxim that the pistol is only there to allow the operator to fight his way to a rifle and there is a lot of truth to that statement. As mentioned earlier, the operator is never going to be using his pistol as his primary weapon unless circumstance has forced his hand. He will be using the pistol to eliminate the closest threats to regain his rifle (or giving him a chance to clear a stoppage for instance) or grab a fallen enemy's rifle and continue the fight.

Even the placement of where SOF operators carry their pistols has changed over the course of the wars in Iraq and Afghanistan. At the start of Operation Iraqi Freedom (OIF), US Army Special Forces operating in customised HMMWVs known as Ground Mobility Vehicles (GMVs) began a trend of carrying their pistols, then almost exclusively the issue M9 Beretta, in holsters attached to the chest area of their body armour. This allowed the Green Berets to rapidly draw their pistol whilst seated and engage targets through the windscreen or side windows if necessary, as the cramped confines of a HMMWV made manoeuvring a carbine difficult. The idea followed standard practice for many tanker and mechanised crewmen who often wore a shoulder holster that placed their pistol on the upper left side of their chest.

This practice later became commonplace amongst SOF units involved in conducting raids as part of the counter terrorism campaign by JSOC in Iraq and later Afghanistan. These units, principally Delta and the British SAS in Iraq, found that carrying the pistol in a chest mounted holster kept it clear of snagging and sped up the transition from dropping a disabled or jammed carbine and drawing the secondary (known as 'transitioning' from the primary). It also kept all of an operator's essential bits of kit – his pistol, magazines, grenades, restraints, chemical lights and such – all centrally located on his plate carrier (a type of body armour favoured by SOF due to its lighter weight and size). This method of carry also cut down on the possibility of items snagging on doors or windows or as they exited a helicopter or ground vehicle.

The position does have its disadvantages. When going prone, the pistol may be exposed to mud or water and it works against a soldier getting as low as he possibly can in the prone position in the same way that chest rigs carrying rifle magazines will. It can also interfere with maintaining a good cheek weld with the primary weapon's stock. Carrying a pistol in a holster on the front of one's body armour (or in fact anything attached to the front of the vest) was actually banned for a time by the UK command in Helmand, Afghanistan as it was felt that this added to the number of potentially lethal items that could cause further injuries in an IED blast.

For SOF teams using chest holsters, many preferred to take the increased risk from IEDs in favour of a faster draw that avoids the pitfalls of drop or thigh holsters. SOF operators conducting night raids were also typically not facing the same level of IED threat as conventional forces. Although some operators were killed by IEDs whilst travelling to or from an objective, their primary concern was being shot or blown up by a suicide bomber on the objective itself. When conducting longer term dismounted operations in Afghanistan, SOF personnel have increasingly relied upon a more traditional waistband holster worn on the hip or kidney.

Drop or thigh holsters are increasingly rare in today's SOF world outside of specialist counter terrorism operations. First pioneered by the SAS in the late 1970s, the technique gained popularity after its use by B Squadron, 22 SAS during Operation Nimrod in 1980. The SAS Counter Revolutionary Warfare Wing developed the holsters specifically so that the pistol could be easily accessed whilst wearing heavy body armour such as the Bristol armour worn during Nimrod. These often included versions with groin protectors that inhibited the deployment of a standard belt holster. The regiment had an additional need for their pistols to be accessible whilst fast roping (abseiling). The drop holster ticked all of these boxes.

Their use by the SAS immediately catapulted them into popularity with both law enforcement and military special operations units. They became so synonymous with SOF that rear echelon types who normally never ventured out from Forward Operating Bases – and thus were known as Fobbits or even more derogatory terms – began to be seen sporting them in dining facilities across Iraq. Police tactical units also adopted them en-masse, apparently without considering their suitability during a foot pursuit or similar situation. The drop holster design generally means that when running, the pistol tends to flop around on the leg, increasing the risk of it coming loose and another good reason many operators attach a lanyard to their sidearm.

Current Trends
Along with the trend back toward 9×19mm pistols with the advent of reliably expanding 9×19mm bullet designs, special operators have also taken major steps to adapt the pistol to their particular operational requirements. Many of the innovations first seen in competition pistol shooting, in particular the practical shooting or IPSC discipline, have made their way onto SOF pistols. In the last few years, Delta have led the way with the adoption of mini red dot sights (RDS) on their sidearms. These work in the same way as the similar larger sights mounted on their carbines or rifles – place the red dot displayed within the optic over the target and fire. If the weapon is properly calibrated (zeroed) to the optic and barring the effects of wind and other environmental factors, the round should strike wherever the red dot is placed. They improve both accuracy and speed of engagement, particularly in interior or low light conditions.

Originally these were mounted directly, and permanently, onto the frame of the pistol but the number of rounds fired necessitated another solution as the sights were failing under the strain. To solve this issue, Delta had a custom system developed by ALG Defense known as the 6-Second Mount. This allows for both a weapon light such as the SureFire X400 series and a mini holographic or RDS: in Delta's case apparently the Aimpoint Micro, to be attached to the frame of the pistol itself rather than directly to the slide. Shooters had also reported that slide mounted sights slowed the process of re-engagement as the sight is brought back onto the target. With the 6-Second Mount attached to the frame itself the RDS does not now move with the slide, meaning it is easier to keep the target in the sight picture.

The 6-Second Mount was designed for use on specific operations in extreme close quarters, such as hijacked airliners, with the name coming from the fact that a firefight in such an environment will literally be over in six

Another unidentified US Army operator firing what appears to be a .40S&W Glock 22 with SureFire light and mini red dot sight, a set-up that mirrors that pioneered by Delta after the Unit trialed .40S&W STI 1991s in Iraq. Unusually, the Delta STIs were later sold on the civilian market giving US civilian shooters the chance to own a unique piece of SOF history. (*Thomas Cieslak, USASOC*)

seconds, one way or the other. It's an ideal choice for the point man in a stack who is also carrying a ballistic shield to protect him and his compatriots during those first vital moments of an opposed entry. Many SOF units have now discovered the merits of the ballistic shield – the British SAS used them extensively in Iraq during house raids and many readers would have witnessed the French RAID counter terrorism officer bravely advancing directly into AK47 fire as his team breached into a Paris supermarket in January 2015. Interestingly, RAID operators, and many others, who are assigned the shield-man position will carry two pistols as it is obviously difficult to reload with one hand. Instead they will transition to the second pistol when the first runs dry.

The pistol mounted mini RDS is considered by retired operator John 'Shrek' McPhee to be '*the way of the future*' but he feels they are currently '*too small to get on target*'. He believes that more attention should be paid to the physical size of the sights used by competition pistol shooters – the larger the sight, the faster the operator can attain a sight picture and begin to engage. Glock have recognised the market for a pistol with just such a mounting mechanism for a mini RDS or Reflex sight both for special operations users and competition shooters. They have recently introduced the Glock MOS (Modular Optic Series) range that features an interchangeable base plate mount allowing the attachment of a number of different sights to the Glock 34, 35, 40 and 41. This will likely become available for more models as the use of the pistol mounted RDS increases.

Along with optics, operators have increasingly required a rail mounted tactical light to be fitted to their pistols. All of the major manufacturers have released versions with under-barrel rails to allow weapon lights to be fitted. Perhaps surprisingly one of the first units to use a SureFire weapon light mounted under the barrel of their pistols was not a military unit, but actually the Los Angeles Police Department's Special Weapons and Tactics team. Lights such as the SureFire X400 series offer a 500 lumens LED white light capability along with a red, visible laser, target illuminator. The light is powerful enough to momentarily blind an insurgent or terrorist during an entry on an objective.

Unlike in the movies where special operators are shown moving through buildings with their weapon lights constantly switched on, actual operators only briefly touch the switch when they need to identify a target or scan a location. Similarly with visible lasers, these are rarely employed as they can easily pinpoint the location of the operator. Infra-red systems are more widely used, however, as only those wearing night vision goggles can actually see the beam. For instance, the even more advanced X400V IRc model is favoured by many SOF units as it combines both visible white light and infra-red light and laser capabilities, making it ideal for use with night vision.

Many units now also routinely fit extended barrels to their pistols or replace issued barrels with specially threaded ones to allow the easy attachment of a sound suppressor. Many of the more recent designs such as the HK45C come factory-fitted with a threaded barrel. Glock has also responded to the market for suppressed weapons with a new range of Glock TB (Threaded Barrel) variants that feature an extended, threaded barrel allowing a detachable suppressor to be quickly attached and high-set suppressor sights. Sights on suppressed pistols need to be mounted higher to be able to see over the suppressor itself.

Some units such as DEVGRU are increasingly issuing two to three pistols to each operator with others available for special purposes; the HK45C for suppressed work, the SIG Sauer Mk25 (P226R) for assaults and the 9 × 19mm single stack P239 for covert carry. There are also evidently some Glocks available as the compact G19 has been seen carried in Afghanistan. Even units without the budgets of these top-tier SOF routinely make available a concealable version of their primary pistol for certain operations. Otherwise their primary pistols feature many commonalities: 9 × 19mm in calibre, rail mounted weapon lights, low light sites and extended magazines.

US Navy SEALs from DEVGRU conduct partnered operations with Afghan Commandos. Just visible in the shot is the pistol worn by the SEAL on the far right which appears to be the .45ACP HK45C or Mk24 complete with suppressor. (*SGT Jessi Ann McCormick, US Army*)

Individual Weapon Summaries

M9 Beretta

The M9 is the military version of the commercial 9×19mm Beretta M92FS double-action pistol. The M92 base model has equipped numerous Italian and Spanish SOF including the NOCS and GOE national counter terrorism teams since the late 1970s. French SOF have also used the M92 in a number of guises including a suppressed version with a custom slide lock reminiscent of the Hush Puppy of the SEALs. The US military version, the M9, controversially won the Pentagon's 1984 Joint Services Small Arms Program pistol trials, allegedly neck and neck with the SIG Sauer P226, until Beretta won by offering a lower per unit cost after two separate sets of rather exhaustive tests were completed.

The Italian design officially equips many special operators within SOCOM including Army Special Forces ODAs, Rangers and Air Force Special Tactics. Amusingly the M9 was also featured in the recent Hollywood film *Lone Survivor* in the hands of a SEAL – accomplished through a product placement company allegedly employed by Beretta rather than any attempt at historical accuracy. The SEALs of course routinely issue the SIG Sauer P226, not the Beretta. The Beretta isn't particularly popular within SOCOM and many

The old and the new – the 9 × 19mm M9 Beretta replaces the .45ACP Colt M1911A1 in 1985 for all branches of the US military, including SOCOM. The M9 will itself be replaced by the XM17, projected for selection by 2018. Along with a new pistol, the biggest change ushered in by the XM17 programme is the acceptance of hollowpoint rounds by the Judge Advocate General's Office. (*Robert D. Ward, US Department of Defense*)

SOCOM units have subsequently found ways to equip themselves with other makes of pistol, principally the Glock in a number of variants. Army Rangers may for example still qualify with the M9 but on deployment to Afghanistan many are carrying Glocks in the field. There are a number of valid reasons for this.

The M9 was developed from the older M1951 design but upgraded to hold a fifteen-round magazine, along with improved sights and controls. It is a solid, if perhaps not outstanding, weapon. Much of the criticism of the pistol has in fact revolved around its magazines rather than the weapon itself. The issue M9 magazines were purchased from a third-party manufacturer and had a tendency to cause stoppages, so much so that experienced Green Berets would privately purchase original Beretta manufacture magazines for their M9s.

In Iraq, the problem was exaggerated as operators found that the fine Iraqi sand and dust would conspire to foul the magazines. The Beretta's slide design was also call into question as some allege it lets in too much sand. In a 2006 study, some 26 per cent of regular US Army personnel who had used the M9 in combat in Iraq or Afghanistan had experienced a stoppage. If those numbers are true, and there is no reason to doubt them, then the M9 is certainly not suitable for SOF use where the pistol must go bang every time.

The M9 is often wrongly criticised by its users as lacking '*stopping power*', an accusation that has more to do with the issue ammunition than the weapon itself or even the calibre, as we have discussed previously. The US military issue M882 Full Metal Jacket round tends to over penetrate and isn't designed to fragment in the target as a hollowpoint or expanding design will. Much better 9 × 19mm bullet designs exist with far better terminal ballistics than the ball round, but the military are constrained from using them. Thus many of the criticisms of the M9 would be levelled at any 9 × 19mm pistol, even the popular Glock, firing the same M882 ammunition.

The Beretta M9 was upgraded in 2006 for the United States Marine Corps (USMC) when it became known as the M9A1. This version featured checkering to assist in working the slide in maritime conditions, a competition-style bevelled magazine well to allow empty magazines to drop free of the weapon, and a Picatinny rail under the barrel to allow the mounting of light and laser options. It also came with a redesigned magazine that was more reliable in sandy environments. In the mid-2000s, a significant number of Crimson Trace laser aiming modules were also purchased and deployed with M9s heading to Iraq and Afghanistan – the visible red light laser was found to be an effective non-lethal means of gaining compliance from rioting civilians, an unexpected but legitimate use for the red dot laser.

SIG Sauer P226, P228, P239

The Swiss-German manufacturer SIG Sauer has a long history of producing fine hunting, target and military firearms. SIG Sauer pistols are well known for their reliability, accuracy and exacting production quality. As mentioned earlier, a SIG Sauer pistol narrowly missed becoming the US military's standard issue sidearm in the 1980s. A number of European police intervention teams adopted the 9 × 19mm SIG P225 in the early 1980s (the P225 being the product of German police trials in the 1970s) before the first significant SOF adoptions began to take place with the US Navy SEALs and later United Kingdom Special Forces, including the SAS and SBS, selecting the P226 and P228.

The SEALs adopted the 9 × 19mm SIG Sauer P226 after they experienced a number of catastrophic slide failures with both Navy-issue Beretta M9s and its civilian Beretta M92SBs that resulted in facial injuries to three SEAL Team operators during 1987 and early 1988. The SEALs had been working with civilian M92s in various configurations including suppressed versions for a number of years before the military contract was awarded to what became known as the M9. Testing by the Army showed that slide cracks could occur on the M9 after between 10,000 and 30,000 rounds were fired. The SEALs, like all special operations units, fire a lot of rounds through their pistols and it was suspected that the type of metal used in the pistol's slide was the culprit for the failures. Beretta redesigned the slide on the M9 so that even if it should fail, it could no longer cause injury.

The P226 was only ever intended to be an interim replacement for the SEALs until the problems with the M9 were ironed out, but the SEALs liked it

A US Navy SEAL trains with his 9 × 19mm Mk25 or SIG-Sauer P226. The current iteration in SEAL service features a rail for mounting a weapon light. DEVGRU versions typically feature a threaded barrel for suppressors. (*MC2 Martin L. Carey, US Navy*)

so much it became their standard sidearm. A later version of the SEAL P226 fitted with a Picatinny rail for mounting a weapon light under the barrel was known in the Navy as the Mk25 Mod0, and in the civilian world known as the P226R. The Mk25 is still their primary assault pistol with SureFire weapon light and fitted with extended magazines. DEVGRU operators have a version of the Mk25 with an extended threaded barrel for mounting an AAC suppressor.

The US military also adopted the P226's little brother, the P228, as the M11 in 1989 to serve as a compact 9 × 19mm pistol for criminal investigators, aviators and officers who required a smaller framed pistol. P228s also became available to US military SOF units with the weapon often finding favour during undercover or plain-clothes missions where concealment was vital. DEVGRU has a number available for use during close protection tasks such as when they protected the then Afghan President, Hamid Karzai, in early 2002. It's not the smallest pistol in the SEAL armoury though; they also have a limited number of the tiny .380ACP Walther PPK available.

Both the P226 and the P228 were also famously adopted by British Special Forces around the same time, replacing the long-serving Browning High Power that had equipped the SAS since the Second World War. As mentioned, the SAS also carried a specially shortened version of the P226 prior to

US Navy EOD personnel firing their 9 × 19mm M11 (SIG-Sauer P228) pistols.
(MC2 Daniel Edgington, US Navy)

the availability of the compact P228, called the P226K. A number of other concealable pistols were also purchased during the 1980s and 1990s for UK Special Forces, principally for use in Northern Ireland. These included the 9 × 19mm Walther P-5 and the .380ACP SIG Sauer P230. Like the SEALs, the SAS P226s are matched with SureFire weapon lights and extended twenty-round magazines.

Another SIG Sauer that has seen recent combat duty with the SEALs has been the P239. A single stack 9 × 19mm pistol that carries eight rounds in its magazine and only just over six and a half inches in overall length, the P239 is carried as a lightweight and handy back-up. SEALs in Afghanistan some-times tuck a P239 away as extra insurance, often without carrying any spare magazines for the weapon.

The SIG Sauer P320 MHS is a new SIG Sauer offering currently available in 9 × 19mm, .40S&W and .45ACP that will be entered by SIG Sauer into the US Army Modular Handgun System competition to identify a replacement for the aging M9. The new weapon is based on the civilian P320 already offered to law enforcement, but has been designed with the military requirement in mind – the weapon can be easily swapped to different calibre and different frames, all without resorting to an armourer or gunsmith. This also allows different sized grips to be quickly fitted, neatly ticking the military's require-ment for the new pistol to fit 90 per cent of the hands of service members. In testing, the pistol is as accurate and reliable as the P226. The P320 MHS could very well be the next US military and indeed SOCOM combat pistol.

Heckler and Koch Mk23, P9S Navy, Mk24, HK45C, USP

The German firm of Heckler and Koch has been developing and producing military small arms since just after the Second World War when a group of former Mauser engineers came together to form the company, initially developing the Bundeswehr's first service rifle, the G3. Their first commercial pistol offering, however, was the diminutive .32ACP HK4. This was a small frame pocket pistol designed expressly for West German police detectives. The HK4 was reasonably successful and saw H&K soon produce a range of pistols, including the selective-fire VP70M (and its semi-automatic only version, the VP70Z), the P7/PSP and the P9. All of these pistols, with the exception of the VP70, were widely adopted by European police and counter terrorist teams including such luminaries as GSG9 and the French GIGN. Whilst the H&K MP5 became the international SOF standard in submachine guns, it wasn't until well into the 1990s that military SOF units began to adopt H&K pistols in greater numbers. The H&K USP in .45ACP and .40S&W had made significant sales within US law enforcement tactical units but it took the Mk23 Mod0, although far from popular itself, to somewhat ironically lead the charge into SOCOM and JSOC.

A pair of .45ACP HK45Cs – the extended barrel, suppressed version at the top as adopted by DEVGRU as the Mk24. Note the raised iron sights for use with the suppressor.
(*Heckler & Koch*)

The classic .45ACP SOCOM Mk23 Offensive Special Operations Handgun shown here bereft of suppressor and Laser Aiming Module – a modern descendant of the wartime Welrod designed for silent sentry removal. *(Heckler & Koch)*

The Mk23 Mod0 was specifically developed for SOCOM by Heckler and Koch in response to a requirement for an *'Offensive Special Operations Handgun'*. The list of required features, developed by committee, appeared almost endless. The new weapon needed a match-grade barrel threaded for a Knight's Armament Company (KAC) suppressor; a detachable Laser Aiming Module (LAM) to include both laser and white light capabilities; adjustable sights and had to be chambered for the .45ACP and specifically able to handle proposed Enhanced +P ammunition that was intended to be of a higher velocity than regular .45ACP ball.

Designed strictly to these requirements with typical H&K efficiency, the result was considered by many to be both prohibitively large and heavy. Not surprisingly the Mk23 proved far from popular within the majority of SOCOM units. The author was told by a long-time US Army special operations veteran that he saw only one outside an armoury during his entire career, and that example was worn by a senior officer in a shoulder holster within the confines of Bagram Air Base. The Mk23 has seen significant use in video games such as *Metal Gear Solid* and in films like *Tears of the Sun* lending it perhaps some added pop cultural significance.

One place that the Mk23 was appreciated was by the SEALs themselves and their brethren in the SEAL Delivery Vehicle (SDV) Teams. These operators spent most of their working life underwater or in over-the-beach operations that required significant exposure to salt water, sand and mud. It was here that the Mk23 really shone. Superbly reliable, the weapon could and did survive the rigours of combat diving and submersibles. Its magazines also functioned flawlessly in the maritime environment, something that is the Achilles heel for many weapons trialled for SOF use. The Mk23 also won over sceptical users with its unmatched accuracy and, when deployed with its Knight's suppressor and Laser Aiming Module, its silent lethality was unparalleled. The Mk23 did what it said on the tin, it was an Offensive Special Operations Handgun.

The Mk23 wasn't the only unusual H&K pistol used by the SEALs however. During the early years of DEVGRU, then known by their more famous title of SEAL Team Six, along with their stainless steel Smith & Wesson Model 66 revolvers – ideal for maritime operations as the water was easily drained from the cylinder and working parts – the SEALs procured a suppressed variant of the 9 × 19mm Heckler & Koch P9S automatic pistol. Known as the P9S-N (Navy), it featured a threaded barrel and adjustable sights along with a redesigned trigger guard for use with gloves. The adoption of the P9S actually started a long association between Naval Special Warfare and Heckler and Koch.

Intriguingly, the original suppressor for the P9S-N, the Qual-a-Tech, was designed to be able to be fitted to the entire complement of 9 × 19mm Heckler and Koch weapons then in the Naval Special Warfare inventory – the P9S-N, the MP5K-N and the MP5-N submachine guns. Prior to the later adoption of

The rare Navy SEAL 9 × 19mm Heckler & Koch P9S with extended threaded barrel ready to accept a screw-on suppressor. A number of these pistols were employed by DEVGRU until SIGs with extended threaded barrels became available. (*Heckler & Koch*)

the Mk23, the P9S-N appears to have been the most widely issued H&K pistol in the US military although numbers were certainly under one hundred units.

Although it was not well received outside of the SEAL and SDV community, the Mk23 had opened a number of doors. When the SEALs were looking for a new compact suppressed .45ACP pistol a number of years later, another Heckler and Koch design was luckily in prime position. Larry Vickers, the former Delta Force operator instrumental in the development of the HK416 rifle, worked again with H&K as a consultant. His input was key in the development of what became known as the .45ACP HK45 and the HK45C full-size and compact pistols.

Vickers and H&K took the best elements from the civilian H&K P2000 and USP designs (the USP had been itself the basis for the original Mk23 platform) and delivered a compact .45 that held ten rounds, was designed for easy on/off suppression and could be equipped with the by now mandatory tactical accessories on an under-barrel rail. In 2010, following trials that included suppressed versions of the SIG Sauer P220 and the Glock 30, again both in .45ACP, the US Navy announced the HK45C as the winner of the SEAL suppressed pistol requirement. The HK45C was officially adopted as the Mk24 Mod0 Combat Assault Pistol.

The Mk24 Mod0 features a detachable AAC suppressor and an infra-red Laser Aiming Module manufactured by Crimson Trace. Unlike its predecessor, the Mk24 can also function as a compact pistol; it has had all sharp edges dulled to allow carry under clothing and with the suppressor and LAM removed is actually remarkably concealable. For units such as DEVGRU, this remains an important consideration.

Apparently suppressed examples of the HK45C were carried during Operation Neptune Spear in Abbottabad, Pakistan. If the mission had gone wrong and a worst case scenario developed, forcing the operators to attempt to escape and evade overland, their HK45Cs could have been hidden under stolen civilian clothes. It was just such a contingency that made President Obama ask JSOC planners to add a Quick Reaction Force to the assault package to give the operators enough shooters to '*fight their way out*' if necessary.

The H&K USP Tactical was another pistol developed in the wake of the Mk23 programme during the 1990s. This took the well regarded USP platform and mated it with key elements of the Mk23, producing the USP Tactical, a .45ACP (and later 9 × 19mm and .40S&W) platform that featured a match barrel for accuracy and a threaded barrel for use with a suppressor. The USP Tactical also featured the H&K recoil reduction system, an additional spring that dampens felt recoil making the pistol even more accurate, all in a far more compact and handier package than the Mk23. The .45ACP version was purchased in a modified variant with suppressors as the P12 for the German KSK and Army Long Range Reconnaissance Patrols Group. German Army

A suppressed 9 × 19mm Heckler & Koch USP again with raised iron sights to clear the suppressor. This pistol has been heavily adopted by European CT units and Australian SOCOMD units. *(Heckler & Koch)*

SOF have traditionally used 9 × 19mm designs and the .45ACP is something of a departure for them.

The USP Tactical in 9 × 19mm was adopted as the sidearm for both the Australian Tactical Assault Groups (TAG) East and West and for use along-side the venerable L9A1 Browning High Power by their respective parent organisations, 2 Commando Regiment and the Special Air Service Regiment (SASR). The USP Tactical has seen extensive operational use with the Commandos and SASR in Afghanistan where it has become the carry pistol of choice over the aging Browning. A second more compact version of the USP Tactical known as the USP-CT or Compact Tactical was also developed for yet another SOCOM tender. It proved popular as a more compact option than the Mk23 but the trials programme was subsequently cancelled and the weapon never advanced beyond prototyping.

M1911

As we've said, many column inches in hundreds of firearms magazines and websites have been devoted to the age old question of .45ACP versus the 9 × 19mm. To briefly recap, the core arguments against the 9 × 19mm are that it is underpowered, particularly when firing ball ammunition, and that it tends to over-penetrate because of its much higher velocity. The arguments against the .45ACP include its inability to penetrate most common body armour and its limited magazine capacity, most .45ACP pistols only have magazine capacities of between seven and ten rounds. Most significantly the .45ACP also features much increased felt recoil over the 9 × 19mm and is a far harder platform to master.

Most .45ACP pistols based on John Browning's classic 1911 design are also single action only. This means that the weapon must be manually cocked by pulling back the pistol's hammer before it can be fired. On double action pistols, and most 9 × 19mm and .40S&W service pistols are double action, pressing the trigger both cocks and fires the weapon. Although some argue that this makes single action pistols more dangerous – as they need to be carried cocked and locked with a round in the chamber and the hammer back to fire instantly – others argue that single action causes less movement in the firing action and thus is inherently more accurate.

Older models of the 1911 platform also featured a grip safety that was designed to block firing unless it was firmly depressed. Delta, one of the more famous recent users of the 1911, often simply taped the safety closed with skateboard tape as they felt this was a superfluous and sometimes dangerous safety feature on a combat pistol, particularly if trying to operate the pistol whilst wounded. Despite these drawbacks, the .45ACP has soldiered on in limited use within American SOF since the replacement of Colt M1911A1 with the Beretta M9 in the mid-1980s.

The US Marine Corps' SOF elements, firstly with Force Recon and Det One and later with the MARSOC Raider Battalions, have never given up on the .45ACP and have been one of its staunchest supporters. During the 1990s, custom built M1911A1s, hand assembled by armourers at Quantico, were

A Force Recon Marine practises with his .45ACP M45A1 CQB pistol. Along with Delta and DEVGRU, Force Recon and MARSOC are some of the only users of the .45ACP platform within SOCOM. Note the lanyard that keeps the pistol attached to the operator.
(MC SA Edward Guttierrez III, US Navy)

issued to Force Recon operators. These M1911A1s were built from old pistols that had been retired when the M9 became the USMC service pistol. These custom .45s were officially designated the M45.

MARSOC's establishment in 2006 led to a dramatic increase in the numbers of .45ACP pistols needed within the Corps. Some 1911 frame pistols were purchased from Kimber to help fill the gap, known as the Interim CQB Pistol. Finally in 2012 a new specification .45ACP pistol was selected for Marine special operators. The new pistol is the Colt M45A1 and now equips all MARSOC operators, although reports indicate that due to a scarcity of .45ACP in the logistics chain in Afghanistan, a small number of 9 × 19mm Glock 17 and 19 models are also being used. The M45A1 builds upon the earlier M45 and is essentially a production version of the Colt competition grade M1911 known as the Rail Gun. It is built largely from stainless steel to support maritime operations, is finished in a desert tan colour rather than the traditional blued finish and fitted with a match grade barrel as standard.

Whilst MARSOC continues to use the M45 and M45A1, the number of other units deploying with the .45ACP diminishes. As noted, the SEALs have adopted the HK45C as the Mark 24 Mod0 where it continues to be popular. The other major unit that was traditionally associated with the .45ACP platform was of course the 1st Special Forces Operational Detachment – Delta. From its very inception, Delta became synonymous with the .45ACP led by its founder, Special Forces Colonel Charlie Beckwith. Beckwith preferred the .45ACP, mentioning in his memoirs that the round didn't tend to overpenetrate – a vital consideration he felt when shooting pistols around hostages or other non-combatants. Delta's original pistols were apparently match grade M1911A1s with the adjustable rear sight replaced by one designed by a Delta armourer.

One story that refuses to die was that individual Delta operators received a stipend to purchase parts for the unit armourers to build their pistol to their individual specifications. The reality appears to be somewhat different in that this may have actually only occurred once with a single squadron. The majority of operators received whatever the issue pistol was whilst conducting the Operator Training Course (OTC). The type of pistol issued during OTC varied and depended much on the direction of unit leadership, for instance both .40S&W Glocks and .45ACP STI pistols saw service during the 2000s.

Prior to this, two .45ACP Caspian 1911s were issued to each operator, one a customised government model, the other a custom build with a compensator. The concept of an H&K 1911 was developed in conjunction with Delta but the weapon sadly never saw production. The idea of H&K producing 1911s for Delta was raised as the unit was finding the maintenance and upkeep of essentially custom 1911s to be prohibitive, although it has to be remembered that this was prior to the events of September 11. After the terrorist attacks on the US homeland, SOF budgets were significantly increased. The 1911s carried by Delta in Iraq and Afghanistan mounted a SureFire weapon light and were carried in holsters designed to accommodate the pistol with the light unit.

Although a superlative pistol, the 1911 platforms – most heavily custom-ised with parts from Les Baer, Wilson, Novak and similar gunsmiths – require intensive armourer work to keep them running as the unit fired over a million rounds through their pistols every year. Tactics were also evolving to meet the threats the operators were regularly facing in Iraq: suicide bombers encountered at close range inside buildings or jihadists drugged up on narcotics or wearing body armour. Delta's requirements in a pistol evolved to match these threats.

Their pistol was used as a back-up when their HK416 ran dry or suffered a stoppage. When the operator transitions to his sidearm, he is already in a seriously life threatening situation and in those kinds of scenarios he needs a pistol that will, above any other consideration, function flawlessly. It also needs to hold enough rounds to kill his opponent as quickly as possible. This often required a larger magazine capacity than the seven or eight rounds in a typical 1911 platform. Even most .45ACP extended magazines only held ten to twelve rounds.

Leadership within Delta also impacted on the decision of what pistol should be issued. Several influential senior members of the unit held differing opinions on what their operators should carry, with one advocating the .45ACP platform and another arguing the case for the .40S&W. Custom STIs with double stack .45ACP magazines were trialled but allegedly suffered magazine related stoppages. STI 2011 Tactical Models chambered for the .40S&W round were also later issued. These particular STI pistols were short lived at Delta and were eventually sold on to the civilian market, again apparently due to magazine issues. The failure of the 1911 framed STIs led to a command-mandated decision to go with the Glock.

Glock 17, 19 and 22

The famous Austrian pistol was first designed for the Austrian Army pistol trials back in the late 1970s. It surprised many observers by beating competition from far more established manufacturers like Heckler and Koch and SIG Sauer. The 9 × 19mm Pistole 80, as it was known in Austrian service, would eventually cause a revolution in combat pistols as the Glock 17. Built with a lightweight polymer frame, the Glock attracted instant criticism from those who had never handled the weapon – and from sensationalist newspapers that claimed the Glock could evade airport metal detectors or that Libya's Colonel Gaddafi was buying them for terrorists. Of course a large number of components of the Glock were and are made from steel that showed up just as easily as any other pistol on a metal detector or X-ray scanner.

Other calibre Glocks were soon added to the range as the pistol gained popularity in US law enforcement – the 10mm Auto Glock 20, the .45ACP Glock 21, the .40S&W Glock 22 and the compact .40S&W Glock 23. A fully automatic Glock, the Glock 18, was also available to law enforcement and military buyers. Glock prides itself on responding to its customers and when US law enforcement wanted a highly concealable Glock, the company responded with a range of sub-compact Glocks. These were literally miniature versions designed as back-up pistols or for extreme concealment, such as the Glock 26 in 9 × 19mm, the Glock 27 in .40S&W and the Glock 30 in .45ACP.

Perhaps surprisingly considering their reputation for reliability (in one well known test a Glock fired over 300,000 rounds without a single stoppage), the Glocks were initially taken up with enthusiasm by law enforcement rather than military users. The lack of an external safety catch was believed to have slowed military adoption as a new training regime would be required and those used to Browning and Beretta designs saw the Glock as fundamentally unsafe. The lack of an external safety is initially somewhat off-putting for some shooters but the unique trigger safety, which is literally a smaller secondary trigger in the centre of the Glock's trigger that also needs to be depressed before the pistol will fire, soon becomes second nature after a couple of magazines.

Glocks were however widely adopted by European counter terrorist units before they began making headway in military SOF circles. French SOF became an early and enthusiastic adopter including the secretive Direct Action unit of the DGSE intelligence service, as did the Czech SOG. Many units with maritime responsibilities appreciated the polymer frame as it was not susceptible to rust but although it was tested, it failed to meet SEAL OTB requirements.

According to several accounts from former operators, the Glock was also in use by Delta during the 1990s with a range of 9 × 19mm and .45ACP models carried in addition to their distinctive custom Caspian 1911s. The US Army Special Forces were probably the first to adopt the weapon on a wider scale, although these were unit purchases rather than being procured directly by SOCOM. Officially the M9 is still the issue pistol for the Green Berets. On deployments however it's increasingly the Glock. Intriguingly even the Russian Tier One special operations unit known as Alpha Group now use the Glock 17 as their primary sidearm. eschewing numerous Russian domestic designs.

As we've seen, Delta eventually transitioned to the Glock 22 in the mid-2000s during the height of the campaign in Iraq. Once Delta made the change, other SOF began to seriously look at the .40S&W Glock platform as a viable alternative. The Rangers, including their secretive Ranger Reconnaissance Company, apparently began a limited issue of Glock 22s and 23s in .40S&W along with a wider availability of the 9 × 19mm version in both 17 and 19

A US Army Ranger aims for the head whilst conducting CQB training with a weapon light equipped .40S&W Glock 22. *(75th Ranger Regiment Public Affairs Office)*

models. Rangers have been seen in Afghanistan regularly carrying suppressed Glocks using the superlative AAC suppressor in custom holsters. In fact, the Glocks have apparently become so popular on deployment that Rangers are swapping Glocks as new companies deploy to Afghanistan, as there were not enough in the inventory.

Twenty two-round extended Glock .40 magazines in .40S&W were manufactured specifically for Delta in Flat Dark Earth colour to allow easy visual recognition of the .40 version versus the 9 × 19mm extended magazines they were also using. Standard fifteen-round magazines with the +1 extender were also produced for the Army unit. As earlier touched upon, Delta have also been innovative in using mini red dot sights on their Glocks along with Crimson Trace infra-red laser pistol grips. The Delta pistols with their extended threaded barrels for mounting suppressors, Aimpoint Micro T1 optics and extended magazines really do more closely resemble high-end IPSC competition pistols than a military sidearm.

Delta's use of the Glock 22 did not come without its own issues, mainly related to stoppages caused by the extra weight of the rail-mounted SureFire X200 weapon light. This caused some slide failures although this was rectified with the latest Generation 4 Glocks. Delta also requested and received the Rough Textured Frame finish from Glock before it became commercially available. Along with the Glock 22, Delta have also apparently been using suppressed versions of the compact .45ACP Glock 30.

Recently, Delta have swung back to using 9 × 19mm Glocks in a range of variants including the Generation 4 Glock 19 and 34, as the amount of rounds they expend in training was literally destroying the frames of their .40S&W Glocks. Remembering the history of the .40S&W, one of the key selling points was its ability to be used in pistols originally designed for the 9 × 19mm round. The level of pressure a 9 × 19mm pistol is built to withstand is far lower than that caused by the firing of the heavier .40S&W round in the same platform. One Army operator remarked to the author that *'the Glock was not made to take the abuse. 9 × 19 will last almost forever with no issues.'*

Consequently Delta's .40S&W pistols were literally falling apart under the strain from the tremendous number of rounds the operators were firing through them. Remember that Delta operators can often be shooting several thousand rounds a week through their pistols. At one point early in Delta's existence, the unit purportedly fired more .45ACP annually than the whole of the United States Army. A purpose built heavy weight .40S&W frame may be the eventual answer but with continual advances in 9 × 19mm ammunition, such as the Black Hill Barnes TAC XP, indications are that the .40S&W ship may have finally sailed.

At the time of writing, the FBI are looking at 9 × 19mm Glocks to replace their .40S&W Glocks. Whilst not an SOF organisation, the findings of their Firearms Training Unit in recent trials of the 9 × 19mm and .40S&W are

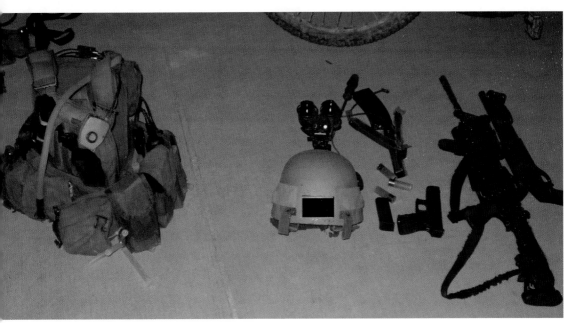

US Army Special Forces assaulters kit from Iraq, 2007. Note, along with the cut-down Remington 870 breaching shotgun and the M4A1, the 9 × 19mm Glock 19 pistol.
(John 'Shrek' McPhee)

illuminating in the context of calibre selection. They compared '*similar sized Glock pistols in both .40S&W and 9mm calibre, to determine if more accurate and faster hits are achievable with one versus the other. To date, the majority of the study participants have shot more quickly and more accurately with 9mm calibre Glock pistols. The 9mm provides struggling shooters the best chance of success while improving the speed and accuracy of the most skilled shooters.*'

Glock have also followed SIG's lead and introduced a concealable single-stack design, the Glock 43 that may well find a place in SOF armouries in a similar manner to the P239 as a lightweight insurance policy. Like the P239, it is also highly concealable and units that employ the full-sized Glocks may well adopt the 43 as it offers increased concealability without the vastly increased recoil of the mini Glocks. Indeed felt recoil in the 9 × 19mm versions is manageable but is noticeably and predictably sharper in the .40S&W models.

Recoil from the compact versions is even more pronounced and rapidly firing the mini Glocks becomes very tiring indeed. United States SOF units have now largely dropped the .40S&W compacts as the recoil was simply too much to outweigh any ballistic advantage over the far more controllable 9 × 19mm Glock 19. In fact, after extensive combat use in Afghanistan the Glock 19 has now been officially accepted by MARSOC as a qualification weapon in lieu of their .45ACP M45A1 or 9 × 19mm M9.

Special Purpose Pistols
We have discussed SOF use of specialised suppressed pistols, but other specialist roles for pistols exist. Amongst these are pistols designed to fire underwater. Intriguingly pistols are among the most effective small arms

The unidentified US Army operator to the left carries what appears to be a .40S&W Glock 22 with Dark Earth round extender magazine and SureFire weapon light indicating he may be from Delta. (*SPC Robin Davis, US Army*)

when fired underwater. A 9 × 19mm pistol round will travel up to a metre or more through water with enough velocity to kill, whilst rifle and carbine rounds will travel perhaps half that distance with any terminal capability. The reason is simple – the longer barrel of the rifle or carbine becomes filled with more water and thus presents more resistance to the bullet's path, slowing its velocity. A pistol's shorter barrel faces less resistance.

SOF units generally only deploy their weapons once they have breached the surface but a special underwater pistol was developed in the 1970s by Heckler and Koch for German SOF combat swimmers, the British SBS and US Navy SEALs. The pistol, known as the P11, fires 7.62 × 36mm darts electrically from a five-round casing and was first adopted in 1976.

The Soviets also developed an underwater pistol, the 4.5 × 40mm SPP-1. Appearing far more like a conventional pistol than the P11, the SPP-1 featured four barrels that sequentially fired specially designed 4.5mm steel darts. Unlike the H&K design, the SPP-1 could be reloaded in action and under-water (the H&K design forced the weapon to be returned to the factory to be reloaded). The Russian design also reportedly had an effective underwater range of some 17 metres, slightly further than the H&K's 15-metre range. Unfortunately no record exists if either design was ever used in combat and indeed if either is still fielded.

One of the most unusual SOF pistols in existence – the 7.62 × 36 Heckler & Koch P11 underwater dart pistol. The fact that this pistol existed was still a well-guarded secret into the late 1980s. (*Heckler & Koch*)

Future Trends

The death knell for the combat pistol has been rung several times over the preceeding century. It was firstly to be replaced as a combat weapon by the likes of the M1 Carbine, then various submachine guns, then the CAR-15 and similar early AR-15 designs and finally by recent Personal Defense Weapons like the futuristic Fabrique Nationale P90 and H&K MP7A1 that we will discuss in the next chapter.

It is interesting to note that both the P90 and the MP7A1 were designed with complementary pistols in the same PDW calibre. The H&K design has never moved past prototyping whilst the FN FiveSeven has been adopted by a mere handful of largely law enforcement organisations. None of these weapons has even come close to eclipsing the pure practicality of the combat pistol in terms of weight and compactness. This applies even more so in the world of special operations.

In 2014 the US Army announced its intention to replace all M9 and M11 service pistols with a new design under the Modular Handgun System (MHS) programme that had been mooted several times in recent years. It will be interesting indeed to see which direction the Army finally chooses to go with the MHS programme. Beretta has, at the time of writing, attempted to unsuccessfully introduce an upgraded version of the M9A1 into the competition. Known as the M9A3 this features a under-barrel rail, an extended seventeen-round magazine and a threaded barrel for attaching a suppressor and all produced in fashionable Flat Dark Earth.

With the recent adoption of the Glock 17 by the British Army, the Austrian design must be a strong contender for the future handgun trials but perhaps in a different calibre. The US Army states in their specifications: *'We are not dictating a calibre during the competition. A vendor may submit multiple calibre of ammunition. However, the ammunition must exceed the performance of the current M882 9mm round'* and later mentions wanting increased *'knock-down power'*. Of course nowhere in the documentation does it stipulate exactly what *'knock-down power'* means and any pistol round that can literally knock down an enemy is defying the generally accepted laws of physics.

It does open up a possible, though unlikely, return to a .45ACP design whilst the .40S&W may yet still be a contender. A 9×19mm design accompanied by a new bullet design that improves terminal effects whilst still abiding by the Hague Conventions would seem a certain winner. The specifications however do not currently allow for new bullet designs, only different calibres. If the US Army does adopt a heavier calibre, it will be to the detriment of personnel who have to actually shoot the issue pistol. As we have seen, the vast majority of those carrying a pistol receive little training or range time with the weapon. Expecting them to now be proficient with an even heavier calibre is asking the impossible.

Marines train on the 9 × 19mm M9 in 2005. The pistol closest to the camera with the light mount appears to be an early M9A1 or else features aftermarket rails. (*JSA Marc Rockwell-Pate*)

A French SOF 9 × 19mm Glock 19 captured by al Shabaab terrorists. It features an extended barrel and detachable suppressor and Glock GTL weapon light. Note unusually the weapon has not been fitted with raised suppressor compatible iron sights. (*Author's Collection*)

Future combat pistol design for SOF use will likely focus on two main areas: one will be the continual evolution of bullet designs to maximise terminal ballistics, including work on a Hague compliant expanding 9×19mm, and the other will be the growth in suppressed heavier calibre pistols. Pistols like the recently introduced .45ACP Fabrique Nationale FNX and the SIG P320 MHS look like likely offerings to be equipping SOF units in the near future, bolstered by the success of the likes of the HK45C with the SEALs. The use of pistol-mounted optics will also increase as more units recognise the advantages in CQB shooting. Glock, SIG Sauer and H&K will continue to dominate the SOF marketplace internationally and will tailor their future offerings to these requirements.

In late breaking news as this book went to press, US Naval Special Warfare, including all SEAL Teams apart from DEVGRU (SEAL Team 6), are officially replacing the 9×19mm SIG Sauer P226R (Mk25) with the 9×19mm Glock 19 following MARSOC's 2015 adoption of the platform. Apparently the timing was tied to the end of the SEAL contract with SIG Sauer and the understandable requirement for a standard combat pistol across SOCOM with MARSOC, some Green Berets and Air Force Special Tactics already using the compact Glock.

The Glock 19 has seen service with JSOC units like Delta and even DEVGRU for many years and is known as a reliable and consistent performer. In SEAL hands, the 19 will replace both the Mk25 and the single stack 9×19mm SIG Sauer P239 that had been issued as a concealed carry option for the teams, although many assaulters adopted it as an emergency back-up that could be more easily tucked away until needed. It is assumed the 19 will be issued with some form of night sights and rail system. In related news, it appears that the HK45C or Mk24 is becoming available across Naval Special Warfare, not just DEVGRU, as their standard suppressed offensive pistol. It is not yet known if the Glocks will be issued with extended threaded barrels for suppressors.

There is also the possibility that following the MHS announcement that new bullet types including hollowpoint and expanding designs are now on the table for more general US military issue, that the SEALs will gain access to more modern 9×19mm bullet designs for their new Glocks. Currently, hollowpoints are only legally allowed to be carried during counter terrorist and close protection tasks (although some JSOC units routinely carry expanding ammunition as all of their missions can be tasked as counter terrorism).

Chapter Two

Submachine Guns and Personal Defence Weapons

Overview

The submachine gun (SMG) is defined as a selective fire weapon that fires pistol calibre rounds like the 9×19mm or .45ACP. Selective fire usually denotes a manual selector switch on the side of the weapon that enables both semi-automatic (one round fired per depression of the trigger) and fully-automatic (continues firing whilst the trigger is depressed until the magazine is expended) but some older or third world designs are fully automatic only. For instance most SMGs carried by the protagonists in the Second World War, such as the famous British Sten or German MP40, were fully-automatic only. This was due to their intended function as a handy, short range weapon that could deliver significant firepower to kill or suppress the enemy during raids or ambushes. The SMG is also perhaps the weapon most identified with the

A Navy SEAL from SEAL Team One trains with a 9×19mm MP5A3 with forward Picatinny rails during operations in Iraq. *(PH1 (SW) Arlo Abrahamson, US Navy)*

commando or special operator due to its long association with SOF units during the Second World War.

The SMG was originally designed during the First World War as a so-called trench broom for the dangerous task of trench raiding. Small teams of infantrymen would make night-time incursions into enemy defensive positions, often with the objective of snatching a prisoner. These raids, sometimes conducted whilst wearing respirators (gas masks) to counter the effects of battlefield chemical agents, often resulted in vicious close quarter and hand-to-hand fighting. Revolvers, pistols and even improvised and decidedly medieval-style clubs like maces and homemade trench knives incorporating knuckle-dusters were employed. Shotguns soon became very popular for this task, including sawn-off commercial models mailed to the troops from home and very early pump-action designs such as the Remington Trench Gun. Introduced in 1918, the Remington was the first true combat shotgun and featured a bayonet lug for precisely this kind of close-range combat. Indeed so effective were these shotguns that the German Army unsuccessfully attempted to have the use of the weapon banned under the provisions of the first Hague Convention.

From the need for a compact firearm that could be used in this deadly CQB environment came the first true submachine guns. Not surprisingly, the Germans were the first to successfully field such a weapon in the form of the 9 × 19mm Bergmann MP18. Examples arrived at the front lines too late to influence the trench war. The MP18 featured the distinctive Luger pistol snail-drum magazine that held thirty-two rounds. The ungainly snail-drum design was replaced after the war with a side-mounted stick magazine that directly influenced later designs like the Sten and the even later L2A3 Sterling. The Germans also saw the usefulness of the famous 'Broomhandle' Mauser C96 and Luger automatic pistols in this brutal form of warfare and experimented with developing the first true machine pistols: fully-automatic pistols with detachable wooden shoulder stocks.

The advantages of SMGs were quickly recognised for employment in what is today known as FIBUA (Fighting in Built-Up Areas) or MOUT (Military Operations in Urban Terrain). Room and building clearances, along with clearing trenches, are amongst the few circumstances where modern armies train their soldiers to fire in fully automatic mode, albeit in short bursts and preferably after posting in a fragmentation grenade. In this kind of environment the SMG excelled. It was assigned to officers, NCOs, radio operators, armoured vehicle crews and other soldiers whose primary role was not to act as a rifleman but who needed a lightweight personal defence weapon. Not surprisingly, the weapon also found favour with the first special operations units like David Stirling's SAS.

Its disadvantages remain largely the same today. SMGs fired a relatively low powered round, had a much reduced range in comparison to service

A Navy SEAL in 1995 conducting VBSS training equipped with a 9 × 19mm MP5 Navy and a SIG-Sauer P226 (Mk25) in a drop holster. Note how his thumb is extended to operate the selector. (*SrA M. Bridget Wright, US Navy*)

rifles, and generally fired from an open bolt. This made them inherently less accurate due to the rapid cycling of the bolt that makes the weapon difficult to fire with any precise accuracy. Many modern SMGs like the MP5 fire from the far more accurate closed bolt. One of the SMG's key advantages however, and something that has kept it in the armouries of modern SOF units to this day, was its suitability for use with suppressors.

Many Allied SOF during the Second World War used the suppressed SMG for covert applications such as eliminating sentries and guard dogs or dealing with the surprise arrival of a troublesome German patrol. The American OSS tended toward the suppressed .45ACP M3 Grease Gun; so-called due to its uncanny resemblance to such a device, whilst the British SOE favoured the domestically produced suppressed 9 × 19mm Sten MkIIS. The suppressed Sten was particularly effective, albeit at very close ranges, when used for single shots only.

The US Army Rangers, the British Commandos, the SAS and the Long Range Desert Group (LRDG) all favoured another submachine gun, the venerable .45ACP Thompson. The original M1928 model made famous by Prime Minister Winston Churchill was used widely in the early days of the war, often equipped with the distinctive fifty-round drum magazine. The M1928 was however difficult to maintain and keep clean in combat environments and was altogether too heavy for commando use. Simplified versions were soon introduced in the form of the Thompson M1 and the M1A1 which were considered more reliable and easier to maintain.

German MP40s were also pressed into service and sometimes favoured by Allied special operators such as the Special Boat Squadron. For many behind-the-lines missions, captured MP40s made sense as 9 × 19mm ammunition and magazines were more plentiful. The Americans even developed a 9 × 19mm barrel and upper receiver for the M3A1 Grease Gun to allow it to use captured ammunition, although the conversion rather curiously used British Sten magazines rather than the far more logical MP40 magazine.

The author has fired a modern Sten MkII reproduction in full auto, although sadly not the suppressed version. Whilst undoubtedly fun to shoot, he found the rudimentary sights (a tiny front post and rear peephole) to do little for accuracy, it was very much a case of point-shooting using the front sight. At close quarters, the range the weapon was of course designed for, the Sten succeeds in laying down an impressive number of rounds in a very short space of time. The author has also fired the M1A1 variant of the Thompson; a far heavier weapon but also very controllable if firing in short bursts which is relatively easy to master due to the M1A1's low cyclic rate. Of the two, the author feels that the M1A1 had the edge despite its weight and can see why the wartime SAS favoured it.

Post-war, suppressed 9 × 19mm MkII Stens continued to be used in limited numbers in Vietnam. The side-mounted magazine was appreciated as it allowed the soldier to go fully prone versus weapons like the M45B with a more conventional design. The suppressed Sten was used by Army Special Forces reconnaissance teams on prisoner snatches – the unfortunate target would be shot in the legs with the suppressed Sten and carried away before his comrades were any the wiser. The Australian SASR used the suppressed version of the British Army 9 × 19mm Sterling SMG known as the L34A1 in a similar fashion. The SASR in Vietnam were also well known for modifying their weapons and mated at least one example of the L34A1 with a 40mm XM-148 grenade launcher! The M3A1 Grease Gun also continued to be employed in Vietnam with US Army and Marine reconnaissance teams, particularly in its suppressed variant with even veteran OSS models still seeing action.

The Swedish 9 × 19mm Carl Gustav M45B or Swedish K was one of the most successful submachine guns deployed by American SOF units and their CIA opposite numbers in Vietnam. The Swedish K was again primarily used with a suppressor. It found great favour with the Navy SEALs and the Army's legendary Military Assistance Command Studies & Observation Group (MACV/SOG). The weapon was replaced with a domestic Smith & Wesson manufactured clone, the M76, after Sweden ceased supplying the M45B and parts and magazines due to their country's political stance toward the Vietnam War. This domestically produced version of the M45B was known to the SEAL Teams as the Mk24 Mod0 and remained in SEAL armouries until the 1980s and the eventual introduction of the MP5.

After Vietnam and the advent of the small calibre assault rifle heralded by the likes of the M16, many predicted the demise of the submachine gun in military use. In fact, the SMG actually saw a great resurgence in the mid-1970s as the scourge of international terrorism increased in Europe. Hostage takings and hijackings suddenly became commonplace and many countries discovered to their peril that their existing police and military resources were not trained, organised or equipped to deal with these types of deadly incidents. The murders at the Munich Olympics in 1972 forced countries to re-evaluate their counter terrorism capabilities. This led directly to the formation of specialist police and military units dedicated to the counter terrorism intervention mission.

As many of these incidents involved hostages, using 5.56×45mm or 7.62×51mm assault or battle rifles was considered to be too risky in terms of potential over-penetration – a round exiting a terrorist and striking a hostage or other non-combatant – particularly since specialist frangible rifle ammunition had yet to be developed. The 9×19mm pistol calibre was somewhat

A pair of operators from the Australian SASR in full black kit and armed with MP5 variants during a counter-terrorism exercise with TAG-East in 2003. The operator to the left carries a 9×19mm MP5A3 with vertical forward grip, Streamlight forearm and Aimpoint optic. The soldier to the right carries the 9×19mm sound suppressed MP5SD3 with Aimpoint and SureFire weapon light clamped under the barrel. (*SGT Troy Rogers, Australian SOCOMD*)

less prone to over-penetrate and could use frangible rounds like the Glaser Safety Slug and Geco Blitz Action Trauma rounds already being developed at the time for Air Marshals.

Many European police forces were also already comfortable with the SMG in a similar way to the traditional use of the pump action shotgun by American law enforcement. Ironically many European nations viewed the police use of shotguns with some trepidation. With its relatively low powered rounds yet with the ability to fire bursts, a key requirement when fighting often fanatical terrorists at close quarters, the submachine gun proved the ideal choice and units were soon equipping themselves with a range of Walther, Beretta and eventually Heckler and Koch designs.

Delta Force's founder, the late Colonel Charlie Beckwith, mentioned the unit's employment of submachine guns during their first mission to rescue hostages held at the American Embassy in Tehran: *'Delta's room cleaners selected as their weapon the Heckler and Koch MP5 9mm Parabellum submachine. Both the Brits and the Germans use it. It feels good in your hand. It is smaller and lighter than a Thompson, and can be used with a silencer. It was ideal for Iran.'*

The submachine gun enjoyed a new lease of life in military and police counter terrorist and hostage rescue teams throughout the 1970s and 1980s. It was not until the 1990s when police tactical units begin to switch from 9×19mm submachine guns to 5.56×45mm calibre carbines, principally to deal with suspects under the influence of narcotics or wearing body armour. Whilst police units began supplementing and sometimes replacing their MP5s with M4s, military counter terrorist units retained their 9×19mm sub-machine guns for two key tasks.

The first of these was for use in certain hostage rescue scenarios where the danger of ricochets and over-penetration negated the employment of short barrelled M4 style carbines. In these situations, the 9×19mm submachine gun was a far safer choice. The second was for missions requiring a suppressed automatic weapon for CQB use. The 9×19mm with subsonic loads, prin-cipally the superb MP5SD3, still outperformed any of its competitors in terms of noise levels. Indeed it has only been in recent years, with the advent of the 4.6×30mm and the .300 Blackout, that the 9×19mm and the MP5SD series has lost its primacy as the suppressed SMG of choice.

Units like Delta actually began to transition away from the MP5 as early as the mid-1980s, instead looking to short barrelled Colt carbines to offer greater range and lethality outside of CQB environments. They were finding them-selves outgunned in range capabilities when fighting 'outside the house'; the 9×19mm MP5 just wasn't cutting it against opponents beyond 100 metres away. An incident during the invasion of Grenada in 1983 effectively began the decline in the use of the MP5 as a standard-issue shoulder weapon among American special operators. An enemy marksman equipped with a rifle of some description kept a team of assaulters suppressed at one of their target

Members of SEAL Team 2 pictured in 1992 carrying a range of then standard SEAL weapons – the 9 × 19mm MP5 Navy, 5.56 × 45mm Colt Carbines and a 7.62 × 51mm M60E3 light machine gun. *(PH3 J. Arthur McLaughlin, US Navy)*

locations with the operators unable to return effective fire thanks to the range limitations of their MP5s. Institutionally the MP5 was then sidelined, apart from a handful of specific tasks.

Popular fiction still arms SOF operators with the MP5 but reality is far different. What happens at JSOC tends to have a trickle-down effect on SOCOM and more broadly across the international SOF community. JSOC and specifically Delta have the budgets and experience to research and develop the finest and most task-oriented weapons for their specific needs – so much so that Delta formally shares its findings with partner units like the British SAS. Significantly, a similar trickle-down effect occurs within UK Special Forces with units following the lead of the SAS and SBS. The shift away from the 9 × 19mm MP5 towards 5.56 × 45mm carbines was soon almost universal in military SOF units.

Calibres and Ammunition

The vast majority of submachine guns are chambered for the 9 × 19mm, a round ideally suited for the roles typically untaken by the SMG. It is manageable in terms of recoil, offers reasonable ballistic effects – particularly if modern hollowpoint rounds are used – and is light, meaning that the operator can carry a lot of 9 × 19mm. Some designs or variants have been produced in .45ACP, .40S&W and 10mm Auto but these are largely aimed at law enforcement and SWAT customers. Only two new calibres have been introduced for military submachine guns and PDWs in the last couple of decades, the 5.7×28mm and the 4.6×30mm. These will both be discussed later in the chapter.

During the War on Terror the submachine gun is rarely seen in SOF hands beyond very limited use in hostage rescue, close protection and suppressed CQB tasks. There are several reasons for this, but nearly all relate to calibre and the operating environments of Afghanistan and Iraq. Like Delta discovered in the 1980s, SOF operators need a platform that can engage targets beyond the limited range of the submachine gun. The MP5 series is superbly reliable, ergonomic and accurate but its 9×19mm round limits its effectiveness. In Afghanistan in particular, an operator may be engaging targets from point-blank range to several hundred metres away requiring a platform that can service targets at both extremes. The MP5 was sadly not the weapon for those kinds of conditions.

Operators also need the incapacitating effects of the heavier 5.56×45 or 7.62×51mm round as it is not uncommon to engage insurgents or terrorists that are either under the influence of narcotics, such as liquid adrenaline, or wearing combat body armour often pilfered from local security forces. During the second battle of Fallujah in Iraq in 2004, operators encountered insurgents using both narcotics and wearing body armour who fought with

Royal Marines of 43 Commando Fleet Protection Group train in CQB shooting with upgraded 9×19mm MP5A3s equipped with Picatinny forward rails and EOTech close combat optics. (*Sgt Esdras Ruano, US Marine Corps*)

almost superhuman strength, only collapsing after being almost literally shot to pieces. In one case a jihadist, who survived a building being brought down around him by tank main-gun rounds, still tried to fire his RPK at Coalition Forces. He required almost a dozen rounds of 5.56 × 45mm to finally put him out of the fight.

In domestic counter terrorist operations, there is rarely the need for shots at longer ranges than 100 metres, however the rise in use of body armour has necessitated the replacement or at least supplementation of 9 × 19mm calibre submachine guns with 5.56 × 45mm carbines. This was recently tragically highlighted in the terrorist outrages in Paris in January 2015. At least one of the terrorists was wearing German Army issue body armour when he was engaged and killed. Indeed he was hit by more than forty rounds according to interviews attributed to members of the French National Police RAID tactical unit that conducted the operation to rescue the hostages held in the kosher supermarket. The 9 × 19mm simply will not reliably penetrate body armour and certainly will not penetrate military level models featuring trauma plates that are proofed against the 7.62 × 39mm round of the AK47.

Tactics and Techniques

Shooting techniques with the SMG have changed dramatically since the Second World War. The SAS and the LRDG along with American Rangers were invariably taught to fire the weapon from the hip. With the rudimentary sights available on many contemporary examples of the class, this was probably not bad advice. Indeed the first version of the Thompson was even designed lacking a shoulder stock at all! Firing the SMG from the shoulder like a rifle and using short bursts to maintain accuracy was really a post-war development that would form the basis of modern SMG techniques.

When SOF units use the SMG in combat, they tend to either fire with the stock fully extended into the shoulder and firing in short bursts of two to three rounds, or semi-automatically to improve accuracy at more distant targets. During CQB operators shoot for the centre body mass and let the natural muzzle rise of the weapon place the rounds into the upper chest and head of the target. One famous SAS technique from the 1980s widely taught by H&K instructors at the time was the so-called 'sling technique'. This saw the operator push the MP5 out from his body supported by the weapon's sling held rigidly tight, aiming the MP5 by pointing the muzzle in much the same way as instinctive or point shooting is taught with pistols. This was apparently developed because of the size and placement of the early weapon lights used on their MP5s. The bulky Maglite and Streamlight weapon lights were mounted on the top of the receiver and thus largely negated the MP5's sights.

With SMGs, standard room clearance drills in CQB are largely the same as for assault rifles and carbines. Two operators make entry to either side of the

Spanish special operators during a VBSS exercise. The operator aims a 9 × 19mm MP5SD3 with magazine clamp. *(Courtesy JO2 Wes Eplen, US Navy)*

US Navy EOD operators train with 9 × 19mm MP5SD3 and MP5K sub-machine guns.
(MC1 Jennifer A. Villalovos, US Navy)

room and clear targets in their arcs. A third man enters slightly behind them who is tasked with dragging any wounded operators or hostages out of the way or stepping in should one of his fellow operators encounter a stoppage or become a casualty. A fourth operator will secure the entrance point and provide rear security. Although units practise their own variations of this, the core techniques remain the same.

Because of the lighter pistol ammunition fired by SMGs, each target will be shot multiple times in short bursts. One of the terrorists killed in Operation Nimrod was shot over thirty times as he was engaged by multiple SAS troopers firing MP5s. He also had a live grenade in his hand that the SAS troopers were keen he had no opportunity to detonate. The SEALS carrying the 4.6 × 30mm MP7A1 in Afghanistan also tend to fire a large number of rounds into their targets as the small calibre does not have the terminal ballistics of the 5.56 × 45mm or even the 9 × 19mm.

Current Trends
The submachine gun is not a common choice for today's special operators. During hostage rescues it remains a viable option, although with many hostage rescues conducted in Afghanistan and Iraq and now Syria, the 5.56 × 45mm tends to dominate as operators need to be able to engage targets

Australian SASR operators conducting a CT exercise in 2004. They are armed with 9 × 19mm MP5A3s fitted with forward grips, Streamlight weapon lights and Aimpoint optics.
(*CPL Darren Hilder, Australian SOCOMD*)

at varying ranges. For hostage rescues in domestic or permissive environ-ments, such as interventions in a Mumbai-style active shooter scenario, the 9 × 19mm MP5 with frangible ammunition is still the preferred option.

Operators will also sometimes still choose the MP5K for close protection duties, particularly when concealment is a requirement, although the latest generation of ultra-compact carbines have begun to replace the SMG in this role. Carbines like the M6 with its 8-inch barrel and 22-inch overall length are tough competition for the MP5K at almost 14 inches without a stock or even the MP7A1: 16 inches with its stock collapsed. There will remain, however, an operational need for a very compact automatic weapon that can only really be met by the likes of the MP5K.

One area where the submachine gun is currently unmatched, although that is changing very rapidly, is in the area of suppressed CQB shooting. The MP5SD series ruled supreme for many years as it combined all the advan-tages of the MP5 with a very effective suppressor. Firing subsonic rounds, the MP5SD was very quiet indeed. The weapon has seen service in SOF hands in Iraq and Afghanistan for use during covert entries upon target compounds and houses. The MP5SD allows any individuals who attempt to get in the way of the assaulters to be dealt with quietly and without awakening the rest of the occupants. They are also excellent in dispatching wild dogs that may betray the presence of an approaching ground assault force, or to quietly shoot out street lights or car tyres.

The disadvantage with older designs like the MP5SD is that its suppressor used a system of internal baffles that slowed the actual velocity of the round as it travelled down the barrel. This effectively took most 9×19mm ammunition under the speed of sound and made them subsonic as subsonic 9×19mm loads were rare when the MP5SD was first designed. With subsonic 9×19mm loads, the MP5SD further reduces the velocity, carving off terminal effect and range as the velocity is again lowered.

Within a small number of SOF units, including the SEALs of DEVGRU, the MP5SD series has been superseded by the MP7A1 firing the unique 4.6×30mm round. Suppressed, it is noticeably quieter than even the MP5SD with subsonic loads. As the pseudonymous Mark Owen formerly of DEVGRU has explained in interviews, the MP7A1 doesn't have the terminal effects of his HK416 but he and his team mates appreciated its diminutive size and weight.

He was also very impressed by its suppressed qualities, even mentioning that operators were able to engage Taliban in one room of a building without waking other sleeping insurgents. Other SEAL Teams have requested the MP7A1 to replace their MP5-Ns and MP5SDs but have been refused as the SEAL command are still wary of the terminal effects of the MP7A1's tiny round. Mark Owen has further explained that within DEVGRU, '*MP5(s) are still in the inventory however the MP7s are light years better so we don't really touch the MP5s anymore*'.

This lack of terminal ballistics has also been criticised by regular German soldiers deployed to Afghanistan where they quickly swapped their MP7s for 5.56×45mm G36 rifles. The MP7 remains divisive with some SOF users stating that long bursts at close ranges are very effective. Others comment that bursts to the target's head are required to ensure the 4.6×30mm performs. The DEVGRU operators involved in the rescue of Captain Richard Phillips of the hijacked freighter the *Maersk Alabama* off the coast of Somalia shot his captors no less than a reported nineteen times apparently with MP7A1s.

The three Somali pirates were each initially engaged with head shots by SEAL recce/snipers from a nearby warship. An assault team that boarded the lifeboat that Phillips and his captors had been confined to fired a number of rounds into each of the pirates until the bodies were no longer moving. This was perhaps not surprisingly absent from the recent Hollywood film based on the rescue.

Individual Weapon Summaries

Heckler and Koch MP5, MP5SD and MP5K
The weapon most associated with SOF in the public consciousness was not even called the MP5. It was originally designated by H&K as the HK54 using

an internal numbering system with the 5 indicating a weapon of the sub-machine gun class and the 4 dictating its calibre; 9 × 19mm. It was adopted by the West German Border Police in the late 1960s to replace their Israeli UZIs which were known as the MP2 in German service. MP5 was thus actually a Border Police designation that was later adopted by H&K. Two versions were initially marketed, one with a traditional fixed stock and the other with a collapsible stock known as the MP5A1. It was immediately praised for its accuracy thanks to firing from a closed bolt. The weapon's inherent ergonomics also helped popularise it as the MP5 handles very well and is a joy to shoot, particularly with the fixed stock fitted.

The weapon was also adopted by the famous Grenzschutzgruppe 9 or GSG9. Their employment of the weapon was instrumental to its later success with military SOF units. It was carried by GSG9 operators during their successful storming of a hijacked Lufthansa airliner at Mogadishu Airport in Somalia in 1977. During that operation, GSG9 were assisted by two operators from Britain's famed 22 Special Air Service Regiment who provided the newly developed and SAS produced flashbang stun grenades. The SAS were suitably impressed by the MP5 (or at that time, the HK54) in action and enquiries were made to H&K for the regiment to evaluate the weapon.

Changes were made including the modification of the standard thirty-round magazine to a curved design, allegedly at both SAS and GSG9 request, to facilitate the feed of specialist ammunition then becoming available for counter terrorism teams like the German Geco Blitz Action Trauma. GSG9 had also apparently had some feed issues with the straight design magazines during the assault on the Lufthansa aircraft, so this was changed to the now distinctive curved MP5 magazine.

Three core products with numerous variations were developed based on the basic MP5 model. The MP5A2 featured a fixed stock whilst the MP5A3 had a collapsible metal stock. Both could be purchased with either the original slimline or larger tropical forearm and variations in iron sights. A compact version for close protection duties was also offered, the MP5K that came in two versions. One, the KA1, lacked any sights at all and minimised external protuberances to allow the weapon to be quickly drawn from under clothing. Both featured no stock and instead mounted a foregrip ahead of the shortened barrel.

The author has shot the MP5K and found the weapon to be more controllable than he imagined although, like the tiny Ingram Model 10, one is constantly reminded of the location of the fingers of the supporting hand lest they stray too close to the muzzle. The MP5K is accurate at the very close ranges it is intended for and recoil is manageable if short bursts are maintained. The old SAS firing technique of pushing the weapon out from the body seems to work well with the weapon, pointing the MP5K somewhat like a large pistol. Compared to the MP5A3, the MP5K is still an uncom-

The 9 × 19mm MP5KA4 featuring the three-round burst option. The MP5K remains popular amongst counter-terrorist breachers and similar specialists and for operations where concealment is paramount, although ultra-compact carbines in 5.56 × 45mm have eclipsed the compact sub-machine gun in many circumstances. *(Heckler & Koch)*

fortable weapon to shoot for very long thanks to its formidable muzzle blast and lack of a stock. A version of the MP5K with a side folding stock was in fact developed for the US Army called the Personal Defense Weapon or MP5K-PDW.

Aircrew from the Nightstalkers, the US Army's 160th Special Operations Aviation Regiment, would routinely carry the PDW version of the MP5K, and apparently sometimes full-size MP5A3s, in their Black Hawk helicopters during the 1980s and early 1990s as the MP5's size made them ideal for the close confines of the cabin. The Nightstalker crew chiefs in the rear of the helicopters with more room to spare would carry full size M16A2s or Colt Carbines. Downed aviator Warrant Officer Mike Durant used an MP5K-PDW in Mogadishu during the infamous Black Hawk Down incident in October 1993. The Nightstalkers transitioned to the 5.56 × 45mm M4A1 soon after, as they were disappointed by the ballistic effects of the 9 × 19mm round from such a short barrel on the Somali militiamen.

The third core version was the MP5SD, the SD standing for Schalldämpfer, German for sound suppressor. Again this version is available with fixed, collapsible or no stock options. The SD, particularly when used with 147-grain subsonic 9 × 19mm loads is remarkably quiet. It has much of the same

The 9 × 19mm MP5K PDW variant originally developed for the aviators of the 160th Special Operations Aviation Regiment in the 1980s. It was also adopted by Delta and DEVGRU who carried it during operations hunting war criminals in the Balkans. (*Heckler & Koch*)

superior handling of the regular MP5 with the added benefit of noise reduction – the author has also fired an MP5SD3 and can attest that the action ejecting the spent casings is indeed louder than the muzzle report! For good reason the MP5SD3 became the default suppressed submachine gun for the majority of the world's SOF units.

Around the same time as Delta Force was conducting its first operation in the deserts of Iran, Britain's SAS were famously storming the Iranian Embassy in London. The operators used the MP5A3 in what was its first public appearance in the eyes of the world's media. The SAS MP5s, known within the regiment as Hocklers, were basic in comparison to later models

The integrally sound suppressed 9 × 19mm MP5SD6, still the standard in suppressed sub-machine guns. Although replaced by the MP7A1 by DEVGRU, the SD6 remains in use with most other units including the SAS, Green Berets and Delta. Advances in suppressed compact carbines in calibres like the .300 Blackout may eventually replace the suppressed sub-machine gun. (*Heckler & Koch*)

with only a handful featuring early Streamlight weapon lights. A number of MP5Ks and MP5SDs were also used in the assault as the regiment had not yet received enough of the basic MP5A3 model to equip all the assaulters. The SAS and Operation Nimrod did more than anything else to put the MP5 on the map.

In the United States, small numbers of the MP5A3 were already in Ranger and Special Forces armouries. DEVGRU, searching for a replacement for their early Ingram Model 10s and aging Mk24s (M76s) purchased a number of MP5s for their assaulters, with the MP5A3 and MP5SD3 becoming their principal shoulder weapons in the early 1980s. The compact MP5K was also purchased for close protection tasks, apparently including the version that fired from within a specially constructed briefcase.

For wider SEAL use, an MP5 variant called the HK54A1 was developed for possible adoption as SOCOM's next generation SMG. This featured a detachable suppressor with a custom gas port system that allowed the user to reduce the velocity of the fired bullet to subsonic levels as required. It also featured a bolt hold open device much like the M4A1 (and something that many American operators seem to prefer) and was fed from a fifty round snail-drum magazine. In addition it had a feature that allowed the bolt to be locked, only allowing the single chambered round to be fired and thus largely eliminating mechanical noise when using the suppressor. Several of these HK54A1s were apparently carried into combat by DEVGRU operators during the intervention in Grenada in 1983, but did not fare particularly well with a number of stoppages reported. Eventually the project was cancelled.

Small numbers of MP5s, including the newer A5 and SD6 models, were delivered for testing to a number of SEAL Teams. During 1984 the SEALs fully adopted the MP5 series as their primary shoulder weapon in a modified form known as the MP5-N for Navy. The SEAL specific modifications made by H&K included a threaded barrel for attaching a suppressor (which, as mentioned earlier, was initially a common suppressor across all SEAL 9×19mm weapons – the P9S pistol and the two MP5-N variants, including the MP5K-N that had seen its barrel extended to allow the use of the suppressor). It had luminous iron sights for low light shooting and a new fire selector that was both ambidextrous and featured a three-round burst setting. The weapon was largely constructed from corrosion resistant stainless steel to better combat maritime conditions. The USMC also favoured the MP5-N as their primary assault weapon for equipping the then newly established Marine FAST (Fleet Anti-Terrorist Security Team) units.

The three-round burst feature deserves further discussion. Logically it should be popular as it takes the trigger manipulation work out of the hands of the operator and does it mechanically. Apparently though, it is seldom used by operators as they are either firing fast semi-automatic shots or short bursts in the fully-auto setting. The SEALs and the highly regarded French GIGN still use versions of the MP5 with the three-round burst option. H&K also offered a two-round burst selector for the MP5 series, to mechanically provide a double tap. These burst options are available on all later A4 and A5 models.

In the 1980s, Heckler and Koch released two further MP5 variants known as the MP5 PIP and the MP2000, both product-improved MP5s. Neither enjoyed much success as most of the units that wanted MP5s had already procured them and the new variants were not enough of an evolutionary step to satisfy the budget expenditure. As we discussed earlier, a third new variant called the MP5K PDW was also developed by Heckler and Koch around this time. The PDW was essentially an MP5K with side folding stock and an exposed threaded barrel for fitting a suppressor. Along with serving as an emergency weapon for Nightstalker aircrews, complete with its own drop holster designed for the weapon, the PDW was adopted in small numbers by the Navy SEALs, DEVGRU and Delta. The PDW remains in their armouries today for CQB and close protection applications.

The MP5 was later modified in the 1990s to accept both the newly developed .40S&W cartridge and the 10mm Auto cartridge. The MP5/10 model was adopted by the FBI for MP5s issued to their agents as carbines. Neither variant was particularly successful, although the MP5/40 sold reasonably well to domestic law enforcement in the United States. Neither are currently offered for sale, but apparently FBI SWAT and HRT still use both weapons.

Heckler and Koch also developed a new submachine gun design called the UMP or Universal Maschinen Pistole. The largely polymer UMP was intended as a cheaper, more modern replacement for the MP5 and was originally chambered for both the .45ACP and .40S&W, marketed again primarily for US domestic police use. A small number of the .45ACP version were apparently purchased by the 5th Special Forces Group and saw some limited action in the early years of the Iraqi insurgency.

The UMP included a central Picatinny rail that ran along the top of the weapon allowing optics to be mounted and a side folding stock as standard. (Incidentally, the Picatinny rail was named after the location where the first such rail, produced by Knight's Armament Company, was tested, at the Picatinny Arsenal in New Jersey.) Despite these upgrades, the weapon made little dent in the popularity of the MP5 even after a later 9 × 19mm version was added to the range.

In the War on Terror, MP5s have seen service with US Army Green Berets in both Iraq and Afghanistan. In Iraq, the MP5 along with captured Iraqi L2A3 Sterlings were hung from bungee cords between the front seats of their Ground Mobility Vehicles. This allowed the driver or passenger to quickly respond to a close range threat by firing the submachine gun through the front windscreen, as early GMVs had no windscreen glass, or out of the side windows. The MP5A3 was also carried by Polish GROM assaulters during joint operations with the US Navy SEALs to seize oil pumping and docking

Romanian special operators training in Afghanistan with a 9 × 19mm Heckler and Koch UMP on the left and a 9 × 19mm MP5SD3 on the right. The UMP is fitted with a suppressor and an Aimpoint optic whilst the MP5SD3 has two magazines taped together to speed up magazine changes. *(ISAF)*

facilities in southern Iraq during the invasion phase of OIF. In Afghanistan, the MP5 was often included in ODA team gear when stationed at remote patrol bases and carried as a lighter and more compact alternative to the M4A1 when moving around within the base. Outside the wire the MP5 was rarely carried due to the range limitations of the 9 × 19mm round.

The MP5K and MP5KA1 are still used principally for high risk close protection and close quarter battle in hostage rescue scenarios. The diminutive little SMG was used by the British SBS to guard Afghan warlords during the early months of the Afghan war, backed up by their longer range 5.56 × 45mm L119A1 carbines. Australian SASR and 2 Commando assaulters from TAG East and West have also been seen using the MP5K fitted with Aimpoint sights during hostage rescue training. It's a particularly handy weapon for the lead breacher. Licenced versions of the MP5K and the MP5A2 from Iran and Pakistan even occasionally show up in the hands of insurgents, but the difficulty sourcing 9 × 19mm ammunition in comparison to Soviet 7.62 × 39mm means that the German submachine gun would thankfully never be widely employed by the enemy.

The suppressed MP5SD series has been largely superseded by the MP7A1, as discussed earlier in this chapter, but the SD is still used by a large number of units including the regular SEAL Teams, often with a rails kit mounted on the forearm to facilitate lights and lasers and fitted with a vertical foregrip. The US Army Special Forces and the British SAS and SBS also still deploy the MP5SD. It soldiers on in the hands of many law enforcement and military counter terrorism teams, including the originators the German GSG9. Despite its now elderly suppressor technology, the SD remains an excellent suppressed submachine gun. A variant even exists within the Australian SASR armoury of an SD3 with a custom shortened suppressor. It's unknown if this was a SASR modification or something produced in a short run by Heckler and Koch, but was seen carried by operators in the last few years.

Walther MPK/MPL, Beretta M/PM12S, UZI and the Ingram

Prior to the development of the HK54/MP5, the most commonly encountered submachine guns used by special operations units were the Walter MPK and MPL, the Beretta M12 (and later PM12S) and the venerable Israeli UZI, all chambered for the 9 × 19mm round. The 9 × 19mm and .45ACP Ingram Model 10, named after its inventor Gordon Ingram, also saw some limited use and offered an extremely high rate of fire in an exceptionally small package, although as we shall see its inaccuracy largely negated its use in hostage rescue missions. All of these weapons were eventually superseded by the MP5 series.

The Walther models were widely adopted by European police forces and both models were evident at the notorious 1972 Munich Massacre. The fledgling Delta Force on Operation Eagle Claw into Iran in 1980 even carried a number of Walther MPK and MPL platforms alongside vintage suppressed .45ACP M3A1 Grease Guns. A small number of the then brand new MP5A2 also equipped the assault elements. The Walther MPK (K for Kurtz or Short) and the MPL (L for Lang or Long) were in fact natural predecessors to the MP5 and the lineage can be clearly seen between the models. Both the MPK and MPL were largely unremarkable if reliable SMGs, firing from an open bolt, although users have commented that both were surprisingly controllable in fully-automatic fire thanks to their low cyclic rate.

The Beretta M12 design was also mainly popular with European police including counter terrorism units like the Italian GIS and NOCS, although some military sales were made to a number of Central and South American nations. Again the M12 and the later PM12S versions were largely unremarkable stamped steel SMGs firing from the open bolt. The Beretta design did feature a unique grip safety along with a more conventional safety setting on the selector. Incredibly, later versions were fitted with a third manual safety on the bolt itself, giving the PM12S the rather dubious distinction of featuring more manual safeties than any other weapon in its class!

The Israeli UZI was, of course, the issue submachine gun of Israeli forces including their Sayeret Matkal special operators. It was also widely adopted across the globe with a version called the MP2 being adopted by the German Bundeswehr, beating out the Walther MPK and MPL at trials. The MP2 itself would be replaced by the MP5. Despite it featuring in the hands of many Hollywood commandos, the UZI was not widely adopted by military SOF units outside of Israel and Central and South America. Unlike the MP5, the UZI and all of these submachine guns, fired from an open bolt that significantly reduces accuracy during semi-automatic fire and increases the chance of foreign matter such as sand or grit entering the weapon through the open ejection port.

The British SAS used the American 9 × 19mm Ingram Model 10, often better known as the MAC-10, for a short period in the late 1970s to equip their counter terrorist Special Projects teams until the MP5 became available. Before the Ingram, the Special Projects operators had a number of UZIs and suppressed L34A1s as their primary shoulder weapons. Compact carbine versions of the British Army issue 9 × 19mm Sterling L2A3 were also supposedly trialled for the role but were never adopted. The SBS also retained the

A grainy image of a captured Iraqi 9 × 19mm L2A3 Sterling sub-machine gun attached by bungee cord for use by the driver of a US Army Special Forces Ground Mobility Vehicle. The captured Sterlings were favoured for this unique role due to their length – compare with the suppressed M4A1 stored to the right. (*Author's Collection*)

suppressed 9 × 19mm Sterling L34A1 until later fully adopting the MP5SD3; like the MP5SD, the L34A1's integral suppressor also lowered the round's velocity to subsonic levels. The Ingram was also used by the SAS, SBS and the covert surveillance operators of 14 Intelligence Company in Northern Ireland before the MP5K became more widely available.

According to some sources, another user of the Ingram was the Israeli Sayeret Matkal counter terrorism unit which apparently carried them in preference to their standard UZIs during the famous Entebbe hostage rescue mission. The reasoning given is that the Israeli operators appreciated the smaller size of the Ingram, however the author has been unable to confirm this, with all photographic evidence he has seen indicating the assaulters carried captured AKMs with a scattering of UZIs. The Ingram, whilst small and compact, had a very high rate of fire, somewhere approaching a cyclic rate of 1,100 rounds per minute with the 9 × 19mm version. Because of its diminutive size, felt recoil was substantial, particularly without the flimsy wire stock extended. The short barrel also made the Ingram something of a dangerous weapon to handle. This could be addressed with the addition of a sound suppressor and most examples employed by SOF were used with suppressors as it significantly enhanced the capabilities of the weapon. In fact a limited number of suppressed Model 10s were employed by the SEALs in the late 1970s and early 1980s before adoption of the MP5.

Indeed concealable submachine guns became something of a fashion trend in the 1980s and even into the 1990s, with various manufacturers trying to sell their ever more compact designs to special operation units. The most well-known was perhaps the Mini-UZI from Israeli Military Industries that sold particularly well with Central and Southern American units that already issued the Israeli Galil assault rifle along with some Israeli police and military units. The tiny Micro-UZI was also produced with dimensions similar to the Ingram and served with undercover Israeli counter terrorist teams. Amusingly in the 1980s action blockbuster *Delta Force*, Chuck Norris' and Lee Marvin's operators are portrayed carrying the Mini-UZI along with their rocket equipped motorcycles. At least the SEALs in the equally atrocious Charlie Sheen film *Navy SEALs* carried actual MP5SD3s in several scenes.

To compete with the MP5 phenomena, Israeli Military Industries even developed a closed bolt version of the UZI and the Mini-UZI. UZIs in .45ACP and .41 Action Express (a short lived pistol calibre competing with both the 10mm Auto and .40S&W) were also produced although the .45ACP UZI featured only sixteen rounds in the magazine due to the larger calibre rounds. Other designs, including the 9 × 19mm Finnish JATI and Italian M4 Spectre, also failed to make much of an impression in military circles although both were rather revolutionary in their ways. The Spectre fired from a closed bolt and featured a four-column, fifty round magazine, whilst the JATI had a unique cocking action; by deploying the weapon's folding forward grip, the weapon cocked itself and placed a round in the chamber. Despite these innovations, nothing could come close to the MP5.

Heckler and Koch MP7/A1/A2

Heckler and Koch developed what many consider to be the successor to the MP5 series in the diminutive MP7. Chambered for the newly developed 4.6 × 30mm round which is roughly ballistically equivalent to the tiny .17 HMR Varmint round, the polymer based MP7 is fed from an UZI-style magazine in the base of the pistol grip thereby reducing its overall length. It is charged by an M4-style cocking handle and features a standard H&K style graphical fire selector above the pistol grip. A folding fore-grip (the same as that featured on the M320 stand-alone grenade launcher) completes the image of some sort of unholy marriage between a Mini-UZI and an MP5K. It also uses a similar action to the G36 rifle and fires from a closed bolt, gas piston system like the HK416. A pistol firing the same round, named the P46 UCP or Ultimate Combat Pistol, was developed but apparently never produced.

The MP7 was never developed specifically for special operations use; it was designed in response to a late-1980s requirement for a NATO PDW. The proposed PDW needed to be able to penetrate Soviet body armour and combat helmets, the then most likely opponent of any NATO force. Along with the MP7, the PDW programme also saw the development of the competing 5.7 × 28mm Fabrique Nationale P90.

Like many SMGs, the P90 has been more widely seen in the hands of celluloid special operators than in the hands of real-life operators. Infamously it was apparently among a number of weapons used by Uday and Qusay Hussein, Qusay's son and their bodyguard against a Delta assault force who attempted to capture them in Iraq in July 2003. One Delta operator was

The 4.6 × 30mm MP7A1 as carried by the SEALs of DEVGRU. This weapon features a detachable suppressor, an extended forty-round magazine and an Aimpoint Micro optic. The MP7A1 has never been widely adopted due to questions regarding the lethality of the 4.6 × 30mm round. SEALs who have used the weapon in Afghanistan have confirmed that they tend to empty the magazine into their targets to ensure incapacitation. *(Heckler & Koch)*

allegedly struck in the leg by a 5.7 × 28mm round from a P90. A suppressed P90 was also used by Peruvian counter terrorists in the assault on the Japanese Embassy in Lima in 1997. This was likely its first combat use and its first use against terrorists wearing light body armour. The Peruvians carried an interesting mix of suppressed Mini UZIs and P90s during the operation.

Questions remain as to the effectiveness of the 5.7 × 28mm round. Its body armour piercing capability is well documented, but sources differ greatly in regard to actual terminal ballistics. Some anecdotal evidence from SWAT teams deploying the P90 indicates that the round has been extremely potent, whilst other decry it as ballistically similar to the .22 Magnum. The performance of the round in the FiveSeven pistol appears to be broadly positive with many end users remarking on the accuracy and low felt recoil, two factors that certainly contribute to good shot placement.

The Heckler and Koch MP7 was also capable of penetrating body armour beyond 200 metres in a platform that was light, compact and suffered very little felt recoil. The author can attest that the MP7 is very pointable and easily handled, its controls are well placed and designed for ambidextrous use, and the folding back-up iron sights are more than adequate. Most shooting with the MP7 will be at extremely close ranges and operators will be using the Picatinny rail that runs along the top of the weapon to affix an EO Tech or Aimpoint Micro optic. Since the weapon was originally conceived, a range of ammunition types has been developed for the calibre and the round is now available in standard ball, a hollowpoint, an armour piercing penetrator and a frangible CQB round.

The MP7A1 was a refinement of the original MP7 to allow the use of thirty- and forty-round extended magazines. The original MP7 only accepted twenty-round magazines that sat flush with the base of the magazine well. The MP7A1 has been adopted by DEVGRU and the German Army KSK, along with a number of European counter terrorist units. It is apparently not favoured by Delta or the SAS as the round is considered underpowered. One Army operator mentioned DEVGRU conducting raids in Afghanistan armed solely with the suppressed MP7A1. The weapon proved very satisfactory during the assault phase but once outside the compound, the SEALs ran the risk of being overmatched by the enemy's 7.62 × 39mm and 7.62 × 54mm platforms. This was apparently where the Navy unit's initial interest in the new .300 Blackout calibre arose. More on that in a moment.

DEVGRU assaulters equipped with the MP7A1 also often carry a heavier back-up weapon along with their MP7A1 and their pistol. This is commonly a unit armourer customised 40mm M79 grenade launcher with a shortened barrel and either no stock or a folding MP5 style stock. Within DEVGRU this M79 is known as the Pirate Gun. DEVGRU have also been seen carrying the M320 stand-alone launcher. Former DEVGRU operator Mark Owen is quoted as saying that the MP7A1 *'works great up close. Over 100 meters ... the ballistics suck. There is a place for it though. When I carried the MP7 I typically carried the M79 pirate gun as well.'* He stated that he would use the M79 if he *'had to engage any enemy past 150 meters'* as he felt that was the maximum range of the MP7A1.

Apparently the US Army Rangers are also supplementing their stocks of the MP5SD3 with suppressed MP7A1s, although this is likely only the Regimental Reconnaissance Company that now reports directly to JSOC. The RRC, once known as the Ranger Reconnaissance Detachment, was part of the Ranger Regiment and conducted surveillance and reconnaissance missions, a role now conducted by dedicated Ranger Recon platoons within each battalion. The RRC itself has long had access to more specialist weapons like the MP5SD3 and suppressed Glock pistols.

The French covert operators of the Direct Action or CQB Unit of the French DGSE intelligence agency deployed the MP7A1 during an aborted hostage rescue in Somalia in 2013. Two MP7A1s were left behind and used for propaganda purposes by the al-Shabaab militia after one of the DGSE operators was killed during the assault. They offer a rare glimpse into how a unit like Direct Action set up their weapons systems. Both captured MP7A1s were suppressed and featured Aimpoint Micro combat optics and SureFire Scout weapons lights. One also mounted an unidentified infra-red laser illuminator above the barrel. Also recovered by the insurgents was a suppressed 9×19mm Glock 19 pistol with rail mounted SureFire light and a number of 5.56×45mm magazines looking to originate from a HK416 and a SIG 551

An image taken by al Shabaab terrorists after an unsuccessful French SOF raid into Somalia in 2013. These weapons were left behind after one operator was killed. The MP7A1s are fitted with extended forty-round magazines, Aimpoint optics (Comp M3 on the right and Micro T-1 as used by DEVGRU on the left) and Scout weapon lights. One also features an unidentified infra-red illuminator. *(Author's Collection)*

series rifle. The DGSE operators weren't the only ones using the MP7A1 in Somalia.

DEVGRU also use a similar set-up on their MP7A1s including AAC suppressors and Aimpoint Micros along with SureFire Scout weapon lights and custom S&S Precision GPS mounts to carry a Garmin GPS receiver mounted onto the stock. In October of 2013, DEVGRU themselves launched a covert seaborne assault to attempt to capture or kill an al-Shabaab military commander in Somalia. The assault force was spotted just as they were about to conduct a silent breach into the target compound and a firefight ensued.

The SEALs blew their way in but ran into unexpectedly heavy resistance and numerous non-combatants, forcing them to fall back to the beach where they were picked up by special operations boats. The SEALs, like the French operators, also left behind a few items. These included a Garmin GPS receiver, expended flashbang grenades, one magazine of 5.56 × 45mm in a Magpul EMAG and one MP7A1 magazine of 4.6 × 30mm. The 5.56 × 45mm ammunition was of interest as it appeared to be the Barnes Optimized 70-grain TSX round supplied to JSOC units: a heavy, open tip, match grade round designed to maximise the potential of the 5.56 × 45mm in short barrel carbines and the most likely round used to kill bin Laden.

Based on the success of the MP7A1, Heckler and Koch have recently added the MP7A2 to their range, the only visible changes being the addition of further Picatinny rails to the weapon, a non-folding foregrip, which is visually similar to the MP5K foregrip, and the colour which has gone from basic black to desert green. The weapon's use by units like DEVGRU inevitably gives the MP7A1 a certain 'cool guy' factor, much like the use of the MP5 all those years ago by the SAS. This will undoubtedly drive wider adoption of the weapon, however the encroachment of the .300 Blackout cartridge, and the new suppressed carbines that fire it, will likely prove stiff competition.

The latest version of the MP7, the MP7A2 fitted with an Aimpoint Micro T-1 and H&K suppressor. Note the new non-folding foregrip and RAL 8000 finish. *(Heckler & Koch)*

Machine Pistols

One class of weapon related to the submachine gun which has almost completely disappeared in military SOF use is the machine pistol. Although examples such as the Czech VZ61 Skorpion and Russian Stechkin APS may be occasionally encountered in terrorist or insurgent hands, the type has never really offered much to the special operator although suppressed Stetchkins were used by Soviet Spetsnaz teams in Afghanistan. The 9 × 19mm Beretta M93R was capable of firing three-round bursts, as was the Heckler and Koch VP70M via the attachment of a Broomhandle style shoulder stock which acted as both a holster and a fire selector. As mentioned in the previous chapter, the most modern machine pistol still in production is the 9 × 19mm Glock 18 that can fire fully-automatic from an extended thirty-three round magazine.

The 93R, the VM70M and the Glock 18 are the best known of the type and although examples were procured for trials purposes none were adopted by any major special operations unit. The Glock 18's enduring claim to fame may be that it was the weapon Iraqi dictator Saddam Hussein was armed with when Delta captured him in late 2003. The offending Glock was later presented to then President George Bush as a gift by unit operators.

Future Trends

New submachine gun and PDW designs continue to be developed. With the MP7A1 and now A2 effectively sewing up the high-end SOF market and the MP5 still the perennial favourite for everyone who isn't using a short barreled 5.56 × 45mm carbine, it's difficult to see both an immediate need and an opportunity for these new entrants, at least outside of law enforcement.

The American .45ACP Kriss Vector is one such design. Also available in 9 × 19mm and .40S&W, the Kriss fires from a closed bolt and is designed to be

The latest iteration of the venerable MP5. Note A5 style three-round burst setting, MP5K style foregrip and RAL 8000 finish. *(Heckler & Koch)*

fired single-handed if required. Its ergonomics, size and accuracy have all been positively commented upon in early trials and possibilities exist for a suppressed version. Heckler & Koch have not rested upon their laurels and have continued to ensure their offerings keep pace with end user requirements. The MP5 for instance has been recently updated with a central Picatinny rail running along the top of the weapon and further rails at the nine o'clock and three o'clock positions on the foregrip.

The MP7A1 is potentially on the way out from DEVGRU as representatives from the unit apparently approached suppressor manufacturer AAC with the idea for a new lightweight carbine design chambered for the .300 Blackout (7.62 × 35mm) round. The .300 Blackout is discussed in some detail in the next chapter, but suffice to say it is ballistically superior to both the 9 × 19mm and 4.6 × 30mm in subsonic loads. The supersonic load has apparently similar terminal ballistics to the Soviet 7.62 × 39mm AK47 round, and all from a 9-inch barrel, integrally suppressed carbine about the size of the MP5SD3. AAC developed a prototype called the Honey Badger that is rumoured to have found much favour with the Navy operators. SIG Sauer have also been

A US Army Green Beret in Afghanistan in 2002 carrying a 9 × 19mm MP5A3 whilst conducting hearts and minds operations with the locals. The MP5 was still sometimes carried as a personal defence weapon as it is lighter and handier than even the M4A1 carbine. *(PH2 (DV) Eric Lippmann, US Navy)*

developing a similar weapon system, this time allegedly for Delta with the SIG MCX in .300 Blackout and 5.56 × 45mm. Both the Honey Badger and MCX will be further detailed in the next chapter.

One nation that has continued to innovate with submachine gun designs for use by both its internal security and military SOF is Russia. A large number of designs have appeared, most aimed at the domestic security market. The most successful of these include the 9 × 18mm PP-19 Bizon which features a sixty-four round helical magazine and is often seen equipped with a sound suppressor in the hands of MVD special units. The Russians eventually adopted the 9 × 19mm as standard in the late 1990s and later designs have been chambered for this round; the Bizon for instance was rechambered and christened the PP-19-01 Vityaz in 9 × 19mm.

Russia has continued to develop unusual SMGs, their 9 × 19mm PP-2000 being a case in point. In limited use by Russian police SWAT units and more widely known from its appearances in the *Call of Duty* video game franchise, it is a closed bolt SMG that is fed from a forty-four round magazine in the grip. Equipped with a Picatinny rail and threaded for a suppressor, it ticks all of the boxes in terms of features for a modern SOF submachine gun.

Chapter Three

Assault Rifles and Carbines

Overview

Assault rifle is a term that is often bandied about in the news media to describe almost any weapon of vaguely military appearance, irrespective of calibre or selective fire capability. Generally if it's matt black and has a pistol-grip, it's an assault rifle. Confusion exists even within the firearms industry itself, typically centred round the definition of the increasingly popular short barrel rifle (SBR) such as the Mk18 CQBR used by the US Navy SEALs.

Is the Mk18 even an assault rifle or is it in fact a carbine? Or does its diminutive size perhaps qualify it as a submachine gun, despite its chambering for the 5.56 × 45mm rifle round? And for that matter what exactly is a carbine? Does barrel length alone make a weapon a carbine or is calibre also a factor?

Operators from the Australian 2 Commando based TAG – East conduct a building assault exercise in 2003. The operator to the left carries a 5.56 × 45mm M4A5 with Aimpoint optic and KAC suppressor whilst the Commando to the left aims a 9 × 19mm MP5A3 with Streamlight forearm and Aimpoint. The optics are mounted deliberately high for use with the vision reducing respirators. (*SGT Troy Rogers; Australian SOCOMD*)

US Navy SEALs train prior to deployment to Afghanistan. This SEAL is shooting a 5.56 × 45mm SOPMOD Block 2 M4A1 with Tango Down foregrip, AN/PEQ-15, Knight's QD suppressor, and EOTech with swing-to-side magnifier (in the image it is clicked out of the way illustrating how the non-magnified EOTech can be used for CQB). *(MC2 William S. Parker)*

It gets even trickier when we look at the latest generation of ultra-compact carbines intended to replace submachine guns in certain specialist roles. Does the intended role of a weapon influence its categorisation?

Sometimes the difference between the submachine gun and the assault rifle, and in particular the modern short barrel carbine, are sometimes more academic than real. The HK53 for example is effectively an oversized MP5 but chambered for the 5.56 × 45mm rifle round. Or the more recent HK416c, developed for a British SAS requirement for an ultra-compact carbine to replace the MP5 in some roles. Its dimensions are far more similar to an SMG but it too fires the 5.56 × 45mm. It gets even more confusing when the tables are turned and an assault rifle or carbine is chambered for a pistol cartridge such as the 9 × 19mm Steyr AUG or the Colt Model 635.

To properly answer these questions, we first need to define and agree what constitutes an assault rifle. The key properties of an assault rifle are that it features selective fire, thus it's capable of both semi (one shot for every press of the trigger) and fully-automatic fire (continues to fire until the trigger is released or the magazine is emptied of rounds) and it is chambered for what is generally known as an intermediate calibre. An intermediate calibre is a calibre of so-called intermediate power meaning it is less powerful than a full power round like the 7.62 × 51mm NATO or the civilian .308 Winchester. Typically these intermediate calibres are of 5.56 × 45mm or similar dimensions or .223 Remington in civilian terms.

Intermediate calibres have a reduced range capability compared to the larger calibres as the bullets are lighter in weight, smaller in size and carry less propellant powder, thus they typically cannot maintain velocity over the same distances as a full power calibre can. Conversely, a weapon chambered for an intermediate calibre produces significantly less felt recoil for the shooter, meaning that such calibres are easier to shoot accurately. They also normally weigh significantly less than their larger calibre cousins. This last factor is a major consideration for the military and for SOF units in particular and was a principal driver for the US adoption of an intermediate calibre assault rifle back in the 1960s.

The concept of an intermediate calibre round for military use first came to prominence during the Second World War when it was discovered through operational research by the Germans that most contacts (the military term for firefights with the enemy) took place at relatively short ranges, far shorter than once presumed, based on First World War experiences. These contacts were also more often than not conducted within close terrain like woods, *bocage* (high, virtually impregnable hedges) or urban areas that broke lines of sight and reduced engagement distances. Simply put, soldiers were shooting at each other at closer ranges than ever before.

These factors typically reduced the average engagement range to between 200 and 300 metres. Indeed beyond 300 metres, human-sized targets become increasingly difficult to identify without the use of a magnified optic like a rifle scope. Helmet camera videos from Afghanistan illustrate this well. The insurgents, when they are seen, are indistinct figures that are difficult to make out with the naked eye.

At close ranges, the submachine gun had proved its worth in both the First and Second World Wars, but it lacked both the stopping power and the range of the full power service rifle. Most submachine guns of the time were lucky to be accurate much beyond 50 metres or so. Small arms developers began to look for a hybrid of the two: a weapon that had the greater range and lethality of the service rifle whilst maintaining the compactness, reduced recoil and selective fire capability of the submachine gun.

By 1942 the Germans had begun developing a Maschinen Pistole (machine pistol, the German term for the submachine gun) that fired a heavier round than the standard 9 × 19mm used in the issue MP40. The earliest experimental version of this new design was the Maschinenkarabiner 1942 or MKb42 that saw some limited action on the Eastern Front. This MKb42 fired a newly developed intermediate cartridge, the 7.92 × 33mm.

This was a necked-down (shortened) version of the standard full power 7.92 × 57mm of the issue Mauser Kar98k bolt-action rifle of the German Army. The developers' intention was to provide a weapon that could fire fully automatic at the close ranges normally associated with the submachine gun, or in semi-automatic mode at longer ranges, all based around a calibre that offered both improved accuracy and terminal ballistics over the pistol calibre submachine gun.

After positive combat trials, the issued rifle began to appear in service in 1944 and was officially christened the Sturmgewehr44 or the StG44 (Sturmgewehr is German for assault rifle). It proved popular on both the Eastern and Western fronts. Allied bombing efforts kept production numbers low so there were never enough available to re-equip entire units, but those units that had the Sturmgewehr appreciated it. The rifle and its unique cartridge also impressed the Soviet Red Army who captured large numbers of examples and eventually seized Sturmgewehr manufacturing facilities.

Although the exact extent that the later Soviet AK47 was based on the StG44 is argued to this day, it is certain that the Sturmgewehr provided inspiration at the very least for the eventual Kalashnikov design and for the development of the now famous Soviet 7.62 × 39mm cartridge. The Soviets were themselves already looking at a similar concept to the Germans since 1943, namely a cartridge that could be used in rifles, SMGs and light machine guns after discovering the same ground truths about combat engagement distances.

On the Allied side, there were a number of carbines but no actual assault rifles, apart from perhaps the odd captured StG44 in the final days of the war. The closest thing to an intermediate calibre weapon in the British and American armies was the .30 M1 Carbine which was used extensively by both the wartime SAS and US Army Rangers who appreciated its compact size and weight, if not its calibre. The M1 Carbine suffered from an underpowered round that limited its effective range to around 200 metres and was widely criticised for its poor performance on human targets.

Many Allied Special Forces of the day favoured the .45ACP Thompson submachine gun instead due to its fully automatic capability although a fully automatic version of the M1 Carbine, the M2, was developed toward the end of the war. The British SAS also favoured one other carbine – the bolt-action .303 MkV Jungle Carbine, a shortened SMLE service rifle that had a fearsome reputation in terms of recoil but one that fired the full power .303 round from a significantly shorter and lighter weight weapon. Besides the M1 Carbine and the MkV Jungle Carbine, wartime SOF relied largely on full size service rifles like the M1 Garand or SMGs like the Thompson and Sten.

After the war, both the US and Britain embarked on separate programmes to develop replacement service rifles incorporating the lessons they had learned during the conflict. Both programmes kept a keen eye on contemporary Soviet developments including the 7.62 × 39mm SKS Carbine and the famous AK47. About the same time, the US-dominated North Atlantic Treaty Organisation (NATO) pushed for a NATO standardised calibre for inter-operability between member nations. As these efforts had a direct and far-reaching effect on the weapons and calibre used by today's special operators, we shall spend a moment examining this important period of firearms history.

The Americans pushed for the adoption of the M14, a magazine fed semi-automatic rifle that was the natural successor to the M1 Garand; indeed the M14 really was a product-improved version of the venerable M1 but with a twenty-round magazine and selective-fire capability. The M14 fired the 7.62 × 51mm round which was itself a development of the wartime .30-06 fired by the Garand and the Browning Automatic Rifle (BAR). The M14 with its full wood stock was also a very lengthy and a particularly heavy weapon, developed with combat in open European battlefields in mind. The Americans still believed that the most likely conflict would be another conventional war – this time of course against the Soviet Union – and thus argued for a longer range full power cartridge with a rifle to match. The British however worked on a calibre and weapon solution that were oddly prophetic and far better suited for the small wars and insurgencies both nations would soon be fighting and would continue to fight until the current day.

According to small arms authority Russell C. Tilstra, the British *'wanted a cartridge that was effective to 600 meters, but they also wanted less recoil than that delivered by the .303.'* The new round was to be fired from a lightweight, compact rifle that would offer selective fire largely mirroring the German Sturm-gewehr concept. The British development team came up with a wholly new calibre too in the form of the .280 or 7mm. This followed previous research during the inter-war years into the flat shooting .270 and .276 that identified them as arguably the perfect military rifle calibres.

To fire this new round an experimental, bullpup design was produced known as the Enfield EM-2. The EM-2 looked for all the world like the grand-father of the later British Army issue L85A1/A2 (SA80) and was only 35 inches in overall length. It weighed in at just over 3.5kg, dimensions that were far closer to the submachine gun designs of the day. In comparison to the competing 7.62 × 51mm designs such as the M14, the Heckler and Koch G3 and the Fabrique Nationale FAL, the EM-2 design was far handier and lighter. It was also the first of the so-called bullpup designs that placed the weapon's action and magazine behind the pistol grip in an effort to shorten the overall length. The origin of the unusual term is still debated but may have originated from the UK Ministry of Defence's project name for the EM-2. Modern descendants of the EM-2 can be seen in the Steyr AUG and the FN 2000 along with the British L85A2 that owes so much to its predecessor.

This .280 round was remarkably prescient as many today argue that calibres in this general spectrum – for example the 6.5mm, 6.8mm and .300

Blackout – are the ideal choice for the modern assault rifle and short-barrel carbine. These modern developments will be examined in some detail later, in particular the development of the 6.8mm by the US Army's 5th Special Forces Group and the use of the .300 Blackout by American SOF in their suppressed carbines. All of these intermediate calibres commonly feature far less felt recoil than the 7.62 × 51mm NATO round whilst still offering increased range and lethality over the later 5.56 × 45mm, or at least according to their supporters. More on this later.

The decision over a new NATO standard cartridge was eventually decided more by politics than by ballistics and the American 7.62 × 51mm, not surprisingly, won the race. In terms of new rifles to fire this new round, the M14 was adopted for the US military in 1957 and the L1A1, a semi-automatic Fabrique Nationale FAL variant better known as the SLR or Self Loading Rifle, was adopted by the British. Other NATO countries were fairly evenly split between the Heckler and Koch G3 – itself a refinement of the experimental Nazi Stg45 whose debut was cut short by the end of the war – and various versions of the Belgian FAL. Curiously, a FAL variant existed in the experimental British .280 chambering, an interesting case of what might have been should sense have prevailed.

In the decade following the M14's adoption – and it is interesting to note that the M14 was not adopted by any other NATO country – the United States military found themselves embroiled in a counter insurgency war in Vietnam, just the kind of small war that required a far more compact, handy and lightweight rifle particularly for use by America's fledgling Special Forces, President Kennedy's beloved Green Berets. That weapon would eventually become the famous M16.

The M16 was derived from an earlier semi-automatic only Eugene Stoner design called the ArmaLite AR-15. The AR-15 had been trialled in limited numbers with Green Beret advisers in Vietnam before the selective fire version, the original M16, was first purchased by the US Air Force as the XM16E1. The AR-15 had performed well enough, although questions were raised about the ballistic efficiency of the 5.56 × 45mm round that remain to this day. This will also be discussed in some detail later in this chapter.

The US military had a history of deploying full power service rifles – the .30-06 Springfield Model 1903, the .30-06 M1 Garand and finally the 7.62 × 51mm M14 – so the 5.56 × 45mm calibre was a significant departure. Its only historical precedent was the .30 M1 Carbine round fired by the wartime M1 and M2 carbines. When the selective fire M16 was adopted on a wider scale across the US Army, the first serious problems arose. The rifles were suffering sometimes catastrophic stoppages in the field including instances that led directly to the deaths of combat troops.

These incidents apparently included cases of the rim of chambered rounds breaking off, leaving the rest of the round in the chamber and necessitating the use of a cleaning rod to clear the stoppage, something that many soldiers did not carry into the field with them. The cause of these stoppages was a new propellant that had been introduced when the weapon became general issue and thus the problems hadn't been seen with the AR-15 or XM16E1 test weapons.

This propellant caused increased build-up of propellant residue and carbon on the weapon's working parts, exaggerating a problem already known to occur with gas impingement actions such as the M16.

Indeed the problem occurs to some degree with all semi-automatic and fully-automatic weapons that are fired rapidly. Coupled with the questionable early advice given to troops on maintenance of the new rifle (including the infamous and preposterous instruction that the M16 was 'self-cleaning'), tragedies occurred that would forever darken the history of the M16.

An improved version, the M16A1, was soon introduced with a chromed bore and chamber to help minimise carbon build-up from rapid and fully-automatic firing and a forward bolt assist was fitted that would manually force the action closed if the bolt itself suffered from a build-up of residue locking the action open. A new cleaner burning propellant was also soon introduced, as was an extensive re-education programme to teach the troops how to maintain their new rifle properly.

Based on field experience by the Green Berets in Vietnam, Colt developed the first version of what would eventually become the M4 and M4A1 carbine. The CAR15 or Colt Commando (type-classified as the XM177E2 in US service) was essentially a shortened version of the standard M16A1 with a new cylindrical handguard, collapsible stock and extended flash suppressor. It also featured an 11.5-inch barrel versus the standard 20-inch, significantly shortening the weapon's overall length. It could also accept the experimental 40mm XM148 grenade launcher which became the predecessor to the M203 and eventually M320 designs. The M16A1 and CAR15 were also adopted by the Australian SASR in Vietnam alongside their highly modified Australian L1A1s, including versions with shortened barrels, XM148 grenade launchers and full-auto sears.

The US Air Force also purchased the XM177E1 for their Special Tactics teams where it was classified as the GAU/5A and featured an even shorter 10-inch barrel and a forward bolt assist like the M16A1. Many years later the GAU/5A was upgraded with a longer M4-style 14.5-inch barrel and new rifling to accept the M885 5.56 × 45mm round. This version, the GUU-5/P, remained in service right up to the early years of OEF in Afghanistan and was only slowly replaced by more recent manufacture M4A1s and a number of Mk16 and MK17 SCAR platforms within Air Force Special Tactics units. Another specialist version of the M16 was also developed during the Vietnam War, this time for the US Navy SEALs. The Mk4 Mod0 suppressed variant was designed with built-in drainage ports to operate after being submerged

A SEAL zeroes his early flat top 5.56 × 45mm M4A1 equipped with a Trijicon ACOG optic and 40mm M203 grenade launcher somewhere in Kuwait in 1998. *(JO2 Charles Neff, US Navy)*

in water, thus becoming the first truly over-the-beach proofed assault rifle designed for maritime operations.

The M16 and its predecessor the AR-15 were adopted, in limited numbers at least, by the British Army several years before the US Army acquired their new rifles. Procured for use in jungle warfare, British SAS operators carried the new rifle in Borneo during the Indonesian Confrontation, as did the Australian SASR soldiers that operated alongside them. In the 1970s in the deserts of Yemen where the SAS was heavily involved in a covert counter insurgency war against communist rebels, the regiment chose to carry a mix of M16s and the 7.62 × 51mm L1A1. This allowed lead scouts to benefit from the firepower of the selective fire M16 to break contact, but with the L1A1 on hand to attain longer range dominance over the AK47 and SKS armed guerrillas.

During the Falklands, the SAS again deployed a mix of M16A1s, CAR15s and L1A1s based on the same concept. This time they found the 5.56 × 45mm to be seriously underpowered at the extended ranges at which they were often operating. Other Special Forces units also deployed a mix of M16s and L1A1s. Royal Marine Mountain & Arctic Warfare Cadre operators at the famous Falklands battle of Top Malo reported dissatisfaction with the lethality of the 5.56 × 45mm round. This may well have had more to do with the physical design of the British L2A1 ball round than their M16s and

A classic image of 1980s era SEALs (complete with regulation moustaches!) emerge from the water carrying a mix of 5.56 × 45mm CAR15s, M16A1 with 40mm M203 grenade launcher and 9 × 19mm MP5 Navy. The SEALs carried a similar weapons mix in Grenada and Panama. *(Courtesy US Navy)*

CAR15s. As we shall examine later, the British standard issue round was, astoundingly, designed to actually minimise fragmentation and yaw, leading to through-and-through wounds that sometimes failed to incapacitate the enemy.

The spectre of international terrorism that saw the MP5 submachine gun flourish also eventually led to a wider adoption of 5.56 × 45mm carbines and SBRs. As we have noted in the previous chapter, counter terrorist units were beginning to encounter enemy who wore soft body armour. Units like Delta were experiencing situations that required a weapon for both close quarter battle within an urban environment and a longer range capability when the battle shifted to outside the target location. Delta was one of the first units to recognise this fact and looked to develop a carbine that accomplished both requirements.

Delta was also the first unit to recognise the potential of pairing Aimpoint Red Dot close combat optics with their carbines following the pioneering use of South African Armscorp OEG sights by the Green Berets during their famous Son Tay PoW rescue mission in North Vietnam. This situation was graphically demonstrated by the Battle of the Black Sea, the infamous *Black Hawk Down* incident. Thankfully the Delta operators were carrying their

A US Army Ranger practises with his SOPMOD Block 2 M4A1 – note the full-length Daniels Defense rail, EOTech optic and suppressor. He also carries a Glock sidearm. This is largely the standard kit of the Rangers serving in Afghanistan post 2009.
(75th Ranger Regiment Public Affairs Office)

custom-built Colt Model 723 Carbines which they still termed CAR15s. Larry Vickers, a highly respected former operator has been quoted that '*the customized CAR15s issued by Delta became the main drivers for the modification/ customization capability available on all M4 Carbines issued today.*'

In 1980, the 5.56 × 45mm round was finally adopted as the NATO standard and European SOF units followed the American example, purchasing CAR15s or adopted the Heckler and Koch 5.56 × 45mm HK33 carbine or the Fabrique Nationale 5.56 × 45mm FNC. During the 1990s many European units moved across to 5.56 × 45mm SIGs and the compact versions of the Heckler and Koch G36, the G36K and even shorter G36C. Most units outside of Europe still carried the M4A1 or Diemaco carbine. In fact, until the advent of the HK416, the only serious contenders to the throne held by the M4A1 was the H&K G36 series.

In the United States, the SEALs continued to issue M16 variants even after the CAR15 and M4 became more widely available, although there were also some domestically imported Heckler and Koch HK33s in their armouries since in the 1970s. The SEALs and US Army Special Forces also carried M16A2 Carbines, mainly the Colt Model 723. By the 1990s the SEALs had received the M16A3 that was simply an M16A2 with the three-round burst

The carbine version of the older 5.56 × 45mm G36 service rifle, the Heckler & Koch G36C fitted with EOTech optic and H&K vertical foregrip and weapon light mount. *(Heckler & Koch)*

US Navy SEALs conduct Shoot House training at Little Creek, Virginia in 2007. They carry the 5.56 × 45mm Mk18 Mod0 CQBR carbine with M68 Aimpoint optics, Knight's QD suppressors and AN/PEQ-2 infra-red illuminators. *(LCDR Keith Williams, US Navy)*

selector replaced with a fully-automatic only setting. Eventually these were replaced by M4A1 SOPMOD carbines and the short-barrelled Mk18 Close Quarter Battle Rifle (CQBR) that was developed specifically for Naval Special Warfare use.

Today most of the world's SOF carry some variant of the venerable M4 carbine, whether that be the Colt M4A1; the Diemaco, or now Colt Canada, C8; or the new kid on the block, the HK416. Indeed even in units where other weapons are frequently deployed such as within the French COS or Special Operations Command, where the SIG 553, the FAMAS and the H&K G36C frequently rub shoulders, the M4A1s are also available. The Mk16 or SCAR-Light was at one time considered to be the most likely successor to the M4A1 platform but its adoption proved limited, particularly after SOCOM declined to adopt the weapon en-masse claiming that it had failed to show enough of a performance improvement over the M4A1. The next generation of SOF assault rifle will have to be a significant evolution as we shall see later in this chapter.

A member of the Asymmetric Warfare Group in Afghanistan carrying a 10-inch barrel 5.56 × 45mm HK416 with EOTech optic and Insight Technology M3X weapon light. Later the AWG were made to hand in their 416s to be replaced by standard M4A1s, although they kept their non-standard Glock 19 sidearms. *(ISAF)*

Calibres and Ammunition

In the on-going debate surrounding the 5.56 × 45mm round we should firstly consider the benefits of the round. The lighter weight of the 5.56 × 45mm ammunition, for example, cannot be underestimated. It enables approximately double the amount of ammunition to be carried in comparison to 7.62 × 51mm. For a practical example, a US Army Ranger on a direct action raid mission in Iraq would routinely carry seven thirty-round magazines for his assigned M4A1 along with an eighth in the weapon itself. He would also routinely carry two fragmentation hand grenades, two flashbang stun grenades, a smoke grenade, a 9 × 19mm Beretta or Glock pistol with a spare magazine, along with spare ammunition for the SAW gunners or Mk48 machine-gun teams.

This is on top of his combat body armour including heavy ceramic trauma plates, ballistic helmet, night vision goggles, at least one radio, ear defenders with communications interface, a combat lifesaver kit, spare batteries for the NVGs and radio, at least a couple of litres of drinking water, zip-tie restraints for prisoners, some infra-red chemical lights and any technical equipment he might need to do his specific job on the mission. This might include a camera,

A Marine Raider in Afghanistan carrying a very nicely camouflaged 5.56 × 45mm M4A1 with EOTech and magnifier and AN/PEQ-15. This image clearly illustrates the use of the magnifier with the EOTech, essentially placing an EOTech red circle on a four power magnification sight picture. When the operator needs to transition to non-magnified close quarter shooting he simply flips the magnifier to the side. (*SSgt Nicholas Pilch; US Air Force*)

Rangers zero their weapons at a range in Bagram, Afghanistan in 2014. Note the controversial 'C-Clamp' shooting hold. The weapons are the SOPMOD Block 2 5.56 × 45mm M4A1s with Elcan Specter variable magnification optics. *(PFC Dacotah Lane, US Army)*

a breaching shotgun or an escalation of force kit to warn away curious civilians who stray too near an operation. As can be seen, that's a lot to carry, and that's only for a very short duration operation where the assaulters will be driven or flown to the objective.

The 5.56 × 45mm carbine itself is also significantly lighter in weight than 7.62 × 51mm platforms. This has been offset to some degree by the implementation of Picatinny rails mounting all manner of accessories, although most of these would also feature on a typical 7.62 × 51mm weapon; 5.56 × 45mm platforms are also commonly more compact in overall length. The round itself makes the rifle or carbine far easier to shoot and shoot well without the punishing recoil of the 7.62 × 51mm, particularly in aimed rapid fire. The smaller cartridge also lends itself to fully-automatic fire, being far more controllable with longer bursts. The author can attest that even short bursts from the H&K G3A3 or the AK47 are difficult to keep on target. The final argument for the smaller round is commonality in the logistics chain as 5.56 × 45mm is after all NATO standard and the most common military calibre outside the former Warsaw Pact.

Now let's consider some of the challenges faced by the 5.56 × 45mm but before we do, let's address an urban myth or two. The tale that the 5.56 × 45mm round was designed to principally wound rather than kill is used to this day to criticise the round. The story goes that the 5.56 × 45mm was

A rare image of UK Special Forces' 5.56 × 45mm L119A1 with 10-inch CQB upper as manufactured by Colt Canada, previously Diemaco. This example mounts the most common UKSF optic, the Trijicon ACOG. *(Kelly Stumpf, Colt Canada)*

intentionally developed to cause non-lethal wounds as this would have an exponential effect on enemy strength as additional soldiers would be needed to carry the casualty from the battlefield and transfer them to a medical facility. Despite featuring in many accounts in books and movies, the 5.56 × 45mm round was never designed to wound. It was designed, just like any other bullet, to strike with the point, increasing range and penetrative potential with the aim to kill the enemy.

One of the key drawbacks with smaller high velocity rounds like the 5.56 × 45mm is that they are inherently unstable and may tumble if they strike any significant barrier on the way to the intended target. If a 5.56 × 45mm round does not expand, tumble or yaw within the target creating a large permanent wound cavity or does not strike a major organ, the round may well zip through the body causing comparatively minor tissue damage.

Lighter bullets like the 5.56 × 45mm also require increased twists in a rifle's barrel to stabilise them in flight. By way of explanation, rifle barrels have grooves known as twists cut into the barrel that contribute to the accuracy of the weapon by spinning the bullet as it travels down the rifle's barrel. The more spins, the more stable and thus more accurate the bullet becomes, although bullet shape and weight also play a part. Heavier rounds and those with pointed noses require a faster twist.

The 1:14 or one twist per 14-inch specification in the original AR-15 barrels contributed to a very unstable round in flight. This twist ratio was likely the source of both Vietnam-era tales of massive wounds as the unstable round would turn upon itself in flight creating a large permanent wound cavity, the so-called 'tumbling' effect, and stories of rounds being deflected by light cover such as intervening foliage. The twist ratio has increased over time to

A US Army Green Beret firing his 10-inch barreled 5.56 × 45mm M4A1, often mistaken for an Mk18 CQBR. This example features a Grip Pod vertical grip incorporating a bipod, an Insight Technology M3X weapon light wit infra-red filter, and an EOTech weapon sight and switch-to-side magnifier. (USASOC)

1:12 in the later M16A1 version and 1:7 on most current designs like the M4 Carbine. This has meant that whilst the 5.56 × 45mm bullet has become more stable in flight and thus more accurate, its increased stability conversely has meant that its ballistic effect on target has been reduced. As mentioned in the introduction to this book, this is particularly pronounced with military-issue ball ammunition that is not designed to fragment or yaw upon impact.

A failure to expand, tumble or yaw is most often attributed to three factors: bullet design, insufficient velocity at extended ranges beyond 400 metres, or insufficient velocity from SBRs and carbines at ranges over 200 metres. In rifles with standard length barrels like the M16A4 or Mk16 SCAR, the 5.56 × 45mm can effectively engage targets out beyond 400 metres in combat conditions. With the addition of improved ammunition like the Mk262 Mod0 we will discuss in a moment, the same M16A4 or Mk16 SCAR can reach even further and still provide solid terminal effects on target, perhaps even out to 800 metres with the right optics.

With the SBRs and carbines that most special operators carry, the shorter barrel lengths severely compromise the round beyond 50 metres, with their effective range envelope closing at around 200 metres. In a standard 14.5-inch barrel M4A1 for instance, most rounds will only reliably yaw with ball

7th Special Force Group Green Berets stack-up on a door. Their Block 2 M4A1s feature EOTech optics, SureFire Scout lights and AN/PEQ-15 illuminators. Note also what appear to be aftermarket Magpul P-MAG magazines. Their carbines also feature the Magpul AFG (Angled Fore Grip) which is finding favour as a more compact alternative to the traditional vertical foregrip. *(USASOC)*

ammunition at ranges under 50 metres. Fired from the SEAL Mk18 CQBR that range decreases to around 30 metres. This performance can be, and has been, improved upon during the last decade with new bullet designs and the use of heavier bullets.

It is interesting to note that the British military's experience with their L85A2 with its longer 20-inch barrel has not resulted in a similar cloud of suspicion over the 5.56 × 45mm. Indeed one is hard pressed to find British veterans criticising the round, which is doubly surprising considering they are shooting the appalling L2A2 ball round. There have been few apparent complaints from UK Special Forces either with their longer barrelled carbine, the 15.7inch L119A1. The fact that UKSF are upgrading their L119A1s to A2 standard at the time of writing is surely a significant show of confidence in the weapon and its calibre.

A quick discussion on combat ranges may be necessary here. Over 50 per cent of small arms engagements in Afghanistan were between 300 and 900 metres. In Iraq the proportion of closer range contacts rose sharply due to the terrain and was far more in line with the findings from World War Two. Indeed in the back streets and alleyways of Iraqi cities, engagement ranges could drop dramatically to under 100 metres. Most SOF firefights tend to be at closer range even in Afghanistan as assault teams are often contacted by the insurgents during building and compound raids, meaning that assaulters could be using their carbines at close to point blank range.

As we've noted before, SOF teams will also run into opposition outside the target location, leading to longer range firefights. Not surprisingly, there is far less criticism of the 5.56×45mm round from SOF units that tend to shoot at close ranges as the shorter barrel of their carbines is sufficient to deliver enough velocity to reliably incapacitate targets (the SOF units also commonly have access to better ammunition designs than their infantry counterparts). Units like the Rangers or British Army SFSG, will also tend to deploy machine-gun, sniper and designated marksman teams around the perimeter of the target site to deal with longer range engagements so the 5.56×45mm carbine tends to be used for what it is good at.

The extended ranges in Afghanistan impacted on the abilities of the 5.56×45mm round, sometimes in ways that weren't readily apparent. We commonly imagine Afghanistan as a land of desert or scrubland but there are snow topped mountain ranges in the country, particularly along the eastern border with Pakistan. Shooting in these kinds of environments can be as punishing to the smaller round as long flat distances. Elevated shooting (firing upward at an angle) causes a dramatic reduction in velocity and consequently range and lethality and is why 7.62×51mm rifles perform better in mountainous terrain – they can afford to lose velocity as they have more propellant and heavier bullets.

The Russians ran into similar challenges during the Soviet Afghan War in the 1980s. The 5.45×39mm round from their otherwise popular AK74 was losing lethality and accuracy over extended ranges, particularly when firing up steep gradients in the mountains. To compensate for this, their Spetsnaz special operations troops began to supplement their AK74s with older 7.62×39mm AKMs, including suppressed versions, and more SVD Dragunov sniper rifles chambered for the excellent longer ranged 7.62×54R.

Conversely Iraq presented unique problems for special operators. As noted, the ranges were generally much shorter due to the built-up urban nature of large areas of the country but long-range engagements were still common to the west and north where the recent concept of the Designated Marksman Rifle (DMR) really came into its own. Teams from all the principal American SOF commands – the SEALs, the Green Berets and Delta – began to carry a mix of 5.56×45mm carbines supplemented by a number of scoped 7.62×51mm platforms to cover these extended ranges. DMRs became increasingly popular in Afghanistan for the same reason.

DMRs are but one answer to a particular capability problem and will be covered in the following chapter to some depth. Many vehicle mounted units such as the 5th Special Forces Group ODAs in the initial invasion of Iraq had

A MARSOC operator firing his 5.56 × 45mm M4A1 mounting an EOTech optic, AN/PEQ-15 illuminator and Insight Technology SU-233 weapon light. He has deployed the bipod fitted integrally to his Grip Pod vertical foregrip. Note also his .45ACP M45 MEU-SOC sidearm.

(LCpl Stephen Benson, US Marine Corps)

the luxury of carrying what amounted to a small armoury on each of their GMV trucks. Most of the operators carried the M4A1 but within their trucks were available the 7.62 × 51mm Mk11 and 5.56 × 45mm Mk12 Special Purpose Rifles, the 5.56 × 45mm M249 Minimi Squad Automatic Weapon and the 7.62 × 51mm M24 and .50BMG M82 (M107) sniper rifle systems, allowing them to choose exactly the right tool for the job. These ODAs obviously also benefited from their vehicle mounted 7.62 × 51mm M240B general-purpose machine-guns, .50BMG M2 heavy machine guns and 40mm Mk19 automatic grenade launchers.

Along with dealing with the range limitations of the 5.56 × 45mm, military users are often disadvantaged in the lethality department by the design of military issue rounds. These rounds are generally Full Metal Jacket or ball design – a construction which enhances penetration but does nothing to increase terminal effects. The use of such designs can be traced back to the first Hague Convention of 1899 that banned the use of *'bullets which expand or flatten easily in the human body'* between signatory nations. As we have seen earlier, the issue also effects pistol rounds and actively forces the use of bullets that aren't designed to incapacitate an adversary as quickly as possible which seems patently ridiculous in a military context.

The United States is not a signatory to the Hague Conventions although they have followed the spirit of the Conventions and have yet to issue explicitly hollowpoint or similar expanding rounds for general-service weapons. JSOC units like DEVGRU and Delta are considered to be operating against terrorists so receive much greater latitude around the types of bullet they can use operationally. Open tip match rounds such as the recently developed Mk262 and Mk318 have both been approved from a Hague standpoint by the US military as neither are *'expressly designed to expand upon impact'*.

The British, who are signatories to Hague, continue not to issue expanding or deforming rounds. Indeed the first version of the standard British 5.56 × 45mm round the L2A1 yawed and fragmented rather reliably and so a heavier jacket was produced to actually inhibit this, resulting in the current issue round, the L2A2. It seems like madness that the British would deliberately design out the very factors that contribute to successfully incapacitating an enemy by gunfire, but there you have it. Thankfully, like the US, units operating on counter terrorism missions such as the SAS are exempted from these restrictions and may use specialist ammunition.

It perplexes many observers that the provisions of the Hague Declaration IV.3 of 1899 continue to be adhered to in the modern day when warfare has so drastically changed, particularly when the Declaration explicitly only applies to war between signatories. Afghanistan and Iraq have never ratified the relevant Declaration so one could argue that the use of expanding or fragmenting ammunition against insurgents or terrorists in these countries does not at all contravene the Declaration either in the letter or spirit of the law.

Adhering to outdated and redundant Hague Conventions can have serious operational impacts – even on the most elite soldiers. In Somalia in 1993 during the *Black Hawk Down* incident, some Rangers and, anecdotally at least, one Delta operator reported having to shoot Somali militiamen multiple times as their rounds, the then-issue 62-grain M885 Green Tip, were over-penetrating and producing non-incapacitating through-and-through wounds. The Somalis were generally far skinnier than their Western opponents and wore light, loose clothing. The M885s weren't getting the opportunity to yaw or fragment as they were exiting the thin bodies of the militiamen before they had the chance to even begin to do so.

The M885 had been designed around a steel penetrator to pierce Soviet Army body armour as at the time of its development the most likely opponent of the American soldier was judged to be a Soviet infantryman. Thus the M885 needed to penetrate both body armour and helmets. Conversely members of Task Force Ranger also found the M885 to be less than optimal in barrier penetration, with serious difficulties defeating light cover such as car doors, a common issue with the 55 and 62-grain 5.56 × 45mm rounds.

The heavier the 5.56 × 45mm round, the better it performs both at extended ranges in full length rifles and from short barrelled carbines. The lighter 55-grain M193 round and the 62-grain M885 or NATO SS109 both rapidly

A MARSOC operator in Helmand carrying a 5.56 × 45mm M4A1 with Elcan Specter sight, suppressor and Grip Pod bipod foregrip. Additionally he carries a unit modified standalone 40mm M203 grenade launcher. (*SSgt Nicholas Pilch, US Air Force*)

shed velocity and become susceptible to any changes in wind direction that can greatly affect accuracy. The heavier 77-grain Mk262 Mod0 rounds discussed below perform far better at ranges beyond 400 metres and reportedly out to over 700 metres in Afghanistan. SOF users have also reported an increase in terminal effects with the heavier design. The US military have also issued an enhanced M885A1 that weighs the same as the Mk262 but features an exposed steel tip that apparently increases barrier penetration.

The Black Hills manufactured 77-grain Mk262 Mod0 and Mod1 were initially designed for use in the Mk12 Special Purpose Rifle carried by US Army Special Forces and Navy SEALs. Black Hills President Jeff Hoffman mentioned in a 2012 interview that the round was found to be so impressive by these operators that '*the assaulters were stealing it from the snipers*'. Both rounds, the Mod0 and Mod1, perform far better than the M885 standard-issue round, increasing effective range by several hundred metres in the right conditions, and consistently hitting far harder when striking human targets. The Mk262 also offers solid barrier defeat capability but the round obviously isn't as barrier blind as the 7.62×51mm. The Mk262's penetration of body armour and helmets is also not as good as the general-issue M885 and

A MARSOC MSOB operator in Helmand takes a knee with his SOPMOD Block 2 5.56×45mm M4A1 fitted with an underslung 40mm M203 launcher. The M4A1 also features a Knight's suppressor, AN/PEQ-15 and Elcan optic. Note the belt of 40mm rounds he carries around his waist. (*Cpl Kyle McNally, US Marine Corps*)

M885A1, although for operations in Afghanistan against Taliban insurgents this is unlikely to prove an issue.

Even the Mk262 is not a panacea. In a contact in September 2003 in Ramadi, Iraq, an insurgent ambushed and killed two 5th Special Forces Group Green Berets with his AK47. Although apparently shot some seven times with the Mk262 round from an M4A1 carbine, the insurgent was finally dispatched by a Green Beret shooting him in the head with his .45ACP 1911 pistol. This incident does not paint the Mk262 in a particularly positive light, although it must be noted that had the insurgent been shot in the head by a 5.56 × 45mm round it would have likely had the same, immediately terminal, effect as the .45ACP. It is also notable that this is one of the only documented potential failures to stop by the Mk262 round.

In Marty Skovlund Jr.'s tremendous history of the US Army Rangers in the War on Terror, *Violence of Action*, a Ranger describes engaging an AK47 wielding Taliban insurgent in 2009 with his M4A1, most likely loaded with the Mk262:

> I squeezed my trigger. The crack of a round leaving my barrel was answered by a puff of dust off of his black shirt. The red reticle of my optic blurred as I loosed thirteen more rounds through him. He remained

Pictured in Afghanistan in 2009, this Ranger's 5.56 × 45mm SOPMOD Block 1 M4A1 features Magpul P-MAGs, a Grip Pod bipod vertical foregrip, AN/PEQ-15 and EOTech with magnifier. *(Walter Reeves; US Army)*

still. The red overt laser from my team leader's weapon bounced on the man's chest as he acquired and engaged with an equal amount of gunfire. We broke trigger rapidly, if wildly, until at last the man fell to the ground, rolling unceremoniously behind a bush.

Even rifle rounds offer no guarantees of immediate incapacitation. Another Ranger recounts in the same book of hitting an Iraqi insurgent in the throat with a single 5.56 × 45mm round that immediately dropped him.

The Mk262 isn't the only development that has improved the range and lethality of the 5.56 × 45mm. JSOC units with their greater budgets and R&D capabilities have widely adopted the 70-grain Barnes TSX Optimized Brown Tip which has exhibited excellent intermediate barrier penetration capabilities and enhanced terminal effects, especially from short barrelled 416 and M4A1 carbines. Indeed the Optimized Brown Tip is alleged to have been the round that dispatched Usama bin Laden and is the load carried in Delta's 10-inch barrel HK416s.

The 62-grain Mk318 Special Operations Science and Technology (SOST) round was developed for wider SOCOM use and issued to SOF units from 2009. The SOST was designed for both the M4A1 and the CQB and Standard

An unidentified US Army special operator runs a course of fire with a 5.56 × 45mm Block 2 M4A1 fitted with aftermarket rails and flash suppressor. He also carries what appears to be a .40S&W Glock 22 with weapon light. (*USASOC*)

versions of the Mk16 SCAR-Light to optimise the 5.56 × 45 round in carbine length barrels. Additionally it was developed to address one of the primary criticisms of the issue M885 and M885A1 rounds, namely their barrier defeat capabilities. The SOST performs far better against intermediate barriers and offers much greater, and more reliable, terminal effects than either the 55-grain M885 or the improved M885A1. The SOST has been adopted by the US Marine Corps in 2010 over the Army issue M885A1 and is widely deployed along with the Mk262 by Army Green Berets and Navy SEALs.

Another recent innovation finding use within the wider SOCOM community is the 5.56 × 45mm Mk255 Mod1, a Reduced Ricochet Limited Penetration Round (RRLP) designed for both CQB training in Kill House environments and operationally in urban or similar close terrain where hostages or non-combatants may be intermixed with hostiles. Beginning in the late 1990s, Crane Division of the Naval Surface Warfare Centre that is tasked with developing and procuring weapons systems and ammunition for the SEALs and SOCOM, surveyed all available commercial rounds for a frangible 5.56 × 45mm CQB offering that ticked the boxes of SOCOM's requirement.

These requirements included zero over-penetration potential, lethality at least as great as the M855 at up to 100 metres, and waterproof for OTB operations. No commercially available round could match these requirements so Crane developed the 62-grain Mk255 Mod0 and later the Mod1 which entered service in 2005. Both rounds were designed with M4 carbines and SBRs like

US Army Green Berets in Afghanistan 2010. The operator in the foreground's 5.56 × 45mm M4A1 mounts a Trijicon ACOG four-power optic with slaved mini red dot sight. Note the 7.62 × 51mm M240B and M134 minigun in the background. (*SSgt Joseph Swafford, ISAF*)

the SEALs' Mk18 in mind. Whilst the round does not totally eliminate ricochet fragments and so-called reverse splatter (when pieces of a bullet fly back toward the shooter after striking a hard barrier), it significantly lowers the risk of both.

In CQB environments, particularly during counter terrorist and hostage rescue operations, frangible rounds are far safer to any hostages or non-combatants caught in the gunfight. In a December 2014 incident, a police assault group stormed a café in Sydney, Australia that had been seized by a mentally unstable individual claiming allegiance to Islamic State. The police assaulters were reported to have fired up to twenty-seven rounds inside the café during the assault, seven of which apparently struck the hostage taker, two in the head. Fragments from some of the other 5.56 × 45mm rounds tragically struck and killed a hostage and wounded three hostages and one of the police assaulters. The fragmentation may have been exaggerated by the largely marble internal design of the café, but one cannot help but think that rounds like the RRLP might have provided a significant advantage.

Along with new bullet designs to improve the combat performance of the 5.56 × 45mm, several wholly new calibres have risen to prominence during the War on Terror, each proposed by their often vociferous supporters as the ideal replacement for the 5.56 × 45mm in special operations use. A 2006 US Army research project into carbine calibres identified the 6.8mm as the optimal round for such short barrelled weapons. A further 2007 trial conducted by a number of members of US military special operations units from SOCOM found that the 6.8mm performed at least as well as the best offerings in 5.56 × 45mm in terms of accuracy and outshone all of its competitors in simulated terminal effects in ballistic gel.

This cartridge, the 6.8 × 43mm Special Purpose Cartridge (SPC) round, was developed in the early 2000s by members of the US Army's 5th Special Forces Group and the Army Marksmanship Unit, with design support from Remington. The Special Forces operators were not particularly happy with the performance of the 5.56 × 45mm in their M4A1s in Afghanistan in terms of both accuracy at distance and terminal effects on target. The operators instead wanted similar ballistics to the Soviet 7.62 × 39mm in a carbine-sized package.

It is interesting to note that Delta, also operating in Afghanistan at the time, were not reporting similar issues. Their rifles, however, were custom-built M4A1s with free-floating handguards. This improves accuracy as the handguard is attached to the rifle at the receiver only and at no point along the barrel. This process stops any minute vibrations from the stock, or any of the accessories mounted on rails, from impeding accuracy. They were also likely firing the then experimental Mk262 Mod0 round. The increased accuracy of Delta's rifles and ammunition, and the fact that they have the opportunity and training budget to shoot more often than any other unit in the world, were apparently overcoming the limitations of the smaller calibre. Perhaps tellingly, the Green Beret operators were carrying standard issue M4A1s firing the M885.

Its supporters claim the 6.8mm SPC has performed better than the 5.56 × 45mm in all key areas – and even apparently beat the Soviet 7.62 × 39mm in some. These requirements included improved barrier penetration, improved accuracy out to 500 metres and improved terminal effects, including from SBRs and carbines. The key challenge identified with the 6.8mm SPC is not one that can be easily surmounted by any large organisation such as SOCOM. Adoption of the calibre requires a new upper receiver and barrel to be installed on all issue M4A1s (and HK416s and Mk16s) and new magazines procured, as modified 5.56mm M4 magazines will only hold between twenty-five and twenty-eight rounds of the larger 6.8mm SPC cartridges.

To offer a counter to these otherwise glowing claims, the author has been told by former operators who have tested the 6.8mm SPC, that the round provides little real improvement in lethality over the 5.56 × 45mm, particularly with more modern bullet designs. The 6.8mm SPC certainly extends the effective range of the M4A1 but one wonders if so much effort would have been expended in developing the new calibre if the Mk262 or Mk318 had been commonly available at the time?

There has been no official, or unofficial, confirmation of the 6.8mm SPC being trialled in combat but it would be most unlikely if the calibre has not seen at least some limited field testing in Afghanistan. A persistent tale of limited US Army Special Forces adoption by one Special Forces battalion that supposedly ordered commercial 6.8mm SPC uppers for a tour in Afghanistan has been questioned by commentators knowledgeable in SOCOM procurement processes.

Competing with the 6.8mm SPC is the longer range 6.5 × 38mm or 6.5mm Grendel. The 6.5mm achieves and retains higher velocities than the 6.8mm SPC and is considered to tip the scales in accuracy at extended ranges. It suffers from the same adoption challenges as the 6.8mm, however, namely a new upper receiver, barrel and magazine are required. The standard thirty round M4 magazine can only accommodate twenty-six of the 6.5mm Grendels. Like the 6.8mm SPC, there is also no official word on field testing although the author would be surprised if the 6.5mm Grendel hadn't been fired in anger at some point in Afghanistan. Even if the 6.5mm Grendel and the 6.8mm SPC have been used to shoot insurgents, have there been enough shootings to start to understand how the round performs in human bodies rather than ballistic gelatine?

The third new cartridge in the frame is the .300 Blackout, or the 7.62 × 35mm as it is apparently now termed, within SOCOM. The .300 Blackout was originally developed in the late 2000s at the behest of a JSOC unit, but first publically unveiled in 2010. The story goes that DEVGRU specifically requested an improved CQB cartridge and matching weapon system that could be used with or without a suppressor and that exhibited good terminal ballistics beyond 200 metres. DEVGRU were dissatisfied with their suppressed MP7A1s in terms of range and incapacitation effects and were looking for a replacement. The result was the .300 Blackout and the AAC Honey Badger.

The great advantage of the .300 Blackout is its flexibility; using a magazine of subsonic rounds a suppressed .300 Blackout carbine with a very short 9-inch barrel will produce sound levels comparable to the suppressed 9×19mm MP5SD3 submachine gun but with far superior terminal effects. With a magazine change to supersonic ammunition, the weapon can then be used to engage targets at extended ranges out to apparently the 400 metre mark with ballistics similar to the Soviet 7.62×39mm.

The first carbine to be developed to chamber this new round was the AAC Honey Badger which, when fired, sounds at least as quiet as the suppressed MP7A1 and MP5SD series. The Honey Badger features an integrated suppressor and thus can effortlessly handle both subsonic and supersonic loads with just a magazine change. The Honey Badger has been supposedly trialled in combat in Afghanistan by DEVGRU elements and received a positive report card. The round has apparently also been tested by UK Special Forces,

A Ranger in Afghanistan zeroes his Block 2 M4A1 in 2013. The weapon is fitted with the full-length Daniels Defense rail, AN/PEQ-15 illuminator, a well-worn Knight's suppressor and an Elcan Specter DR optic. Note the Ranger to his right carries an American flag secured to his MOLLE straps in case of a casualty. (*1LT Tyler N. Ginter, US Army*)

but these results are unknown. The .300 Blackout of all of the new cartridges offers the greatest chance of at least a limited adoption amongst some SOF units. Whether it will eclipse the 5.45 × 45mm seems unlikely and its role will remain largely specialist.

Tier One SOF units like the SAS and Delta can and do test and evaluate whatever weapons they wish. They have their own budgets and procurement systems that allow them to purchase any weapon, ammunition or equipment they think will increase their effectiveness. Yet despite this incredible latitude, they continue to choose 5.56 × 45mm calibre rifles and carbines as their principal shoulder weapons. With their formidable combat experience over more than a decade, and remembering that operators from these units often conducted three to four raids a night in Iraq and Afghanistan, why would they continue to do so if tales of the gross ineffectiveness of the 5.56 × 45mm were true?

Tactics and Techniques

The biggest misconception around assault rifles is the use of selective fire. Put simply, special operators (and most infantrymen) will use aimed single shots, reserving bursts for clearing rooms or trenches. Operators will often fire so quickly that the string sounds like a short burst. The special operator must be able to quickly and reliably engage and put hostiles out of action. Often these lethal encounters are conducted at night at extremely close quarters and with non-combatants in the immediate vicinity. As we have seen with other weapons, all combat shooting revolves around fast and accurate placement of shots at those areas of the body most likely to incapacitate the foe.

Many books and films claim the so-called double tap is the preferred shooting technique of the special operator when firing his carbine or rifle. There is some truth to this in that most professional armies are trained to fire aimed pairs or double taps at their targets. It increases the likelihood of a hit and is a good drill, encouraging aimed fire. Some police training includes firing two rounds and then pausing to assess their effect before continuing to fire if necessary. As discussed in the pistol chapter, neither of these techniques takes into consideration the nature of the opposition the special operations soldier often faces.

Sometimes the terrorist or insurgent will be wearing body armour; sometimes they will be wearing a suicide bomb vest; and sometimes they will be under the influence of amphetamines or similar narcotics. The operator is trained to instantly recognise the threat and respond appropriately. Some units train for centre of body mass hits, others for the pelvic girdle followed by the chest. Some still train for a pair to the chest followed by a pair to the head.

Former SEAL Mark Owen:

> . . . I started to shoot. Tracking from one fighter to the next, I pumped two
> or three rounds into each blur's chest, pausing only for a second to make

Australian Commandos preparing to deploy back to Iraq in 2014 train on a timed course of fire. The operator is firing an M4A5 with 40mm M203 grenade launcher, a Troy vertical grip mounted on the M203, Scout weapon light, what appears to be an AN/PEQ-15 and a newly issued Elcan Specter optic. Also of interest is his holstered, weapon light mounted 9 × 19mm H&K USP Tactical. (*SGT Hamish Paterson, Australian Defense Force*)

sure the fighter went down. There was no yelling or screaming, just the muffled sound of my rounds cutting into the enemy fighters.

Owen was using a suppressed 5.56 × 45mm HK416 on this operation. He later describes moving into the room and with a teammate '*making sure they were no longer a threat*' by re-engaging the insurgents until there was no visible movement. Such 'insurance' or 'security' rounds may seem callous but when dealing with an enemy that may have a bomb strapped to themselves, there can be no room for doubt.

Technology has also affected how operators shoot. The close combat optic has sped up engagement times and improved accuracy. There are several principal types and the most common are the Aimpoint, the EO Tech, the Short Dot and the ACOG. All operate slightly differently and provide the shooter with distinct advantages and disadvantages. All of these optics offer the ability to keep both eyes open, unlike with traditional magnified telescopic scopes.

The Aimpoint is arguably the oldest type and normally features a non-magnified optic that superimposes a red dot over the target. This is not a laser as the dot is contained within the optic itself. The operator places the red dot

A Norwegian Marinejegerkommandoen (MJK) special operator aiming a Colt Canada
5.56 × 45mm C8SFW carbine with Aimpoint CompM4 red dot optic. (*Kelly Stumpf, Colt Canada*)

over the target and theoretically his bullet should strike where the red dot is
positioned. The Aimpoint is available in a myriad of types and sizes but the
two most common in SOF hands are the M68 and the Micro and have traditionally been favoured by the Navy SEALs, although the British SAS also
deploy the later. The Aimpoint offers a very fast sight picture at close to
medium ranges and is a reliable and well-liked design.

EO Tech Holographic Weapon Sights have become the choice for the
majority of the world's SOF for a number of reasons. The EO Tech doesn't
require the shooter to look down a tube or scope. If he can see the target reticle
on the EO Tech, he can fire. This means the EO Tech is exceptionally well
suited for CQB work and shooting accurately from stress positions and poor
angles, over or around barricades or while wearing respirators or other
hazardous material protective equipment. It will also operate if the glass is
broken and does not fog or be affected by temperature variations.

Later models are also night vision capable, meaning the reticle is viewable
through night vision goggles. EO Techs will also work with another recent
innovation that has seen extensive use with SOF in Afghanistan, the switch-
to-side EO Tech Magnifier. A similar system is also available for the Aimpoint
and is basically a three-power magnifier that sits behind the EO Tech or
Aimpoint and uses the optic to provide the reticle or dot whilst magnifying
the field of vision. It allows a primarily CQB sight to be used for longer range

Australian Commandos from 2 Commando Regiment in Afghanistan in 2010. The lead Commando carries the 5.56 × 45mm M4A5 with Grip Pod bipod vertical foregrip, Trijicon ACOG with RMR mini red dot, AN/PEQ-2 and Knight's QD suppressor. *(Australian Defense Force)*

shooting. Both the EO Tech and Aimpoint variants also swing out of the way when not required, so an operator can use the magnifier when fighting their way into a target compound, for example, and then flip it out of the way to use the primary CQB sight at close quarters to engage hostiles inside the compound.

Delta and the Rangers discovered in Mogadishu in 1993 that Aimpoints did not allow for target positive identification at longer ranges as they lacked any magnification. A civilian optic called the Microdot was used for the interim period, a variable power sight that projected an Aimpoint-like red dot. Former Delta operator Larry Vickers was instrumental in designing a new optic that would allow shooters to use it at CQB distances as a red dot whilst having variable, user set, magnifications to allow longer range target identification and engagement. That optic is the Schmidt & Bender CQB Short Dot and allows dial-able magnification between one and four power in a similar fashion to the Elcan Specter DR we'll look at in a moment. It also computes bullet drop for several weapons systems including the M4A1 and the SR-25.

The final principal type is the Trijicon ACOG or Advanced Combat Optic Gunsight. The ACOG is a magnified sight that offers four power magnification in a rugged, optical tube. It has found much favour amongst SOF units in

A MARSOC Raider in Afghanistan with a 5.56 × 45mm M4A1 equipped with 40mm M203 launcher, Elcan Specter DR optic and, unusually as the Specter offers both an ×1 and ×1.5 magnification CQB setting, off-set RMR red dot sight for close quarter shooting.
(*Sgt Pete Thibodeau, US Marine Corps*)

Afghanistan including amongst UK Special Forces who tend to deploy either the ACOG or the Aimpoint Micro. The ACOG is often matched with a much smaller red dot optic that is mounted on top of the ACOG, offering a close combat optic when the ACOG's magnification is not needed. US Marines in Fallujah reported a steep increase in headshots against insurgents when the ACOG was deployed.

The ACOG, EO Tech, Short Dot and Aimpoint may be the most common but they are certainly not the last word in combat optics. The US Army Rangers and Special Forces have been deploying to Afghanistan with another type of optic, the Elcan Specter DR (Dual Role) or SU-230/PVS in SOCOM terms. The Specter allows the user to set the magnification, up to four power, in the field using a simple lever. At one and one-and-a-half power magnification, the sight shows a red dot; as the magnification is increased, the red dot is replaced by the more familiar targeting reticle. Like many current optics, the Specter is also designed to work in concert with clip-on thermal and night vision viewers that can be mounted to the Picatinny rail in front of the optic to provide a night vision capability to the sight.

As the majority of SOF operations are conducted at night, one of the most important attachments on an operator's carbine is his infra-red illuminator.

The small arms of Afghan special operations, the Police Partnered Units. Seen here are Hungarian AMD-65s in 7.62 × 39mm with aftermarket rail kit and what appears to be M68 Aimpoint optics. Other units use a range of AKs, M4s and M16A2s. (*Australian Defense Force*)

Various makes are used although the AN/PEQ-15 or LA-5 Advanced Target Pointer Illuminator Aiming Laser (ATPIAL) is one of the most common amongst SOF. Along with a visible spectrum red dot laser (which is most commonly used to zero the system), the ATPIAL can project an infra-red beam only viewable through night vision goggles. Along with improving accuracy at night, the system can be used to mark targets for other units or air support. Aircraft such as some helicopters, including the MH-47E Chinook, the AC-130 gunship and UAVs like the MQ-1 Predator, mount an onboard infra-red searchlight that can be used to illuminate an area as if it was daylight, as long as you are wearing night vision goggles. For an insurgent enemy without such technology, they are none the wiser.

If you remember the scene in the film *Zero Dark Thirty* when the SEALs are approaching the target house in Abbottabad, the green beams visible were their ATPIAL infra-red lasers, although the Hollywood origins of that scene are betrayed by the fact that the operators keep their lasers on (and occasionally 'painted' each other in a display of poor muzzle awareness). In reality, operators are trained only to switch on the laser as they identify an enemy, in a similar manner to their weapon lights. The shot is taken and the enemy is engaged. The laser is switched off immediately as the enemy may be equipped with night vision themselves and the beams will betray the operator's location.

A US Army Green Beret trains Afghan partnered units in room clearing techniques in Kabul, 2013. His weapon appears to be a CQB barrel M4A1 fitted with AN/PEQ-15, scout light and Elcan Specter optic with RMR mini sight. (*SFC Brehl Garza, US Army*)

This image graphically illustrates the use of the AN/PEQ-2 and AN/PEQ-15 infra-red illuminators. Only visible through night vision goggles or optics, the infra-red beam can be used to identify targets or in extremis to mark locations for air support. (*SSG Jeremy D. Crisp, US Army*)

Current Trends

The biggest trend amongst the special operations community during the War on Terror has been the rise to prominence of the 5.56 × 45mm short barrel carbine. It is carried as the primary shoulder weapon by most units and, with the right ammunition, is ideal for operators conducting raids or similar operations in confined spaces. These operators are often deploying from helicopters or ground vehicles where any reduction in weapon size is of benefit. They are very handy, compact and lightweight and can engage targets out to 200 metres or more. They can also accept a myriad of accessories and the now near mandatory sound suppressor.

For all their benefits to the SOF shooter, the carbines also offer some drawbacks, some we have already discussed. The short barrel carbines use a shorter gas system than their full-length assault rifle cousins and this increases the felt recoil. It also increases pressure and heat build-up inside the weapon that can lead to stoppages after extended periods of firing. Along with reducing the range and accuracy of the carbine, the short barrel also increases the muzzle blast – one of the reasons why suppressors have become so popular.

Despite these disadvantages, the short barrel carbine just keeps getting shorter. Even taking into account the drop in velocity and resulting effect

An Australian SASR operator in Afghanistan trains with his hand-painted 5.56 × 45mm M4A5. It is fitted with a range of accessories including a Troy full-length rail, LWRC folding foregrip, VLTOR stock, Surefire light, Trijicon ACOG with mini red dot sight and what appears to be an AN/PEQ-2 infra-red illuminator. (*CPL Chris Moore, Australian Defence Force*)

A US Army Special Forces operator in Afghanistan in 2010 carrying a 5.56 × 45mm M4A1 with Elcan Specter DR optic. Note the vertical foregrip fitted to his underslung 40mm M203. (*SPC Nicholas T. Lloyd, US Army*)

on incapacitation potential, a short barrel carbine in 5.56 × 45mm is still more effective ballistically than a 9 × 19mm MP5. We have earlier noted the advancements in bullet design for the 5.56 × 45mm with rounds now designed to wring the most performance capable from short barrels. We've also mentioned the development of several new calibres. The most promising in SOF terms is the .300 Blackout that we will look at it further detail at the close of this chapter.

Along with short barrel carbines, the biggest current trend is the adoption of further rail mountings on operator's carbines like those produced by Troy, Daniel Defense and Knight's. These are now generally free-floating to avoid any contact with the barrel that may impinge upon accuracy and often extend out right to the carbine's muzzle, making the best use of the available real estate. The prevalence of Picatinny rails now sees a typical SOF carbine mounting an infra-red laser illuminator, a white light tactical flashlight, a sound suppressor or aftermarket flash hider, a forward vertical foregrip (some combining a retractable bipod) and, at the minimum, a close combat optic such as an EO Tech or Aimpoint. These optics are often slaved with a magnifier, as described earlier, that can be flipped away when not needed. Of course the weight of all these accessories often negates the point of carrying a

A MARSOC Raider pictured in Afghanistan in 2013 with a SOPMOD Block 2 M4A1 platform mounting an EOTech optic and magnifier, AN/PEQ-15 illuminator, Surefire white light and Knight's QD suppressor. *(Sgt Pete Thibodeau; US Marine Corps)*

lighter weight weapon like a carbine in the first place, but they have become relatively standard issue amongst special operators.

Individual Weapon Summaries

Colt M4A1

The M4A1 is a selective fire (fully and semi-automatic) 5.56 × 45mm carbine fed from a thirty-round detachable magazine. Without any accessories mounted, the M4A1 weighs in at 3.4kg with a loaded magazine fitted. In comparison, the full-sized M16A4 rifle weighs some 4kg loaded and is around 6 inches longer at 39.5 inches, versus the M4A1's 33 inches with its collapsible stock extended. This reduction in length and weight makes the M4A1 far preferable when operating within vehicles and during CQB in urban environments and is one of the key reasons for its success within the US military's SOF units.

For a recent example, Marines carrying the full length M16A4 found it unwieldy whilst clearing insurgent occupied buildings in Fallujah in 2004 and stated a preference for the carbine version. The Rangers of Task Force Ranger in Mogadishu, Somalia had a similar experience with their M16A2s during the Black Hawk Down incident in 1993 and almost immediately transitioned

Australian Commandos provide security for a US Army MEDEVAC flight in Afghanistan in 2010. Both operators carry 5.56 × 45mm M4A5 (the Australian designation for the M4A1) fitted with M68 Aimpoint optics and AN/PEQ-2 illuminators. (*LT Aaron Oldaker; Australian Defence Force*)

to the M4A1, then known as the Colt Model 927, in the year following the fateful battle. Although the M4A1 has its detractors, and we will discuss some of its drawbacks in a moment, it is generally well liked amongst operators who carry and use the weapon in combat, particularly at the range envelopes it was intended for.

The M4A1 used by SOCOM is complemented by what is known as the SOPMOD Kit, now in two variations known as Blocks or Increments: the SOPMOD Block I and SOPMOD Block II (with a Block III on the drawing board). SOPMOD stands for Special Operations Peculiar Modification and these kits offer a range of Picatinny rail mounted accessories that the shooter can select from based on specific operational requirements or mission type. According to the Special Missions Project Office at Crane Naval Warfare Surface Centre who developed the initial SOPMOD Kit, the intention was to *'increase operator survivability and lethality by enhanced weapon performance, target acquisition, signature suppression, and fire control.'* Its development was ushered in by the until then ad-hoc attachment of weapon lights and Aimpoint optics to carbines by JSOC units such as Delta.

A poster displaying a range of accessories offered in the SOPMOD Block 1 Kit. Many are known by their military designations rather than their commercial names- the ECOS-N is the Aimpoint CompM for instance and the 4X Day Optical Scope is the Trijicon ACOG. *(USSOCOM)*

The initial SOPMOD Kit, the Block I, came with a bewildering array of items. In terms of optics to mount on the M4A1's flat-top receiver rail, there were four Trijicon four-power magnification ACOGs and two Trijicon Reflex sights, along with four non-magnified Aimpoint M68 red dot sights. The Block I Kit also came with a number of Knight's Rail Adaptor Systems (RAS) to replace the cylindrical forearm of the M4A1, vertical handgrips (the first examples of the so-called 'gangster grips' that became so prevalent amongst US infantry), folding back-up iron sights in case the optic was disabled, two Knight's Quick Detachable (QD) sound suppressors and a number of infrared, white light and laser illuminators. The kit was topped off with an AN/PVS-14 passive night vision scope. It also included a specially adapted 40mm M203A1 grenade launcher and mounting system with a shorter, 9-inch barrel to accommodate the M4A1's reduced overall length.

The M4A1's success has seen it and the M4 base model replace the M16A2 throughout the US Army with every soldier now receiving the same rifle as many of the SOF units of SOCOM, albeit without many of the custom

The later SOPMOD Block 2 Kit offering Daniels Defense full-length RIS rails and a range of upgraded optical, white light and night vision accessories. Block 2 is still being rolled out across SOCOM with units like the Rangers and Special Forces receiving the kits as a priority. (*USSOCOM*)

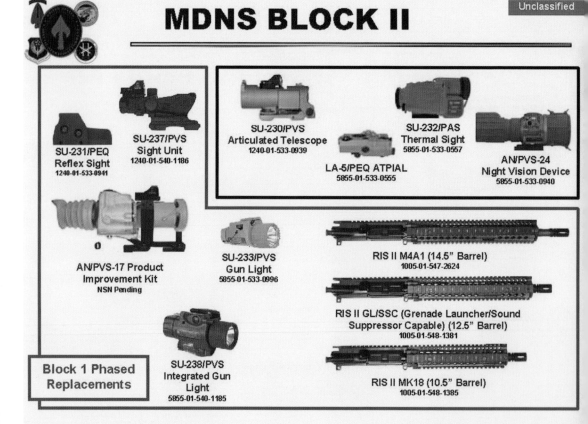

accessories of the SOPMOD kits. The major differences between M4 and M4A1 is the barrel, which is heavier on the M4A1 to better reduce operating temperature when firing the weapon on fully-automatic, and the fire selector that offers automatic rather than the M4's three-round burst setting. Both weapons feature a distinctive step cut into their barrels to allow the mounting of the M203A1 grenade launcher and are otherwise visually very similar.

The M4A1 SOPMOD is issued to all SOCOM units to include the Army Rangers and Special Forces, the Navy SEALs, Marine Raiders and Air Force Special Tactics. Each Special Forces ODA A-Team, for instance, was issued two full SOPMOD kits prior to the initial infiltrations into Afghanistan in October 2001, whilst each sixteen man SEAL Platoon was issued four kits to divide between them. The M4A1 SOPMOD is also seen extensively deployed in the hands of special operators around the globe, from the French 1er RPIMa to the Australian Special Forces.

Australian Special Forces use M4A1s with Troy TRX Picatinny rails that are known locally as the M4A5 and visually resemble an American Block II. The Australians, including 2nd Commando Regiment and the SASR, chose the M4A1 platform due to its capability for mounting rail accessories and its over-the-beach performance, along with commonality with Coalition SOF they are likely to be operating alongside. The Australian Army issue 5.56 × 45mm F88, a locally produced Steyr AUG variant, has only been relatively

A Special Forces operator providing overwatch in southern Afghanistan 2014. He carries a Block 1 M4A1 with suppressor and Elcan Specter optic. *(ISAF)*

recently retrofitted with a Picatinny rail capability. The latest version, just being issued at the time of publication of this book, is the EF88 and features multiple rails along with other enhancements.

As discussed earlier, the very factor that makes M4A1 carbines so attractive to the special operations community is also its greatest failing: the short barrel. The M4A1, with its 14.5-inch barrel firing the standard issue M885 or NATO SS109, suffers from a rapid loss of velocity at ranges beyond 200 metres. This and the ineffectiveness of the M885 and similar ball designs, as we have covered, has led much of the current negative press surrounding the suitability of the M4A1 and M4 designs for current conflicts.

Both the M4 and M4A1 also suffer in sandy conditions, as indeed do most weapons, and they need to be carefully maintained – somewhat confusingly, they shouldn't be over lubricated as this will attract sand that may cause stoppages, but conversely dry lubricant options often don't work in the Iraqi and Afghan heat. In a series of Army tests in 2007, the M4 was subjected to increasing amounts of dust. It came last in these tests against the HK416, the Mk16 SCAR and the experimental Heckler and Koch XM8. All of the test M4 barrels required replacing whilst none of the other weapons' barrels did.

The carbine was not designed for prolonged rapid firing either. At Wanat in Eastern Afghanistan in July 2008, a US Army Patrol Base was almost overrun by insurgents resulting in the deaths of nine servicemen. Part of the blame was placed on the M4 with accounts mentioning soldiers firing until the barrels were white-hot and at least one soldier firing a dozen magazines rapidly through his M4 until it suffered a catastrophic stoppage and failed. The soldiers also suffered stoppages with their M249 Squad Automatic Weapons. A staff sergeant present at the battle later explained:

> My M4 quit firing and would no longer charge when I tried to correct the malfunction. I grabbed the Engineers' SAW and tried to fire. It would not fire, so I lifted the feed tray, tried clearing it out and tried to fire again. It would not.

The M4 is designed to be fired safely up to fifteen times a minute semi-automatically and, for brief periods, up to three magazines can be fired fully automatically again in one minute (with the M4 obviously, these need to be fired using the three-round burst setting). Anything much beyond this limit and the weapon's barrel and receiver will heat up to unacceptable levels, potentially causing dangerous cook-offs after approximately 140 rounds are fired at this rapid rate.

SOCOM defines a cook-off as *when a live round is left in the chamber or in contact with the chamber of a hot weapon and heats to the point that the propellant is ignited*. Continued rapid firing beyond this point will eventually cause the barrel to droop and the receiver to lock up completely unless the weapon is

A Green Beret with an M4A1 showing how carbines can be set-up in widely differing ways, even within the same small unit. This soldier's M4A1 features older Knight's rails but matched with an Elcan Specter DR optic and now standard AN/PEQ-15 illuminator. The operator also uses Magpul PMAGs with round count window. *(SPC Connor Mendez, US Army)*

cleared and ceases firing. An M4 takes approximately thirty minutes to cool to ambient temperatures.

As noted, the M4A1 was designed with fully automatic fire in mind and features a heavier barrel than the M4 which helps reduce, but does not eliminate, this heat build-up. This barrel is known as the SOCOM Profile Barrel. This is of considerable importance to special operators as, for instance, they will routinely fire several magazines on fully auto during a break contact drill as they attempt to suppress enemy firing points. Ranger Lieutenant Nate Self, leader of the Ranger Quick Reaction Force (QRF) that had their Chinook helicopter shot down in eastern Afghanistan during an attempt to rescue a trapped SEAL recce team, experienced a potentially fatal stoppage with his M4A1 during a close range gunfight with insurgents:

> My red dot reticle floated center of mass of his green jacket. Squeeze the trigger straight back. Click. No round fired, no recoil. Just the clicking of the firing pin against an expended casing already in my rifle's chamber. I dropped to the ground. My rifle had malfunctioned, and I had to clear it.

Lieutenant Self had experienced a failure to eject and attempted to clear the stoppage with his cleaning rod. As Murphy's Law intervened, as it will often do at the most importune times in combat, the cleaning rod itself broke leaving Lieutenant Self with an inoperable rifle and no way to get it back into the fight. He subsequently braved enemy PKM machine-gun fire to return to their downed Chinook to recover another M4A1 from a fallen Ranger.

Self wasn't the only operator to experience a dangerous weapons failure during the operation. A Black Team recce-sniper element operating under the call sign MAKO 31 inserted onto a nearby peak as part of the larger Operation Anaconda. Tasked with establishing a covert observation post, the SEALs instead discovered a 12.7mm DShK heavy machine-gun position manned by Chechen or Uzbek insurgents perched upon the location selected for their observation post. Co-ordinating with a circling AC-130 Spectre gunship, the SEALs engaged the insurgents with their suppressed rifles before suffering not one, but two stoppages, after firing only a single round each. As the two SEALs desperately cleared their weapons, a third kept the enemy suppressed until the others could re-join the battle. After a surviving insurgent attempted to suppress the SEALs with his PKM, the operators fell back and called in the might of the AC-130 that decisively ended the contact with several rounds from its 105mm howitzer.

These stoppages may well have been caused by the freezing temperatures encountered high in the Afghan mountains, although Lieutenant Self's incident may also have been pure bad luck. Weapons maintenance was clearly not the culprit here due to the pedigree of the Rangers and SEALs involved as they are hardly the types to shirk such essential duties. Indeed the Rangers took their weapon maintenance so seriously that many, including Lieutenant Self, zip-tied cleaning rods to their weapons. What exact rifles the SEALs of MAKO 31 were carrying is unknown but have been described in accounts as M4s, however due to their role as recce-snipers, suppressed 5.56 × 45mm SEAL Recce Rifles are the much more likely option. Discussed in detail in the next chapter, the Recce Rifle was something of a predecessor to the 5.56 × 45mm Mk12 Mod0 and Mod1 Special Purpose Rifles. These Recce Rifles were custom built from the ground up for the SEALs by Crane and should have been very reliable.

Delta used rather distinctive M4A1 carbines in Afghanistan and later Iraq until the HK416 became available. These M4A1s featured the Knight's Armament Company More Real Estate (MRE) proprietary Picatinny rails on a 16-inch barrelled M4A1 that actually appear visually somewhat similar to the SEAL Recce Rifle. The MRE rails became a Delta favourite as it extended side grip rails right out to the muzzle allowing forward grips to be mounted, along with lights and visible spectrum and infra-red lasers. Knight's Armament Company was the first to offer a range of non-floating and later free floating rail kits, allowing operators to mount accessories to their rifles. Prior to the invention of these Picatinny rail kits, Delta operators used a clamp mount to

A SEAL from SEAL Team One zeroes his ACOG equipped 5.56 × 45mm M4A1 which is also equipped with a Knight's suppressor, older AN/PEQ-2 illuminator and aftermarket Harris bipod. This is a similar set-up to the SEAL Recce or Recon Rifles that later led to the development of the Mk12 SPR although the Recce tended toward longer 16-inch, free floating barrels. *(PH1 (SW) Arlo Abrahamson)*

affix weapon lights under the barrels of their Colt Carbines. Indeed according to Larry Vickers, early Delta carbines featured SCUBA flashlights clamped under the barrel, whilst the Rangers affixed a Mini Maglite under the barrels of their M16A2s and carbines.

The other distinctive characteristic of the Delta carbines from this time period was the custom made forward grip fitted with a red button on/off switch for their weapon light. This forward grip was so popular within the unit that examples were later ported across to the HK416. Former operator John 'Shrek' McPhee explained that it was originally made from an M4 pistol grip and later machined to include two buttons that could trigger both the SureFire tactical light and the infra-red laser unit. Two versions of the grip existed, one angled and one vertical, dependant on operator requirements. The Polish GROM SOF unit that has operated closely with Delta and the SEALs since its earliest days also purchased a number of these grips from Knight's.

Delta carbines almost universally mounted EOTech models, a combat optic that they have used for many years and continue to do so although other types such as the Schmidt & Bender Short Dot have also gained prominence since the introduction of the HK416. The Rangers have continued to carry the

A historical image of a Delta operator providing close protection in the Balkans in 1996. The genesis of later innovations can be seen in his weapon – a 16-inch free-floating barrel M4A1 with Knight's vertical foregrip and what appears to be an Aimpoint red dot sight. *(USASOC)*

M4A1 although now built to SOPMOD Block II standards. The current speci-fication for the majority of Rangers is the M4A1 fitted with the Daniel Defense RIS II extended rails out to the muzzle, an EO Tech 553 holographic sight (some variable magnification Elcan Specter DRs are also used), an LA-5/PEQ infra-red illuminator, Tango Down or Grip Pod vertical foregrip, and an Insight M3X Scout or WMX200 weapon light. Ranger dog handlers and other operators who require a more compact weapon carry the M4A1 with a SOPMOD Block II 10.3 inch barrel upper receiver. These shorter carbines are often also carried by the designated Ranger assaulters who will conduct the actual entry and exploitation of a target location.

The SEALs also deploy the M4A1 alongside their shorter Mk18 CQBR uppers. Indeed SEALs deployed to Iraq and Afghanistan routinely brought along two uppers, one with a standard 14.5-inch barrel and equipped with an Aimpoint or Elcan, and the CQBR mounting an EO Tech. The Marine Raiders of MARSOC carry Block II equipped M4A1s that are very similar to those carried by the Rangers, although their weapons are officially termed the

M4A1 Close Quarter Battle Weapon (CQBW). The Raiders and Marine Force Recon also deploy the 10.3-inch barrel when conducting VBSS (Visit-Board-Search-Seizure) missions as the shorter barrel is ideal for shipboard CQB.

The Army Special Forces purchased a number of commercial 10-inch M4A1 barrels soon after the beginning of OEF as the requirement for a compact carbine to use whilst clearing Afghan compounds quickly became evident. Since then the ODAs have used M4A1s equipped with both barrel lengths and the full suite of SOPMOD accessories. Today they often use suppressed Block II carbines mounting the Elcan Specter or ACOG. The Special Forces are often operating as mentors in the field to Afghan or Iraqi Army units and need a magnified sight for both positive target identification and, with the Mk262 round, to allow engagement beyond typical carbine distances.

Despite various products and calibres loudly vying to replace the M4A1, the carbine is not going anywhere just yet. M4A1+ is the name of the latest US military request for a product improved M4A1. Apparently this M4A1+ will act as a mid-life extension for the venerable carbine until a truly evolutionary replacement becomes available. The M4A1+ shopping list reads like a custom SOF M4A1 the likes of which Delta were carrying in the late nineties – a match grade, free-floating barrel, an extended set of Picatinny rails, an enhanced trigger pull, an enlarged charging handle and folding back-up iron sights. All of which, combined with the improved range and lethality of the

Two unidentified US Army special operators conducting a dynamic course of fire with 5.56 × 45mm SOPMOD Block 2 M4A1s with 10.3-inch uppers mounted with EOTechs, M3X weapon lights and AN/PEQ-15s. (*SGT Marcus Butler, USASOC*)

A very clear shot of a typical Ranger weapon set-up circa 2014. His 5.56 × 45mm Block 2 M4A1 is relatively spartan with only an EOTech, Surefire weapon light and AN/PEQ-15. Note how the weapon has been hand-painted but has chipped through extensive operational use. *(PFC Dacotah Lane, US Army)*

Mk262 and the Mk318 cartridge, may mean that the M4A1 can finally shrug off its detractors and the baggage that has accompanied its M16 heritage.

Mk18 CQBR

As mentioned previously, the US Navy SEALs currently issue both standard length M4A1s and the Mk18 CQBR upper receiver. The only SEALs to be currently issued the Heckler and Koch 416 – and the MP7A1 submachine gun – are DEVGRU. The most common SEAL rifle is the Mk18 Mod0 which features a 10-inch CQB barrel and measures only 32 inches in overall length with the stock collapsed, making it ideal for use in the narrow confines of ships. In all respects the Mk18 Mod0 is essentially an SBR version of the M4A1 and in fact was originally made from simply cutting down M4A1 barrels and mounting a new flash hider. Later versions featured custom Colt and LMT barrels in both 10.3 and 10.5-inch lengths.

The Mk18 CQBR was developed by Crane specifically for the SEALs as an upper receiver and barrel unit that could be easily swapped out with their standard M4A1 upper, although it is also now deployed as a complete carbine by naval boarding parties and Navy EOD (Explosive Ordnance Disposal). It was developed largely to replace the 9 × 19mm MP5-N SMG in SEAL service. Some early Mk18s fitted with Crane developed stocks were deployed by

A very clear image of the US Navy issue Mk18 Mod0 CQBR carbine in 5.56 × 45mm carried by a Navy SEAL. The optic is the Aimpoint CompM. SEALs deploy with both the CQBR upper and the full-length 14.5-inch M4A1. (*Naval Special Warfare*)

A Navy SEAL emerges from the sea carrying his fins and a 5.56 × 45mm Mk18 Mod0 CQBR carbine fitted with an Aimpoint red dot sight, Tango Down foregrip, Surefire weapon light and Knight's suppressor. (*Naval Special Warfare*)

DEVGRU in Afghanistan when they were tasked with providing close protection to then Afghan President Hamid Karzai. These Mk18s were unusual in appearance in that the stocks featured several rubber bands fitted to keep the stock from accidentally collapsing – a low tech solution to a potentially fatal problem that was solved in later models.

The Mk18 is now typically employed with the Aimpoint Comp M2 red dot optic although some SEALs have switched the Aimpoint out for various models of the EO Tech holographic sight. The Mk18 can also be equipped with the Knight's Armament Company QDSS-NT4 suppressor. As noted earlier the Rangers, MARSOC and Special Forces are often seen carrying short barrel M4A1s that are sometimes misidentified as the Mk18 CQBR. In fact these 'shorties' are SOPMOD Block IIs with the optional 10.3-inch barrel.

Heckler and Koch 416

The Heckler and Koch 416 is the rifle that killed Usama bin Laden. That should be enough to impress even the harshest critics of the 5.56 × 45mm and the basic M4 platform. It has also killed a large number of terrorists and insurgents since it was first deployed in 2004. Originally known as the HKM4 prior to a lawsuit from Colt over the use of its trademark, the 416 emerged from an outstanding SOCOM Confined Spaces Carbine requirement that had

A Force Recon Marine test fires a 5.56 × 45mm HK416 with underslung 40mm M320 grenade launcher during joint training with Malaysian special operators (who issue the 416). Note the forward mounted Trijicon RMR optic. (*LCpl David J. Adams, US Marine Corps*)

existed prior to 2001 looking for an ultra-compact, side-folding stock carbine for JSOC units.

H&K already had an excellent relationship with Delta and with Larry Vickers who was serving at Delta at the time in charge of small arms development and testing for the unit. The German firm offered to carry out a product improvement project on the M4A1 to address Delta's specific needs, following on from their successful programme for the British Army's L85A2. One of the principal requirements was for the carbine to be made far more reliable, particularly after extended fully-automatic or rapid fire. Instead of a product improvement, H&K literally built Delta a brand-new weapon platform, the HK416.

The new carbine's short-stroke gas piston operating system was developed from the type used in the H&K G36 rifle. It didn't heat up like the M4A1's direct impingement system and it didn't create the same levels of carbon build-up from continuous firing. Indeed it was claimed the 416 deposited only 10 per cent of the carbon build-up of an M4A1. Even with a suppressor, the new carbine generated something approaching only 25 per cent of the carbon a suppressed M4A1 would. All of this, along with a new H&K magazine from the L85A2/SA80A2 product improvement programme, resulted in a more reliable weapon than the M4A1. The new weapon could also handle rapid firing more safely and for much longer periods than the M4A1.

As a final test before being issued to a Delta squadron departing on operations to Iraq in 2004, one of the first production carbines fitted with the CQB 10-inch barrel was subjected to a 15,000 round torture test. The newly christened HK416 passed with flying colours without a single stoppage. By 2006, all of Delta and DEVGRU had swapped out their M4A1s for the 416. Other units adopted the 416 if they could bypass military bureaucracy like the then recently formed Asymmetric Warfare Group (AWG). The AWG were forced in 2008 to hand in their 416s thanks to that very same military bureaucracy although they did manage to keep their 9 × 19mm Glock 19 pistols.

A 16.5-inch barrel 5.56 × 45mm Heckler and Koch HK416A5, the latest iteration of the classic 416 which introduced ambidextrous controls and a gas regulator designed for use with suppressors. *(Heckler & Koch)*

A battalion of the 1st Special Forces Group placed a unit order for HK416 uppers in 2007 but other than that and the JSOC adoption, the 416 remains a specialist weapon within SOCOM. Other nations have evaluated the weapon and it has been adopted by the Polish GROM and the German KSK and GSG9 as the G38. It was evaluated by Canadian and Australian Special Forces but so far has not been adopted. The 416 is perhaps surprisingly also in use by the Russian Tier One unit, the Alpha Group, along with a number of M4A1s of unknown origin.

The story of which weapon was used to kill Usama bin Laden became an internet guessing game immediately following the Abbottabad raid in May 2011. Rumours focused initially around a pistol, most likely the SEAL issue 9×19mm P226/Mk25, a weapon they most likely carried along with their suppressed HK45Cs. The P226 was soon discounted by the internet pundits and the focus shifted to the 7.62×51mm Colt CM901, the fact that the rifle was

A 5.56×45mm HK416 in the hands of an Asymmetric Warfare Group operator in Iraq in 2006. It appears to be fitted with a Schmidt & Bender Short Dot optic as developed for Delta. *(PH3 (AW) Shawn Hussong, US Navy)*

not yet in service with any US military unit didn't seem to matter. The guesses got a little more educated when the 4.6 × 30mm MP7A1 – a weapon that at least some of the operators, including the dog handler and some team leaders actually carried on the operation – was raised as a likely suspect, before reliable sources finally confirmed the 5.56 × 45mm HK416, probably firing the Barnes Optimized load.

The 416s DEVGRU carried on the mission were custom in every way. Apparently the 416s were fitted with custom AAC suppressors incorporating a glass-breaker device, SureFire Scout weapon lights, Magpul vertical forward grips, EO Tech optics and flip-away three-power magnifiers and the AN/PEQ-15 Advanced Target Pointer Illuminator Aiming Laser (ATPIAL) infra-red and visible laser illuminator. The Navy 416 is also often equipped with a Magpul forty-round extended magazine. DEVGRU have even used the SureFire sixty-round magazine for some time on specific Direct Action operations, although the length of the magazine makes firing from the prone position difficult.

Delta continues to provide operational feedback on the 416 in much the same way as they contributed to the continual development of the Knight's SR-25 which will be covered in a later chapter. In fact recent examples of the 416 carried by Delta feature a newly designed rail system from Geissele that now comes standard from Heckler and Koch on any 416s ordered for JSOC. Delta assaulters today most commonly carry the 10.4-inch barrel, often equipped with a SureFire suppressor with some operators providing close-in security on the objective carrying the 14.5-inch model. The SureFire suppressors Delta now uses were designed with a range of their weapon platforms in mind to minimise point-of-impact shift between weapons of the same calibre.

In terms of 416s chambered for new intermediate calibre, prototypes of a 416 chambered for the 6.8 × 43mm were built but as the round was never

An 11-inch barrel 5.56 × 45mm Heckler and Koch HK416A5 in RAL 8000 finish and fitted with EOTech optic and suppressor. The older model 10-inch version is apparently preferred by units such as Delta and DEVGRU. (*Heckler & Koch*)

adopted no production manufacture was begun, although the author would be surprised if a 6.8 × 43mm and a .300 Blackout variant hadn't already been tested at Fort Bragg and at Credenhill. The 416 has apparently not been formally trialled by UK Special Forces, however, the weapon has been tested. A UK Special Forces requirement for an Ultra Compact Carbine produced the first major 416 variant – the HK416C. The 416C was a 9-inch barrel model with a sliding MP5 style stock. It suffered reliability issues and was never produced in any numbers after it failed to win the UKSF Ultra Compact Carbine contract.

Mk16 Mod0 SCAR

The Mk16 Mod0 is the 5.56 × 45mm variant of the SCAR weapons family developed by Belgium firm Fabrique Nationale, SCAR standing for the rather ungainly Special Operations Forces Combat Assault Rifle. The Mk16 and its 7.62 × 51mm cousins the Mk17 and Mk20 – both of which will be discussed in

A rare image of the 7.62 × 51mm Mk17 SCAR Heavy converted to 5.56 × 45mm using the issue conversion kit. This Ranger unusually mounts his switch-to-side magnifier forward of his primary optic, just behind his AN/PEQ-15 and above his Scout weapon light. Note also how he has additionally secured all of the weapon's accessories with parachute cord to ensure none come loose during operations. *(PFC Dacotah Lane, US Army)*

the next chapter – all stem from a 2004 SOCOM contract to FN for the development of a modular assault rifle designed to accept different barrels and upper receivers in multiple lengths and calibre and including a replacement grenade launcher for the aging M203.

The Mk16 Mod0 is a 5.56×45mm short-stroke gas piston design that weighs in at some 3.29kg. It is thus comparable to the M4A1 at 35 inches overall length with its stock extended in its standard configuration. The Mk16 accepts 10, 14 and 18-inch barrels allowing the rifle to be configured as a CQB weapon, a standard length carbine, or a full length rifle for designated marksman roles. The author has fired the Mk16 with the standard 14-inch barrel and found it an exceptionally accurate and enjoyable rifle to shoot. Felt recoil was minimal and the weapon pointed and handled very well, including its ambidextrous controls.

Combat trials for the new weapon began in 2009. The Mk16 Mod0 and the heavier calibre Mk17 Mod0 were both issued to 1/75th Rangers during their 2009 Afghan deployment with C Company, the first to engage and kill a Taliban with one. The Rangers reportedly had mixed feelings about the 5.56×45mm weapon but were positive about the capabilities of the Mk17 as a marksman rifle. The SCAR in all variants proved popular with the SEALs who adopted the weapon enthusiastically, replacing their M4A1s and Mk18s for most tasks. It also saw widespread service with Air Force Special Tactics and some more limited use with Army Special Forces ODAs in Afghanistan. In 2010 however SOCOM announced that no further examples of the 5.56× 45mm version would be adopted. According to a statement at the time:

> After completing testing, US Special Operations Command decided to procure the 7.62mm Mk17 rifle, the 40mm Mk13 grenade launcher and the Mk20 Sniper Support rifle variants of the Special Operations Forces Combat Assault Rifle (SCAR) manufactured by FN Herstal. The command will not purchase the 5.56mm Mk16. The Mk17 will fill an existing capability gap for a 7.62mm rifle.
>
> The Mk16 does not provide enough of a performance advantage over the M4 to justify spending limited USSOCOM funds when competing priorities are taken into consideration.

Additional 7.62×51mm Mk17s were instead purchased by SOCOM along with 5.56×45mm conversion kits that effectively rendered the Mk16 obsolete. Only a year later however, Naval Special Warfare announced a further purchase of Mk16s along with more Mk17s, Mk20s and the Mk13 grenade launcher component to replace worn out examples in SEAL armouries. The Mk16 will certainly continue to see combat with the SEALs for the foreseeable future. Ironically it does mean that within SOCOM and JSOC there are effectively three different primary assault rifles/carbines in common use – the 416, the Mk16 and the M4A1.

Like the 416, few large scale adoptions of the Mk16 have yet taken place. Finnish Special Forces have recently adopted it as a *'reconnaissance weapon system'* and the rifle is not surprisingly used by the Belgian Army Special Force Group. It has also been adopted by a number of French COS units along with the National Police RAID unit and Germany's GSG9. A shortened version debuted in 2011 called the SCAR PDW. This ultra-compact carbine features a tiny 6.75-inch barrel and is only just under 25 inches long with its sliding stock fully extended, making it smaller than an even MP5 but certainly far less controllable when firing on fully automatic. The PDW has since been redesigned and upgraded several times and is currently known as the SCAR-P.

Colt Canada C8SFW, L119A1 and L119A2

As noted previously, the UK Special Forces have carried Armalite and Colt designs since the early 1960s when the semi-automatic AR-15 first became available. Since that time they have used a range of models including the original M16, the M16A1 and the Colt Commando carbine. In Northern Ireland UK Special Forces units carried the 5.56 × 45mm Heckler and Koch 53, a carbine length version of the HK33, along with the 7.62 × 51mm G3K. Trials began for a new rifle and carbine to replace their aging collection of M16 platforms during the 1990s. Apparently, more money was spent on the weapon trials itself than on the actual procurement of the successful weapon.

The three contenders in the UKSF trials were the Diemaco C7 and C8, the H&K G36 and the SIG 551. The winner was the Diemaco. Quantities of both the Canadian Diemaco, now Colt Canada, 5.56 × 45mm C7A1 rifles (similar to the M16A3 with a flat-top receiver allowing optics to be mounted via a Picatinny rail) and C8 carbines (similar to the M4A1) were purchased with some specific refinements requested by the UK Special Forces customers. This version of the C8 carbine was called the L119A1 Special Forces Individual Weapon (SFIW) in British service.

The full-length UK Special Forces Individual Weapon, the 15.7-inch barrel 5.56 × 45mm L119A1 mounting a Trijicon ACOG. The 15.7-inch barrel straddles the divide between the traditional M4 with its 14.5-inch barrel and the so-called Recce Rifles with their 16-inch barrels, offering an excellent compromise in range and compactness. (*Kelly Stumpf, Colt Canada*)

Royal Marines practise with the Colt Canada 5.56 × 45mm L119A1 with CQB length upper used by UKSF including the SAS and SBS. Note the Trijicon ACOG with Docter mini red dot sight. (*MSgt Chad McMeen, US Marine Corps*)

The British Army standard issue L85A1 bullpup rifle was not part of the competition as it was then considered unreliable. This was years prior to the Heckler and Koch refurbishment programme that produced the incredibly reliable and accurate L85A2 and had then no easy means to attach accessories, another issue only partly solved years later with an aftermarket rails kit adopted after experiences in Afghanistan. The L85A1 and the later A2 also immediately identified its users as British Army as no other military issued the weapon in any numbers, something the likes of the SAS would prefer to avoid.

The SAS have, however, carried the L85A1 in at least one conflict – in former Yugoslavia, the regiment deployed with the L85A1 to blend in with other British troops and not identify themselves instantly as Special Forces. The opposite can also be true. In Iraq in 2003, SAS operators who were attempting to pass themselves off to the local civilian population as Royal Military Police failed in their efforts when they were seen carrying Diemaco C8 carbines, a distinctive UK Special Forces weapon.

Other units within UK Special Forces have carried the L85A2 out of necessity, including the Special Forces Support Group (SFSG) who carried the weapon before sufficient stocks of the L119A1 became available. The identity of the SFSG operators was already fairly obvious despite the L85A2s as they wore MultiCam uniforms, Paraclete plate carriers and carried HK417s. Some Diemaco C7 rifles saw service with the Parachute Regiment's Pathfinder Platoon in both Iraq and Afghanistan although these have since been retired as the weapons were wearing out after almost two decades of hard service.

Amongst the requirements for the Diemaco carbine, since christened the C8 SFW (Special Forces Weapon) by its manufacturer, was a heavyweight barrel similar to the SOPMOD Profile barrel to assist with extended rapid fire. It was also fitted with a longer 15.7-inch barrel, versus the M4 style 14.5-inch, and a redesigned front sight base to accommodate use of the Heckler and Koch AG36 grenade launcher mounted to the weapon using a dedicated Knight's rail system, known predictably enough as the UK-SAS Rail. The 15.7-inch barrel appears to have functioned well for the SAS and SBS although it is unknown what particular rounds are issued. The safe bet would be on something other than the general issue L2A2 and more likely the Mk262 or the Barnes TSX is used thanks to their close collaboration with Delta in Iraq. The British Army is currently developing an enhanced performance 5.56 × 45mm bullet to replace the L2A2 that will allegedly feature increased range and lethality capabilities drawing on their Afghan experiences.

The British Army officially describes their Special Forces Individual Weapon as:

> The L119A1, C8 is a versatile 5.56mm assault rifle developed for the Special Forces with a range of 600m. It can also be assembled with a short barrelled upper receiver to make the Carbine which can be used at up to 300m range. When fitted with a Picatinny rail hand guard it can be adapted for various uses with the addition of lasers, lights, UGLs, down grips, in fact almost anything with a Picatinny fitment. It is usually used in conjunction with the ACOG 4 × optical sight or EOTech holographic sight.

The SAS has since purchased new 10-inch uppers for their L119A1s based on their experience conducting raids in Iraq. When fitted, the shorter barrel L119A1 mirrors the likes of the Mk18 CQBR carried by the SEALs and the 10.3-inch Block II M4A1s carried by specialist Rangers. The 10-inch upper, dubbed the L119A1 CQB Carbine, is sans bayonet lug to allow SureFire suppressors to be easily fitted.

The longer 15.7-inch standard barrel was appreciated in Afghanistan and when operating in western Iraq due to the extended engagement lengths encountered. The majority of L119A1s in service today are equipped with suppressors and most have had their stocks replaced by unit armourers using both LMT and VLTOR models. Aimpoint Micro T1 and EO Tech optics have become popular for close quarter battle, including the use of the swing-arm Aimpoint magnifier behind the EO Tech; but for longer ranged encounters the Trijicon ACOG remains British standard with a co-witnessed Docter mini RDS sitting above it for CQB.

A planned procurement of a replacement rifle in 2014 was shelved in favour of a 2013 Mid Life Improvement programme by Colt Canada to produce a new variant from existing stocks of the L119A1. This new version of the rifle, termed the L119A2, features an ambidextrous selector, a new Vortex-style flash suppressor, a full length upper Picatinny rail, additional rails at the three, six and nine o'clock positions on the forearm, fold-down back-up iron sights and a new VLTOR style collapsible stock. The weapons are being delivered with uppers in two dedicated barrel lengths – a 10-inch CQB variant and the standard 15.7-inch barrel Carbine variant.

A second dedicated 5.56 × 45mm ultra short barrel carbine has also been recently adopted in limited numbers by UK Special Forces: the LWRC M6A2 UCIW or Ultra Compact Individual Weapon. The carbine features an 8-inch barrel and measures only 22 inches in overall length. This 22-inch specification was a key requirement for the UKSF trials that produced the weapon, which competed successfully for the British contract against the HK416C. The UCIW is apparently intended for use by UKSF dog handlers, team leaders, signallers and for use in vehicles and whilst conducting covert reconnaissance and close protection, replacing the 9 × 19mm MP5K in the latter role. The weapon is often seen in Afghanistan matched with a SureFire suppressor and either Aimpoint Micro or EO Tech optics.

UK Special Forces are not the only users of the Colt Canada carbines. The New Zealand SAS Group also issue the C8 SFW to its operators, as do the Norwegian FSK/HJK. Perhaps not surprisingly, the platform is also deployed by the elite operators of Canada's own JTF-2. The L119A1/A2 and the UCIW are also perhaps not the only assault rifles deployed by UK Special Forces. At least one intriguing image from Afghanistan shows what appears to be a wooden stocked AK variant fitted with a Grip Pod bipod lying next to an SBS operator. Perhaps the SR-47 concept is not yet dead (and more of that in a few paragraphs) but in all likelihood the weapon is, rather more prosaically,

The replacement for the L119A1 CQB, the Colt Canada 5.56 × 45mm L119A2 CQB upper. Instead of procuring an entirely new weapons system, the British SAS and UK Special Forces decided upon a mid-life upgrade for their tried and true L119A1s. *(Kelly Stumpf, Colt Canada)*

The full-length upper version of the L119A2 procured by UK Special Forces. The new weapons feature ambidextrous selectors, Magpul stocks, folding back-up-iron-sights, full-length upper Picatinny rail and a new tri-rail foregrip along with a Vortex flash suppressor. *(Kelly Stumpf, Colt Canada)*

simply being carried by an operator engaged in mentoring local security forces.

Heckler and Koch G36

The famous HK33 was Heckler and Koch's first foray into 5.56 × 45mm assault rifles. It was used in limited numbers by the SEALs in Vietnam who appreciated the weapon's thirty and forty round magazines, as at the time the M16 and CAR15 were limited to twenty rounds. The German firm also produced one of the first true compact assault rifles in the form of the HK33K with a 13-inch barrel and later the HK53 with an even shorter, just under 9-inch, barrel.

The author has fired the HK53 in both semi and fully automatic modes and can confirm that the felt recoil is far stronger than a modern M4A1 or short barrel SCAR. Despite the generous recoil and muzzle blast, the 53 was an accurate and handy carbine to shoot and feels more like an over-sized MP5, it's easy to understand its popularity with the SAS in Northern Ireland. Indeed one of the rarest of H&K weapons is a prototype based on the HK53, but chambered for the Soviet 7.62 × 39mm, termed the HK32K. Unfortunately the HK32K is one the author hasn't seen, let alone fired!

The G41 was H&K's next offering in 5.56 × 45mm and competed with the likes of the M16A2 and the Belgian FNC (not to be confused with the Second World War 7.92 × 57mm semi-automatic design) for various NATO contracts. The G41 was based largely on the 7.62 × 51mm G3 and was one of the first H&K designs to feature the three-round burst selector setting. The three-round burst setting was a requirement for the US military trials that eventually, and perhaps predictably, selected the M16A2 as the replacement for the M16A1. The G41 was used by several European counter terrorist units and was set to become the new service rifle for the West German military before reunification.

Heckler and Koch's next design was perhaps their most successful yet. The G36 is a short-stroke, gas operated rifle with an almost 19-inch barrel in its standard configuration. Like almost all weapons of its type it is fed from a thirty-round box magazine. At 3.63kg it is comparable to but slightly heavier than the M16A2. In common with the Steyr AUG, the G36 features an integral, three-power magnification optical sight along with a CQB reflex-style sight mounted on top. These features made the G36 certainly ahead of its time. It was developed as a modern replacement for the Bundeswehr's G3 and to replace the aging HK33 and was adopted in 1996 by the German military and later by the Spanish and by the Saudis. In perhaps its most unusual role, the G36 has also been supplied to Kurdish irregulars operating against ISIL/ISIS in northern Iraq.

Two shortened versions, the G36K and the G36C, were widely adopted by military SOF units in Germany, France, Spain, Sweden and police tactical units across the world. The G36K features a 12.5-inch barrel whilst the G36C is even shorter with a 9-inch barrel. Both feature side folding stocks and offer the now-standard Picatinny rails and both are widely liked by users. Certainly an acquaintance of the author, with many years of experience in tactical policing at a national level, prefers the G36C over M4 style platforms, including the vaunted HK416, for his primary shoulder weapon. He ascribes the G36C's success to its reliability and accuracy at typical CQB distances up to 100 metres.

The G36 became embroiled in controversy in 2015 when the Bundeswehr claimed that their rifles heated up when operated in rapid fire in the harsh Afghan climate, affecting accuracy and apparently reducing reliability. The German Defense Ministry announced that the G36 would be immediately replaced within German military SOF units (potentially with the HK416 or even the 417) whilst another rifle would be sought to replace the G36 across the whole of the German military. The German KSK special operations unit had in fact already been trialling a new 5.56 × 45mm platform since 2010, with both the 416 and the SIG 516 in the running, along with a domestically designed M4 variant from Schmeisser GmbH.

It appears the G36 issue had been known since 2010 when German soldiers allegedly experienced significantly reduced accuracy due to heat build-up during a prolonged firefight in Kunduz, Afghanistan. Some reports say that the weapon becomes drastically inaccurate after rapid firing in hot climates like the Afghan summer where temperatures can easily reach over 40 degrees. Questions have been raised about the composition of the synthetic frame of the weapon, but at the time of writing the issue had descended into a series of claims and counter-claims. One report suggests that problems begin after as little as two magazines have been rapidly fired through the rifle, with serious degradation in accuracy past 100 metres in range. It's difficult to sort the wheat from the chaff on the G36 controversy and it may take several years until a true version of events is established although independent testing has not uncovered any problems with the weapon if deployed as intended.

A German instructor trains a US Army Special Operations Command soldier on the 5.56 × 45mm Heckler and Koch G36K fitted with EOTech above the integral three power optic and H&K light mount. Note the US soldier carries a 9 × 19mm H&K P8, the German Army version of the USP. (*Martin Greeson, US Army*)

Other Designs

A number of other assault rifles are used across the world by military SOF units but none are as common the M4A1. In Israel, IDF special forces like the Sayeret Matkal deploy the 5.56 × 45mm Galil along with the ultra-compact Galil MAR with its 7.7-inch barrel and side folding stock. The Austrian Steyr AUG is also used by a number of European SOF units, whilst some SIG variants of the SIG 550 series have been adopted, again mainly by European counter terrorist teams, but also by elements of the French COS special operations command. The French GIGN carry the SIG 551 along with the 416 and the French service rifles, the FAMAS F1 and the upgraded FAMAS G2.

GIGN use limited numbers of the FAMAS platform due to its ability to launch rifle grenades and, more precisely, the Israeli developed Simon Door-Breaching Rifle Grenade that can penetrate both wooden and steel doors from a distance of up to 30 metres. The uniquely French design has been hampered by its inability to use NATO STANAG magazines and like the British L85A2 has not been adopted outside its homeland. French Army operators in Mali are currently carrying a unique mix of weapons including the FAMAS. In a ten-man section there are six FAMAS supported by one grenadier carrying a

G36KV with underslung AG36 grenade launcher, one marksman with the HK417 and two gunners, one carrying the 5.56 × 45mm Minimi and the other the 7.62 × 51mm Maximi.

Special Purpose

SR-47

Before we talk about one of the most unusual assault rifles ever designed for SOF use, it's worth shooting down another recurring myth, specifically the hoary old tale of special operators carrying captured AK47s. The AK series is not carried into combat by Western SOF as its distinctive report can draw friendly fire. Despite protestations that soldiers will always make sure their target is identified before they open fire, the reality is that during a firefight areas likely to contain enemy firing points will be engaged speculatively to suppress those potential firing points. And if that potential firing point is near to a friendly operator carrying and firing an AK47, the risk of fratricide increases dramatically.

This is not the only reason special operators don't carry enemy weapons. Ammunition availability, reliability and compatibility, along with different weapon controls make carrying an AK problematic.

Remember that operators spend hundreds of hours training to develop muscle memory using a particular rifle or carbine; change the weapon and that muscle memory is seriously degraded. The AK series is also a poor choice as the weapon is simply not technologically as advanced, nor nearly as accurate as the HK416, L119A1 or the M4A1 platforms.

Occasionally AKs will be carried for specific missions or in areas where a deniable presence is required; for instance CIA SAD teams carried sterile AKs (and 9 × 19mm Browning High Powers) into Afghanistan in September of 2001, or during covert reconnaissance missions such as the December 2001

The latest iteration of the legendary Knights' SR-47 in 7.62 × 39mm Short – the famed 'M4 using AK mags'. This version features full RIS mounts, a SOPMOD stock and angled foregrip. Knight's have continued development of the platform since the original 2001 requirement, improving reliability and functionality. *(Knight's Armament Company)*

solo operation into Tora Bora conducted by Army operator, John 'Shrek' McPhee. McPhee traded in his much loved 7.62 × 51mm HK21E general purpose machine gun for a folding stock AK47 to blend into his environment. Another circumstance may be SOF training teams operating alongside Iraqi or Afghan soldiers who choose to carry the AK either in solidarity with their charges or as a training tool.

The US Army Rangers continue to provide a brief familiarisation with the operating principles of the AK series during their training, as do the Special Forces and SEALs. These units may encounter friendly forces carrying the weapon or in extremis they may be forced to use a captured AK to defend themselves in a last-ditch scenario. The only other circumstance where carrying enemy weapons makes any sense is deep behind enemy lines, far away from friendly troops.

Long Range Reconnaissance Patrols in Vietnam and the South African Recces and Koevoet would sometimes carry AK47 assault rifles and RPD light machine-guns as they made them look like insurgents at a distance; the sound of Soviet weapons firing would also at least momentarily confuse the opposition as they decided whether they were being mistakenly fired upon by other insurgents. Ammunition resupply could also be accomplished from dead enemy, a consideration on long term operations in enemy base areas. Apart from this and situations where sterile weapons are carried to obscure a particular nation's involvement in an operation, there are few sensible reasons for anyone to carry an enemy weapon.

Having said all that, one of the most intriguing purpose built SOF assault rifles ever developed was the 7.62 × 39mm Knight's Armament Company SR-47. The rifle was designed in the closing days of 2001 as Coalition SOF conducted combat operations in Afghanistan. SOCOM issued a requirement for an M4A1 platform that could fire the Soviet 7.62 × 39mm. Army Special Forces were beginning to experience the long-range engagement distances that would continue to plague the 5.56 × 45mm in Afghanistan. The 7.62 × 39mm would go a long way toward solving this issue. The ability to use captured AK magazines, or to be able to tap into the local supply chain from friendly Afghan forces, was considered a definite requirement.

This stipulation caused challenges for the original designs as these were initially intended to be replacement uppers for the M4A1 that could safely chamber and fire the larger 7.62 × 39mm. Instead a new weapon that could accommodate AK magazines would have to be designed. David Lutz, then vice president of military marketing at Knight's has been quoted as saying:

> Actually this program was kind of on a back-burner until US special operations guys were going into these complex of tunnels that were so deep, expansive and target-rich that they couldn't take enough loaded M16 magazines. So they wanted a weapon that had all the muscle

memory of an M4 – safety, grip, everything that's familiar to the soldier or the SEAL – but capable of using battlefield pick-up magazines.

According to Lutz there was already an existing requirement as part of the SOPMOD programme for a so-called Special Purpose Receiver that would use a drop-in receiver chambered for the 7.62 × 39mm for the M4A1.

Three firms responded to the tender: Knight's, Robinson Arms and LMT (Lewis Machine & Tool). Of these, Robinson's RAV02 and the Knight's SR-47 (Stoner Rifle-47) went forward for further trial but only examples of the SR-47 were delivered to SOCOM. The SR-47 was combat tested allegedly by DEVGRU elements deployed to Afghanistan. Knight's commented at the time about the accuracy and flexibility of the design:

> This particular 7.62 × 39mm is probably the most accurate 7.62 × 39mm in the world because it's got a really fine free-floated barrel, and, of course, it has the rail system so all of the other SOPMOD accessories off the M4s are compatible.

Seven examples were produced, six of which were transferred to SOCOM complete with KAC suppressors and one that resides at Knight's head-

A Navy SEAL in Baghdad 2007 scans for insurgents. His weapon is the 5.56 × 45mm M4A1 fitted with an EOTech close combat optic, AN/PEQ-2, and Surefire integrated weapon light and foregrip. (*MC1 (Naval Air Crewman) Michael B.W. Watkins, US Navy*)

quarters. A second SOCOM tender for a variant designed to handle the 5.45 × 39mm never eventuated. Knight's mentioned this in a 2003 interview:

> There's also a possibility, although they haven't let the contract yet, that there could be another variant that we'd call the SR-74. That could be used if our special operations guys go to a country that has the 'newer' 5.45mm former Soviet weapons. Then they would also have the same ability to pick up magazines.

Knight's debuted an improved and modernised version of the platform in 2014 apparently in response to renewed SOCOM interest so perhaps the SR-47 may finally see combat, more than a decade after its development. This new version features a full-length Picatinny rail along the receiver and is obviously designed from the ground up to accept a suppressor. Indeed with the right ammunition, such a suppressed platform could prove a serious contender against the likes of the .300 Blackout.

Future Trends

There are three principal but interrelated areas of development in the SOF assault rifle and carbine field. These are new calibre, modular designs and the continuing quest for reduction in size. A new calibre that can provide 7.62 × 39mm-like performance in a 5.56 × 45mm sized weapon will continue to be the Holy Grail for many. If it can do so with both subsonic and supersonic open-tip, and Hague compliant, bullet designs, it may well revolutionise SOF small arms. Indeed an experimental prototype HK417 in 6.5 × 47mm was developed that would have been perhaps the answer to many of the concerns and perceived challenges regarding the 5.56 × 45mm in SOF use. In the larger small arms field, efforts will continue with a similar intermediate calibre to replace the 5.56 × 45mm, such as the .264 USA developed by the US Army Marksmanship Unit that appears in testing at least to offer significant promise. Whether the 5.56 × 45mm actually needs replacing in general service is another question entirely!

Modularity will see individual rifles or carbines able to swap between barrel lengths, and indeed calibre, in the field, dependent on operational needs. Continual reduction in size for both covert and CQB applications will see 5.56 × 45mm (and .300 Blackout) weapons of a size comparable to submachine guns like the MP5. Indeed all of these things are happening now with significant research and development behind them. All three factors will feature in any new, successful design for SOF units. Integration of combat optics, offering both magnified and close combat sights in the one packag will continue to improve and become smaller and more effective.

In terms of calibre and modularity, the most likely candidate to partially replace the 5.56 × 45mm (and the 9 × 19mm and 4.6 × 30mm in some tasks) in American hands is of course the .300 Blackout. We have covered the evolu-

An unidentified US Army special operator fires his 10.3-inch barrel 5.56 × 45mm M4A1 fitted with EOTech, AN/PEQ-15 and M3X weapon light. His sidearm is a .40S&W Glock 22 with Surefire weapon light. Note the Dark Earth magazine extender on the Glock, originally developed for Delta. This operator's weapons and equipment give a good indication of what today's Green Beret carries on Direct Action missions. (USASOC)

US Army Green Beret in Afghanistan in 2013 practising his marksmanship with his SOPMOD Block 2 5.56 × 45mm M4A1 carbine. His optic is marked as the SU-231 A/PEQ, the military designation for the EOTech 553. (*SPC Connor Mendez, US Army*)

tion of this cartridge earlier in this chapter, but the latest developments at the time of writing could see it in the ascendency. SIG have developed the MCX LVAW (Low Visibility Assault Weapon), an integrally suppressed carbine that closely follows the dimensions of the MP5SD3.

The MCX's improved integral suppressor means its report is allegedly ten decibels lower than the already quiet AAC Honey Badger. The MCX can also be quickly and simply equipped with the user's stock of choice although it comes standard with a side folder. Unlike most SBRs and carbines, the MCX doesn't run its recoil buffer tube into the stock, allowing for side folders and all sorts of innovative stock options. As noted previously, Delta had this as an early requirement when they were collaborating with Heckler and Koch in developing the 416, but the requirement fell by the wayside.

Additionally the MCX offers a truly quick-change barrel option so operators could conceivably use a 9-inch CQB version for the building assault, whilst swapping out for the 16-inch rifle version to cover the egress from the target and gain maximum advantage of the .300 Blackout at extended ranges. It also features, importantly for many US users, a hold open device which locks the action open after the last round from the magazine is expended, allowing the shooter to visually check that the weapon is empty – a key requirement from many M4A1 users.

The MCX, also known as the Black Mamba, benefited from design work by a former AAC employee who designed the competing Honey Badger but ceased employment with AAC. According to comments attributed to SIG, the MCX was developed at the request of an Army Special Mission Unit which would indicate Delta. At the time of writing, an unspecified number of MCXs have been purchased by SOCOM and the rumour mill suggests these are heading to Fort Bragg for testing. The SOCOM bound MCXs are apparently equipped with both 5.56 × 45mm and .300 BLK upper receivers.

The MCX and the .300 Blackout could become the assaulter's weapon of choice to cover both the CQB and the intermediate distance requirement although John McPhee believes that a new calibre isn't necessary, '*5.56 was always doing this. I think there is no room for .300 on the battlefield. Mixing ammo will break guns and every nation has 5.56*', commenting on the ease of resupply for operators equipped with 5.56×45mm platforms. McPhee notes that having some weapons chambered for 5.56×45mm and some in .300 Blackout will inevitably result in dangerous mistakes when a .300 Blackout magazine is accidentally fitted to a 5.56×45mm weapon and a round is chambered: '*In a combat scenario if a .300 mag got placed in a 5.56 gun, the round will chamber then blow up the gun. Seen this before. So logistically .300 is the worst option.*'

Fully modular systems are the future – the idea of the SCAR with its 5.56×45mm and 7.62×51mm variants in several barrel lengths and configurations but in one weapon. The SCAR has come somewhat toward achieving that aim by the use of the 5.56×45mm adaptor kit that has seen service with the US Army Rangers amongst others. The new Remington design, the ACR, was developed as a fully modular system from the ground up. The latest SOCOM issue sniper rifle, the Mk21, is also fully modular, enabling the sniper to swap out barrels for 7.62×51mm, .300 Winchester Magnum or .338 Lapua Magnum. A similar concept in carbines is needed.

European firm B&T have recently developed the APC300, a suppressed G36C style assault rifle chambered for the .300 Whisper, a competitor to the.300 Blackout. The Swiss SIG 556XI is based on their popular SIG 550 platform in use with French SOF and many European counter terrorism teams. The new SIG 556XI, however, can be swapped from 5.56×45mm to .300 Blackout or to Soviet 7.62×39mm relatively simply, giving a lot of options in the one, combat proven, basic design. The new Beretta offering, the ARX160, can also be rechambered from the 5.56×45mm to the 7.62×39mm in a straightforward manner. These types of rifles, offering the best of all calibre in the one package, certainly seem to be the trend of the future, although with this modularity comes increased risks as outlined by McPhee.

The Russians have also continued to quietly innovate in terms of both ammunition and carbine length rifles. During the 1990s, a new calibre known as the 9×39mm (made by marrying a 9×19mm bullet with a 7.62×39mm casing) was developed. The bullet itself was heavy at 250 grains and was already subsonic, making it easy to suppress. The new round was significantly better than the 5.56×45mm from an M4A1 and far exceeded anything possible with a 9×19mm weapon. It was apparently similar to recent results obtained with the .300 Blackout. An armour piercing load, the SP6, could penetrate common body armour at ranges up to an impressive 400 metres.

A number of weapons were designed for the new round; the AS and VSS and the 9A-91 and VSK14 saw widespread adoption within Russian military and police Spetsnaz. The AS and VSS are integrally suppressed carbines with the VSS designed as a short range sniper rifle. The 9A-91 can also be suppressed and fitted with the compact 40mm GP95 grenade launcher. Its sister weapon, the VSK14, is an integrally suppressed sniper version, all firing the same round for ammunition compatibility in the field.

Other enhancements that will see future adoption include concepts such as Fabrique Nationale's electrically powered Picatinny rails currently available for their SCAR series rifles. As the name suggests, these provide power to compatible sights, lights and other devices attached to the weapon negating the need for numerous batteries to be carried for each device. Instead the accessory draws its power from the Picatinny rails themselves. The RIPR or Rail Integrated Power Rail from ATK operates on a similar principle.

New Picatinny mounted accessories continue to gain favour too. A recent innovation led by Magpul has been the Angled Foregrip or AFG. This is designed to replace the standard vertical foregrip manufactured by the likes of Tango Down and KAC. The AFG provides a far more compact grip that stands less chance of snagging on equipment or obstacles, whilst still providing a strong point of contact with the weapon. One area in which the AFG lacks is replicating the options available to a user with a vertical foregrip and an EO Tech or similar sighting system; with this set-up, the weapon can be

An operator from the US Army 10th Special Force Group fires his modified 5.56 × 45mm M4A1. The weapon features a Viking Tactical VTAC free-floating rail, a Cadex folding vertical foregrip and the SOCOM issue EOTech and AN/PEQ-15. (*Ronald L Miller, US Army*)

The 14.5-inch barrel 5.56 × 45mm Heckler and Koch HK416A5 heavily employed by Dutch and French SOF and by Germany's KSK as the G38. *(Heckler & Koch)*

fired at almost any angle, away from the body if necessary. This is a difficult tactic to conduct with an AFG as the grip pressure is simply not available.

What will the future look like? A future SOF carbine will likely be integrally suppressed; perhaps be chambered in a new intermediate calibre like the .264 USA or 6.5 × 47mm; will have a number of interchangeable uppers including an ultra-compact carbine length under 10-inches; will be easily modified in the field to a range of other calibres most likely to include 5.56 × 45mm, 7.62 × 39mm and 7.62 × 51mm and will have integrated optics with independent night vision and range finding capabilities.

As a postscript, it appears the integrally suppressed SIG Sauer MCX has been adopted by Delta in both the 5.56 × 45mm and .300 Blackout variants filling their Low Visibility Assault Weapon requirement, including the option of a side folding stock. In related news, the London Metropolitan Police's SCO19 CT-SFO or Counter Terrorist Specialist Firearms Officer team have also adopted the MCX although apparently in 5.56 × 45mm (along with the SIG 516 carbine) to replace a range of MP5 and G36 variants. Their adoption of the platform has led to speculation that UK Special Forces may also be adopting the MCX to replace their MP5s and potentially their M6A2s.

Chapter Four

Battle Rifles, Special Purpose and Designated Marksman Rifles

Overview

As has been discussed at length in the previous chapter, SOF and conventional military units in Afghanistan in the opening years in the War on Terror experienced what is known as weapon overmatch. This is when an enemy possesses weapons that match or exceed your own in terms of range and capability. In this case, overmatch related to the insurgent use of 7.62 × 39mm and 7.62 × 54mm small arms and rocket-propelled-grenades versus the principally 5.56 × 45mm small arms of Coalition Forces. This overmatch is often dictated by the terrain as the mountains and wide plains of Afghanistan

A SEAL aims a 7.62 × 51mm Mk17 or SCAR Heavy battle rifle equipped with a Elcan Specter variable magnification optic and ATPIAL AN/PEQ-15 infra-red laser illuminator. The SEALs have remained the heaviest user of the SCAR family, even ordering replacements after SOCOM declined to continue with a planned acquisition of 5.56 × 45mm Mk16s. *(US Navy Special Warfare)*

exaggerated the deficiencies of the lighter calibre weapons systems. In Iraq too, outside the cities, this overmatch occurred with insurgents engaging Coalition SOF at anywhere from 500 to 800 metres and making the most of the capabilities of the heavier Soviet calibre.

Iraq and Afghanistan were not of course the first time this had occurred. During Operation Corporate in the Falkland Islands, UK Special Forces found the 5.56 × 45mm lacking in terminal effects at extended ranges and the high winds and rains common on the islands significantly affected the round. Delta also later experienced a similar situation in the western deserts of Iraq during Operation Desert Storm in 1991. They, along with the British SAS, had been dispatched to stop Iraqi SCUD missile launches that threatened to bring Israel into the war and destroy the fragile Arab coalition.

During their 'Scudhunting' operations, Delta found their 5.56 × 45mm Colt 723 carbines to work well within a few hundred metres, but beyond this range they were forced to resort to sniper rifles and heavier crew-served weapons. Modified 7.62 × 51mm M14s were available but a lighter, more modern alternative was needed. This development would eventually lead to the Knight's Armament Company SR-25 and the adoption of the Mk11 across SOCOM almost ten years later.

Indeed there has also been a constant need for heavier calibre weapons during most modern conflicts, whether they are conventional warfighting,

A MARSOC Marine provides overwatch with his suppressed 7.62 × 51mm M110 SASS in Afghanistan, 2012. *(Cpl Kyle McNally, US Marine Corps)*

counter insurgency or counter terrorism in nature. In some circumstances a heavier calibre weapon is required for penetrative reasons rather than engaging targets at extended ranges. During operations in Northern Ireland for example, the British SAS found that the 5.56 × 45mm of their Colt Commando and HK53 carbines was not reliable enough to penetrate through vehicles.

A request was made to Heckler & Koch to produce a shorter barrel version of their 7.62 × 51mm G3 battle rifle with a collapsible stock, as the weapon was also intended to be carried within, and if necessary fired, from within cars. In the meantime whilst they awaited the new G3K, a quantity of captured Argentine 7.62 × 51mm Fabrique Nationale FALs with folding stocks was shipped to the SAS Troop which apparently proved successful. This wasn't the first time the regiment needed increased penetration. Indeed, the SAS had adopted the HK53 to increase penetrative capabilities over their standard 9 × 19mm MP5s.

The need for longer-range firepower at the squad/section and platoon level had been recognised by the US military back in the 1990s. Both the US Army and the US Marine Corps instituted a fledgling programme alternatively named Designated Marksman (DM) or Squad Designated Marksman (SDM). The concept was to provide an organic precision weapons system that serviced the gap between assault rifles and carbines and the dedicated sniper rifle. This was typically between the 300 and 500 metre marks. These rifle-men would receive an abbreviated version of sniper training, focusing on the fundamentals of advanced shooting rather than on sniper field craft and stalking. Ironically the Soviet Army had been following a similar tactical doctrine since the Second World War with the 7.62 × 54mm Dragunov SVD equipped marksman attached to every squad.

Following on from Delta's experiences in Iraq during Desert Storm, the unit began working closely with Knight's Armament Company on a scoped 7.62 × 51mm semi-automatic platform that could engage out to 800 metres if required. The Navy SEALs were also looking at a similar requirement, but based on a 5.56 × 45mm platform that would eventually become known as the Special Purpose Rifle or SPR. The first formal requirement for the SPR was

The original 7.62 × 51mm Stoner SR-25, serial number 000001 from Knight's Armament Company. Note the original AR-10 magazine. The SR-25 name came from a combination of the AR-10 and AR-15 (10+15 = 25) and in tribute to AR-10 and AR-15 designer, the legendary Eugene Stoner, thus Stoner Rifle-25. (*Knight's Armament Company*)

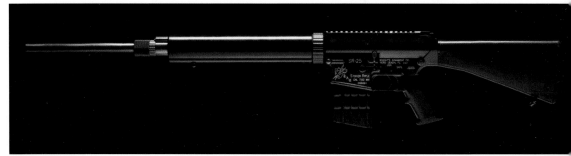

A SEAL Team 8 operator displaying his 7.62 × 51mm M14 battle rifle prior to operations in support of Operation Desert Storm in 1991. Barely visible is the early model Aimpoint optic and armourer fashioned forward grip. Before the SR-25, the M14 was still deployed by a number of SOF units including the SEALs and Delta. *(PH2 Milton Savage, US Navy)*

drafted back in 1991. The 5th Special Forces Group began work with the Army Marksmanship Unit in the late 1990s on a similar concept.

As mentioned, the regular Army and Marines were also working on the DM/SDM concept but it was not until the war in Afghanistan and later in Iraq that the project became fully realised. In fact some observers would argue that it took until around 2005 before the training and dedicated weapons caught up with the thinking. Prior to this, DMs and SDMs were often simply the best shots in the platoon and received little if any specialist training.

They were equipped with a mixture of stockpiled 7.62 × 51mm M14s and sniper-grade M21s with a range of military and commercial optics: 5.56 × 45mm M16A4s with match grade barrels and Leupold optics and standard 5.56 × 45mm M16A2s, again with match barrels and the Trijicon four-power ACOG optic. Later the 7.62 × 51mm Mk14 Mod0 and M39 became available to both conventional and SOF units, as did the 7.62 × 51mm Mk11 and 5.56 × 45mm Mk12 SPRs. As we will discuss in a moment, the Mk11 eventually morphed into the US Army and now US Marine issue M110 Semi-Automatic Sniper System (SASS).

The DM and SDM concept proved successful in both theatres with the shooters providing both an extended precision fire ability and an intelligence

A Det1 Marine, the forerunner of MARSOC, in Helmand in 2008 carrying a camouflage painted 7.62 × 51mm M14 with Leupold optic and Harris bipod. These M14s were replaced by the Mk14, the M39 and eventually the M110. *(SSgt Luis P. Valdespino Jr., US Marine Corps)*

The latest iteration of the Knight's 7.62 × 51mm SR-25 complete with suppressor and ATPIAL infra-red illuminator. Note the full-length upper rail and Flat Dark Earth finish. *(Knight's Armament Company)*

gathering capability using their enhanced optics. Units like the US Army Rangers and the British SFSG adopted the concept in parallel with their conventional counterparts. In Army Special Forces ODAs, the Weapons Sergeants often carried the DM rifle, whilst in the SEALs they were used to provide tactical overwatch. The rifles were often also employed by SOF snipers and their spotters when a bolt-action platform was not required.

Calibres and Ammunition

Whilst the battle rifle has always been traditionally chambered for the 7.62 × 51mm NATO round, designated marksman and SPRs have appeared in both 7.62 × 51mm and 5.56 × 45mm. This is largely due to the way their issuing organisations see the rifles being employed. In some cases it's also historical, such as the development of the SEAL Recce Rifle. The 5.56 × 45mm can be employed reliably out to 400 metres, or sometimes further, depending on the rifle, optics and ammunition combination, whilst the 7.62 × 51mm takes up the slack at the 400 metre mark and reliably covers out to around the 800-metre mark, again dependent on the exact weapon, optics and ammunition used.

The DMR has breathed new life into the 7.62 × 51mm just as the calibre was beginning to be restricted to the medium or general purpose machine gun. In

A US Army Special Forces operator returns fire with a 7.62 × 51mm Mk17 SCAR Heavy during a firefight in Helmand Province, Afghanistan in 2010. The Mk17 is fitted with an Elcan Specter optic, Harris bipod, AN/PEQ-15 illuminator and M3X weapon light.
(SPC Audiffred Laboy-Cruz, US Army)

fact one advantage of the 7.62 × 51mm round is that in an emergency, belted link ammunition for the 7.62 × 51mm machine guns can be broken down and used with the DMR. Although, as the machine gun ammunition will be standard NATO ball and not the match-grade ammunition normally fired in DMRs, accuracy will suffer dramatically. New bullet designs have also been developed including the 130-grain Mk319 Mod0 SOST round. The Mk319 was originally designed for the Mk17 SCAR with its 16-inch barrel but it has been successfully adopted in a wider range of platforms. The Mk319 was designed to improve accuracy, terminal effects and to better penetrate intermediate barriers between the rifle and the target with the objective of being so-called barrier-blind.

In Afghanistan two insurgents in a car were engaged and killed by a single round from an Mk17 after it penetrated the car door using the Mk319 ammunition, an excellent example of its barrier-blind performance. The round is effective out to 600 metres making it a solid choice for the marksman and closing the capability gap with the insurgents. Other rounds such as the 175-grain Mk316 have been designed to improve the long-range accuracy of 7.62 × 51mm ball and increase reliability in gas-operated platforms like the SR-25 and M110.

The US Army's 7.62 × 51mm M110 SASS (Semi-Automatic Sniper System) complete with suppressor which supplemented the Mk11 within SOCOM units like the Rangers until the Mk20 SSR was adopted. *(Knight's Armament Company)*

The same Crane programme developed the Mk318 Mod0, also known as the 5.56 Enhanced. The Mk318 features a 62-grain projectile in a design that was built from the ground up for consistent performance from the 14-inch barrel Mk16 SCAR and similar SBR length rifles and carbines. The Mk318 and Mk319 are both specifically designed not to be yaw dependent, instead the rounds have a Hague and Laws of Armed Conflict compliant open tip with a copper base that acts as a penetrator, punching the round through intermediate barriers. Both also excel at shooting through vehicle windscreen glass, a task that SOF cordon teams are sometimes forced to do.

The other round that has found widespread popularity amongst SOF units was actually developed specifically for one of the first marksman rifles developed by Crane, the Mk12 SPR. This was of course the Black Hills manufactured 77-grain Mk262 Mod0 and Mod1 that was detailed in the previous chapter. To summarise, the Mk262 increased range, accuracy and lethality from both carbines and DMRs and is still the most likely round to be found in the magazines of Navy SEALs or Green Berets in Afghanistan or Iraq.

Tactics and Techniques

Marksman rifles are deployed in a number of operational circumstances. Primarily they are employed on raiding missions or building assaults by overwatch elements who will be positioned to cover the entry and egress points of the assault teams. They will engage any hostiles who attempt to interfere with the assaulters. These overwatch teams will also be watching for any squirters – the nickname given to any insurgents or terrorists who attempt to escape the target.

They will also be carried by several members of the assault teams themselves who will peel off to cover likely avenues of approach as the assaulters move toward their breach points. On Operation Neptune Spear for instance, a DEVGRU marksman armed with a HK417 covered the approach of the assaulters into the main building. In Iraq, overwatch teams would even be inserted by Little Bird helicopters onto the rooftops of buildings overlooking the target location.

As we will see in Chapter Six, these rifles also often equip spotters in sniper teams and are increasingly employed by the snipers themselves. The rescue of

The latest version of the 5.56 × 45mm Heckler and Koch HK416A5 with 20-inch barrel, Schmidt and Bender PMII scope and RAL 800 finish. This variant of the HK416 is intended as a marksman or sniper support/spotter's rifle. (*Heckler & Koch*)

Captain Phillips from Somali pirates was accomplished by DEVGRU snipers using 16-inch barrel HK416s with AAC suppressors, not the 7.62 × 51mm SR-25s or even .50BMG platforms as claimed in most accounts. The snipers used the same set-up in Afghanistan. Also unlike in the film, the real operators shot in complete darkness wearing night vision goggles and employing the infra-red lasers on their 416s to invisibly mark their targets.

Marksman rifles will often be pooled into a support-by-fire element, along with snipers and heavy weapons teams, to provide direct fire support to

A US Army Ranger marksman with a suppressed 7.62 × 51mm M110 SASS in Afghanistan 2014. The M110 has become the primary designated marksman rifle in both US military conventional and special operations units. (*1LT Tyler N. Ginter, US Army*)

assault teams from an overwatch position. Sometimes these teams are inserted covertly hours or even days before the assaulters arrive at the objective. In all these tactical roles, the weapons will be employed as precision rifles to engage identified targets either beyond the range of the assaulters or out of line of sight of the assaulters, for instance whilst they are inside the target location clearing it of hostiles.

On Special Reconnaissance missions, marksman rifles are often carried to provide greater range capabilities and for the surveillance capabilities inherent in the rifle's optics, such as during the infamous Operation Red Wings recounted in the book and film *Lone Survivor*. Two of the SEALs on the mission carried suppressed 5.56 × 45mm Mk12 Mod1 SPRs whilst the others carried ACOG equipped M4A1s with underslung 40mm M203A1 grenade launchers. Green Beret reconnaissance teams, during the initial stages of OIF, also carried both the 7.62 × 51mm Mk11 and the 5.56 × 45mm Mk12 for similar reasons as they offered extended range capabilities, particularly during operations conducted in the Iraqi desert.

Current Trends

At the beginning of the War on Terror, three rifles dominated in the SOF marksman and battle rifle space – the 7.62 × 51mm Mk11 Mod0, the 5.56 × 45mm Mk12 Mod0 and the rifle the Mk11 was largely conceived from, the Knight's SR-25. Arguably, a fourth could be mentioned, the venerable 7.62 × 51mm M14. Over a decade later, there have been refinements and upgrades; optics, suppressors and ammunition have all been improved, a few new entrants like the Mk17 SCAR and the HK417 have emerged, but largely the playing field is still dominated by those four basic weapon platforms.

Today's marksman or battle rifle is likely to be a specialist Stoner based system firing the 7.62 × 51mm and equipped with a Nightforce or Schmidt & Bender optic mounting a back-up Docter style mini CQB sight. In the early years of the war in Afghanistan and Iraq, however, numerous other rifles were employed. The New Zealand SAS Group for instance carried a modified L1A1 Self Loading Rifle for a number of years, apparently scrounged from NZ Navy stocks before being refurbished by SAS armourers. This L1A1 featured aftermarket Picatinny rails replacing the forward grip, a Harris folding bipod and was equipped with both a suppressor and an ACOG four-power optic.

These L1A1s were used in Afghanistan to serve as a designated marksman rifle to engage targets beyond the range of the issue 5.56 × 45mm C8 SFW until a Lewis Machine & Tool MWS design was eventually adopted. Apart from the very occasional use of semi-automatic FN FAL types by private military contractors in Iraq, this is the last known deployment of the veteran battle rifle during the War on Terror.

A US Army Green Beret weapons sergeant zeroes his Flat Dark Earth finish 7.62 × 51mm M110 SASS. *(SSG John Bainter, US Army)*

A New Zealand SAS Group operator in Afghanistan in 2005 carrying a unit modified 7.62 × 51mm L1A1 Self Loading Rifle (SLR) with Trijicon ACOG optic, unidentified suppressor and Harris bipod. These were used to engage targets beyond the range of their Diemaco (now Colt Canada) carbines until the 7.62 × 51mm Lewis Machine & Tool MWS was procured as a designated marksman rifle. *(Photographer Unknown)*

John 'Shrek' McPhee carried a number of 7.62 × 51mm platforms during his extensive career with JSOC and SOCOM. Famously he carried a HK21E general purpose machine gun as a battle rifle in the mountains of Afghanistan in December 2001 whilst on the trail of Usama bin Laden. He explained to the author that it offered the capability of accurate single shot or fully automatic fire and could reach out to the distances encountered in Afghanistan, things that the M4A1s or even the SR-25s carried by other operators could not do in the one package. It also offered the flexibility of magazine (by adaptor) or belt feed and could function as a very respectable battle rifle or as a machine gun with commendable accuracy, thanks to the closed bolt H&K design.

Even McPhee's HK21E wasn't unmodified as it mounted a Trijicon ACOG and ITPEL infra-red laser on a Knight's rail. McPhee also carried a collapsible stock 7.62 × 51mm Heckler and Koch G3A3 battle rifle in Afghanistan a few years later, mounting an EO Tech 551 and ITPEL laser. He explained that at the time it was one of the few offerings available if an operator wanted to carry a reasonably compact 7.62 × 51mm rifle. Although the G3 has been criticised for not being the most accurate of platforms, McPhee found it more than satisfactory.

Knight's Armament Company SR-25, Mk11 Mod0/1, M110 Semi-Automatic Sniper System (SASS)

The SR-25 (Stoner Rifle-25) is a 7.62 × 51mm Armalite AR-10 based design developed by Knight's Armament Company. It is a gas operated semi-automatic rifle that weighs almost 5kg in its standard 20-inch barrel configuration. Like the AR-10 it is fed from a twenty-round box magazine although many special operators today use aftermarket PMAG twenty-five-round magazines. As noted previously, Knight's have had a long and close relationship with SOCOM and JSOC units. After Delta's experiences in Iraq during Desert Storm, they began looking at possible 7.62 × 51mm platforms with Knight's. From this work, the first SR-25s were procured in the early 1990s by Delta. These initial models were a 24-inch barrel model. The 20-inch standard version followed which soon found favour with the unit's recce/sniper operators.

The SEALs were also interested in a 7.62 × 51mm semi-automatic marksman rifle and DEVGRU procured a number of early examples that accompanied their sniper element as part of Task Force Ranger in Somalia in 1993. The SR-25 was heavily modified based on feedback from Delta, in full over thirty changes were made based on operator reports. For a time, the SR-25s operators were carrying were a mixed bag with no two weapons being exactly the same, as each featured varying numbers of improvements based on the feedback and were truly custom rifles. Based on a long-standing requirement from Crane, these changes and improvements were eventually all incorporated into the SOCOM production version type classified the Mk11 Mod0.

Army Rangers in Afghanistan zeroing a 7.62 × 51mm M110 SASS (Semi-Automatic Sniper System), the US military designation for its modified version of the Mk11 itself developed from the SR-25. A 7.62 × 51mm Mk20 SSR (Sniper Support Rifle) is being fired behind the Ranger in the foreground. Also of interest is the operator to the extreme right of the photograph who carries a suppressed Glock complete with extended magazine and RMR mini red dot sight in a waistband holster. (*PFC Codie M. Mendenhall, US Army*)

A US Army Ranger designated marksman providing overwatch for a ground assault force in Baghdad 2006. He is using a 7.62 × 51mm Mk11 Mod0 with Leupold scope.
(*75th Ranger Regiment Public Affairs Office*)

The 7.62 × 51mm Mk11 Mod0 was adopted by the SEALs in early 2000 with some 300 rifles purchased in the 20-inch barrel variant and equipped with the Leupold Mark 4 Mil-Dot scope. The Mk11 Mod0 is, for all intents and purposes, a product improved SR-25. Later Mk11s would see collapsible stocks fitted to trim several inches from the rifle's 45-inch overall length. Along with the SEALs, the Mk11s were taken to Afghanistan with the first Army Special Forces ODAs on the ground and were soon much prized. The Mk11s remained popular amongst the Green Berets although recently the 1st Special Forces Group has purchased a number of 7.62 × 51mm LaRue OBRs. The Mk11 Mod0 was also adopted as both a marksman's rifle and a sniper system by the Rangers and MARSOC where it has seen extensive action. In fact a Marine Force Recon sniper in Farah Province, southeastern Afghanistan, chalked up twenty kills with his Mk11 Mod0 holding back a Taliban assault on fellow Marines trapped in an immobilized HMMWV.

The Mk11 Mod0 and Mod1 later became the basis for the US Army issue M110, a weapon which has performed reasonably well but that has received its fair share of criticism from users. According to those involved in the development of the M110, many of the complaints stem from poor maintenance and care of the rifle, although early examples suffered from barrels that were being quickly shot out. The Rangers and Green Berets now deploy the M110 as both a spotter's weapon and as a designated marksman rifle, replacing the older Mk11s in many cases. DEVGRU continued to use their modified SR-25s with suppressed examples proving pivotal in the hands of SEAL snipers in Afghanistan (the DEVGRU operators would often carry the sawn-off 40mm M79 known as the Pirate Gun as a back-up to their SR-25s as an M203 could not be easily attached).

In Iraq and Afghanistan, Delta was conducting operations that often saw their operators engaging targets at CQB distances at one moment and at ranges exceeding 400 metres the next. The SR-25, although widely adopted by the unit, was too cumbersome for CQB and the alternative, their custom M4A1s, did not have the necessary reach to engage long distance targets due to their calibre. Their solution became known within the unit as the SR-25K.

The SR-25K was first developed by a unit armourer in Afghanistan who took the Knight's SR-25 and cut the barrel back to 16-inches. A later version was developed with an even shorter 14.5-inch barrel. One story contends that Delta asked Knight's for such a weapon who replied that it couldn't be done. In response an operator produced the unit-produced prototype. The SR-25K mated with a Short Dot scope became another unit favourite, particularly useful for sniping from helicopters, including interdicting insurgent vehicles (one operator mentioned that the first five rounds in the SR-25K's magazine were always armour piercing to defeat the engine block of target vehicles) and operating in close confines where the full-length SR-25 barrel may have snagged on obstructions.

Former Unit operator John 'Shrek' McPhee with his 7.62 × 51mm SR-25K in Iraq. The SR-25K was developed to give recce operators a platform that could be used in CQB or extended range shooting. *(John 'Shrek' McPhee)*

The production version of the 7.62 × 51mm SR-25K with 16-inch barrel and Leupold scope. The first SR-25K was produced by a Delta armourer literally sawing down the barrel with a hacksaw in Afghanistan. (*Knight's Armament Company*)

With the right ammunition types and the expert marksmanship of the unit operators, the SR-25K became virtual standard issue. The SR-25K is now produced commercially as the SR-25 E2 Advanced Combat Carbine, with a military version known as the M110K2 also available. Delta operatives today still use a 16-inch barrel SR-25 made to their very particular specifications. SR-25s have also been widely employed by Australian SOCOMD units including SASR and 2nd Commando Regiment since the late 1990s. SASR operators

An Australian Commando aims his Knight's Armament Company 7.62 × 51mm SR-25 during an urban warfare training exercise. The SR-25 was heavily employed by both Australian Commandos and SASR operators in Iraq and Afghanistan.
(*CPL Chris Moore, Australian Defence Force*)

carried SR-25s into Afghanistan and Iraq and the rifle has proven very pop-ular within the regiment.

SEAL Recce Rifle, Mk12 Mod0/1 Special Purpose Rifle (SPR)

The Navy SEALs of DEVGRU were carrying a unit-developed M4A1 during the early 1990s known simply as the 'M4 Sniper', a 16-inch barreled M4A1 fitted with a magnified optic to deliver precision fires during assaults. Examples were first used operationally in Mogadishu by DEVGRU operators attached to Task Force Ranger. These were 16-inch barrel models mounting Leupold 2.5-10 optics, an Ops Inc. suppressor and a PRI forearm, although at least one account mentions a Trijicon ACOG being used in Somalia by the SEAL snipers. Delta were also experimenting with 16-inch (and some 14.5-inch barrel) carbines with rails developed by unit armourers. As seen, these eventually featured the Knight's MRE (More Real Estate) free-floating rails that allowed maximum use of the space on the forearm.

The SEAL Recce concept was driven by the need for a weapon that could engage out to 400 metres or further, whilst still retaining the compactness to transition to CQB use if required. The 16-inch barrels were found to be the ideal compromise. The first Recce Rifles (sometimes also termed Recon Rifles) featured custom 16-inch stainless steel barrels and both collapsible and full length stocks. The collapsible stocks, like the LMT SOPMOD, caused some issues with the carbine length gas systems and made the weapons unreliable in fully-automatic fire. As the role of the weapon was as an 'M4 Sniper', reliable full-auto fire was not a primary requirement and the Mk12's selector was often replaced by operators with a semi-auto only version. As noted, many of the early Recce Rifles were fitted with either Trijicon ACOGs or Leupold ten-power scopes.

A formal requirement was raised for SOCOM and Crane Division of the Naval Surface Warfare Centre developed the Mk12 Mod0 Special Purpose Rifle – originally Special Purpose Receiver – over a number of years. These featured 18-inch barrels in a free-floating PRI forearm. They were built from M16A1 lower receivers and custom built upper receivers and fitted with Ops Inc. suppressors. To confuse the issue further, some Mk12 Mod0 rifles had their 18-inch barrels swapped out for 16-inch ones once they arrived at DEVGRU.

After a number of versions were built based on operator feedback, in a similar manner to the refinement of the SR-25, a second official variant known as the Mod1 was produced. It replaced the PRI forearm with a Knight's RAS based on the SOPMOD model along with several other component changes. The Rangers and SEAL Teams largely adopted the Mk12 Mod1 version. A rarer variant of the Mk12, known as the Mk12 Mod H or Holland, featuring an Ops Inc. suppressor was also developed for a US Army Special Forces Group as a unit purchase. As detailed earlier, the Mk262 5.56×45mm round was developed at the same time to take advantage of the longer barrel of the Mk12 and wring out as much performance as possible from the 5.56 × 45mm platform.

The Mk12 in both variants has been deployed successfully in Afghanistan, effectively engaging hostiles out to 800 metres with the 77-grain Mk262 Mod1 ammunition. The SEALs still carry the Mk12 although the Mk16 and Mk17 SCAR are often more commonly seen. The Recce Rifle requirement has been filled at DEVGRU in more recent years by the 14.5-inch Heckler and Koch 416 mounting a Nightforce optic which Delta also use along with their 16-inch SR-25s.

M14, Mk14 Mod0/1

Prior to the development of the SR-25, Delta were using modified 7.62 × 51mm M14s as were some SEAL teams, including DEVGRU, as a longer range marksman rifle to supplement their 5.56 × 45mm carbines. In fact the SEALs had experimented with a number of folding stock equipped M14s purchased from Italy – the Beretta BM59 – during the late 1970s and early 1980s. They retained these in their armouries along with more conventional wooden stock versions, but with custom forward grips fitted by unit armourers.

Australian SASR aerial sniper team in 2010 in Afghanistan, including VC recipient Corporal Roberts-Smith, prepare to embark on a mission providing aerial overwatch for an SASR assault force. Note the interesting mix of weapons platforms carried – Roberts-Smith's 7.62 × 51mm Mk14 Mod0, a 7.62 × 51mm SR-25 at the rear and a scoped 16-inch M4A5 variant to the right. (*LT Aaron Oldaker; Australian Defence Force*)

A stunning shot of Marines of the 1st Recon Battalion returning insurgent fire in Afghanistan in 2010. The Marine to rear fires a 7.62 × 51mm M14 DMR, still preferred over more modern systems by some users. (*Sgt Ezekiel Kitandwe, US Marine Corps*)

The 7.62 × 51mm M14 was the standard issue service rifle for the US military from 1957 replacing the M1 Garand and serving until the introduction of the M16 and M16A1 in 1967. The US Marines kept the M14 and its selective fire squad automatic version the M14E1 even later and were among the first to begin reissuing the M14 as an interim Squad Designated Marksman Rifle in 2003. Despite being an older design, the M14 remained an accurate rifle which, when coupled with good optics and ammunition, could reliably engage targets out to 800 metres.

Legendary Delta recce/sniper Randy Shughart carried a custom M14 during Operation Gothic Serpent in Somalia in 1993, later immortalised in the film *Black Hawk Down*. His desert camouflage painted M14 featured an early Aimpoint 7000 red dot optic. Prior to inserting at the second crash site, Shughart and his partner Gary Gordon – using an Aimpoint equipped carbine based on the Colt M733 with an Ops Inc. suppressor fitted – had been providing aerial sniper cover for the assault and blocking teams. Incidentally, Shughart was only reportedly carrying seven magazines for the rifle as he was not expecting to be involved in protracted ground combat. Even today, many DEVGRU SEALs only carry three extra magazines in pouches on their plate carriers, in addition to the magazine in their 416, when they conduct night raids in Afghanistan.

Although it is assumed by many that with the advent of the SR-25, the M14 fell into disuse with Delta, this was not actually the case. The veteran rifle soldiered on with a variant being developed in-house by Delta's recce/sniper community and used operationally for the first time in 2002 in Afghanistan. This was an M14 with a barrel chopped back to the gas block, the wooden stock removed and replaced with either an under-folder or side-folder stock from an AK47 (apparently the choice depended largely on whether the operator was left or right handed). Significantly lighter than the SR-25, the weapon was used successfully in combat in Afghanistan and was apparently the genesis for the later Springfield Arms civilian model M1A SOCOM 16.

Crane also developed an M14 modification during the same time period at the urging of the SEALs who wanted a compact 7.62×51mm battle rifle. Crane modified the M14 with a completely redesigned chassis and pistol grip with collapsible-style shoulder stock. The new weapon's barrel was 4 inches shorter than the standard M14 at 18 inches before the addition of flash hiders or suppressors (the original prototypes were even shorter at 16 inches). It featured four Picatinny rails around the forearm and a folding Harris bipod.

A US Air Force Special Tactics PJ or Para Jumper rescue-man fires a 7.62×51mm Mk14 Mod0 SEI Enhanced Battle Rifle at Bagram Air Base, Afghanistan in 2010. The PJs used both the Mk14 and Mk17. (*SSgt Christopher Boitz, US Air Force*)

Early models mounted Leupold Mark 4 optics or either the M68 Aimpoint or EO Tech. Later models used the SEAL standard Nightforce optics.

The weapon was christened the Mk14 Mod0, with later Mod1 and Mod2 variants, and first saw combat with the SEALs in 2004. It was highly prized by the Navy operators in Iraq as it was compact enough for urban operations but packed the punch and distance of the 7.62 × 51mm round. It was also adopted by Army Special Forces ODAs, Air Force Special Tactics and MARSOC operators. The most recent iteration, the Mk14 Mod2, was developed with a 22-inch barrel for SEAL use as a marksman rifle. It is scheduled to be replaced eventually by the Mk17 SCAR within the SEAL Teams.

A number of Mk14 Mod0s have also been deployed by Australian SASR operators in Afghanistan. It is understood these weapons were officially on loan from United States SOF, most likely the SEALs who have operated extensively with the Australians. An Mk14 Mod0 was indeed used by Victoria Cross winner Trooper Ben Roberts-Smith when he engaged a number of insurgent machine-gun positions and cleared several structures single-handedly, killing a large number of Taliban insurgents.

Victoria Cross winner Corporal Ben Roberts-Smith of the SASR pictured carrying a 7.62 × 51mm Mk14 Mod0 apparently borrowed from US Navy SEALs the SASR had been working alongside. Roberts-Smith used this Mk14 to kill a large number of insurgents and silence several machine-gun positions. Note the use of the forward mounted EOTech and magnifier. (*FCE MMT Sgt Paul Evans, Australian Defence Force*)

It is understood that the Mk14 Mod0 has found favour with the SASR including with their aerial sniper teams who have deployed it alongside their suppressed SR-25s. In the United States, although the SEALs and Air Force Special Tactics have been the units to most embrace the Mk14, the regular US Army have also adopted a version of the rifle called the M14EBR-RI as a DMR, whilst the USMC developed the visually similar M39 Enhanced Marksman Rifle.

Heckler and Koch G3 and HK417

Heckler and Koch's 7.62×51mm G3 has long been considered the very model of a battle rifle. Although now over fifty years old, the basic design can still be found in the hands of special operators. It even featured in a recent magazine advert for MARSOC that showed a Marine Raider with a slung Mk13 sniper rifle carrying the distinctive G3 in his hands (although the advert was likely using creative licence as unfortunately no evidence suggests MARSOC operators are actually using the G3 operationally).

It has been carried by German KSK special operators in Afghanistan prior to the fielding of the HK417, the 7.62×51mm big brother of the HK416. Some shorter barreled G3Ks, fitted with aftermarket Picatinny rails systems, folding Tango Down foregrips and Trijicon ACOGs, were also deployed by UK Special Forces in Afghanistan in the early years of the war. These G3Ks were also largely replaced with the HK417 after the rifle became available in 2005.

The HK417 was initially available in three variants and even their names suggested their lineage to JSOC and the first units to adopt the 416. The 12-inch carbine was named the Assaulter; the 16-inch rifle was termed the Recce and the 20-inch was the Sniper. Both the 416 and 417 have been continually product improved by Heckler and Koch based on operator feedback and in 2013 three variants of the HK417A2 were launched with 13, 16.5 and 20-inch barrel versions.

The original 12-inch barrel 7.62×51mm HK417 marksman rifle fitted with an Aimpoint CS red dot optic (equipped with an integral Picatinny rail and originally developed for the Swedish Army). It is also fitted with an H&K suppressor and vertical foregrip. The 417 is now in use with many SOF units including UKSF, Australian Commandos, French Army COS, DEVGRU and the Dutch KCT. *(Heckler & Koch)*

The veteran 7.62 × 51mm Heckler and Koch G3 still soldiering on in Afghanistan where it has been employed by the KSK as a marksman rifle, known as the G3ZF, prior to wider adoption and availability of the HK417. *(MC2 Nicholas A. Garratt, US Navy)*

The HK417 was evaluated but apparently didn't meet the grade at Delta who kept their SR-25s although DEVGRU adopted it as their principal 7.62 × 51mm marksman rifle. They have continued to carry the HK417 in a number of barrel lengths utilizing it both as a dedicated sniper's weapon and as a marksman's rifle. UK Special Forces, including the SAS and the SFSG, have purchased the 417 as have the KSK as the G28 and numerous European units such as GIGN who deploy the 417 as a marksman rifle with the 16-inch barrel Recce version.

Australia's 2nd Commando Regiment adopted the HK417 in 2010 after using SR-25s for some years previously in Afghanistan. The Australian 417s are equipped with the 16-inch barrel and six-power ACOG along with AN/PVS-26 clip-on night vision optics. Several examples of the Assaulter model with 12-inch barrels were also procured for the Commandos to employ as close support during compound raids. These have since been fitted with Elcan Specter DR optics and Grip Pod vertical bipod grips and have served with the Special Operations Task Group in Iraq, training Iraqi forces for the fight against Islamic State.

Fabrique Nationale Mk17 SCAR-H
The final major battle rifle/marksman rifle in current SOF service is the 7.62 × 51mm Fabrique Nationale Mk17 or SCAR-Heavy. As outlined earlier, the

Australian operators from 2 Commando prepare their equipment prior to their return to Iraq in 2014 as part of the Special Operations Task Group mentoring Iraqi forces against Islamic State. In the foreground is a beautifully camouflage-finished 7.62 × 51mm HK417 with 12-inch barrel resting on its GripPod bipod. The rifle is fitted with an Elcan Specter DR optic and a recently acquired AN/PEQ-15. Note the cable ties to ensure the device doesn't come loose in combat. (*SGT Hamish Paterson, Australian Defence Force*)

An US Air Force Combat Controller trains with a 7.62 × 51mm Mk17 SCAR Heavy with Elcan Specter optic, AN/PEQ-15 infra-red illuminator, M3X weapon light and Tango Down vertical foregrip. Air Force Special Tactics, along with the SEALs, use the SCAR family widely. (*A1C Kyla Gifford, US Air Force*)

Mk17 formed one part of a family of modular weapons developed by the Belgian firm for a SOCOM contract. These weapons included the 5.56 × 45mm Mk16, the 7.62 × 51mm Mk20 and the 40mm Mk13 Enhanced Grenade Launcher Module. The Mk17 was developed to accept a range of barrel lengths; a 13-inch CQB barrel, a 16-inch Standard and the 20-inch Long Barrel (LB) variant, allowing the weapon to be easily configured for particular operational requirements. The LB variant was designed as a spotter's rifle or as a DMR.

As we've seen, the Mk17, along with its 5.56 × 45mm little brother the Mk16, was first fielded for combat trials in Afghanistan in 2009 with the Rangers and later the SEALs. Reception was mixed with regards to the Mk16 in the hands of the Rangers but overwhelmingly positive about the Mk17, noting in particular the versatility of the folding rather than collapsible stock and the rifle's light weight along with its inherent accuracy. Post the SOCOM decision in 2010 (as detailed in the last chapter) to only continue procurement and fielding of the Mk17, Mk20 and Mk13 EGLM, the Rangers adopted the Mk17 SCAR as both a DMR and sniper observer weapon alongside their Mk11s and now M110s. The SEALs as noted are keen proponents of the entire SCAR family with SEAL elements deploying on operations in Afghanistan entirely equipped with Mk16, Mk17 and Mk20 SCARs.

A US Army Green Beret scans for insurgents using the Elcan Specter DR mounted on his 7.62 × 51mm Mk17 SCAR. This image provides a good view of the co-located RMR mini red dot sight fitted above the Elcan. (*SPC Connor Mendez, US Army*)

A US Navy SEAL in Afghanistan in 2010 scans for targets with his 7.62 × 51mm Mk17 SCAR Heavy fitted with an ATPIAL AN/PEQ-15 and Leupold scope with RMR mini red dot. Note the tape around the buttstock that likely secures his 'DOPE card' or Data-On-Previous-Engagements. (*CMC Jeremy L. Wood, US Navy*)

A Navy SEAL with a fully accessorized and suppressed 7.62 × 51mm Mk17 SCAR Heavy. Note he also wears a 9 × 19mm Mk25 (SIG-Sauer P226) in a Kydex holster.
(MC2 Martin L. Carey, US Navy)

According to several media sources, the British SAS were looking at a new 7.62 × 51mm (or 6.8mm, depending on which story you believe) platform to supplement or replace their 5.56 × 45mm L119A2s during 2014, apparently due to dissatisfaction with the lighter round. Versions of the Mk17 SCAR were supposedly under consideration. As usual with British SOF, until inadvertently captured on film there will be no hard proof of any of these claims. These tales surface regularly in the tabloid media and should be taken with a rather large grain of salt. As mentioned, the regiment has been using the HK417 as a designated marksman rifle for a number of years and it's difficult to imagine they would be in the market for a new rifle having only just signed off on the L119A2 upgrade.

Future Trends

Marksman rifles will remain an integral tool in the SOF armoury. In a similar manner to assault rifles, the biggest trends will be increased modularity and new intermediate calibre along with advances in optics and ammunition. The SCAR family certainly had the right idea in offering a range of calibre in a range of barrel lengths and configurations. Certainly this will be the future of the marksman rifle.

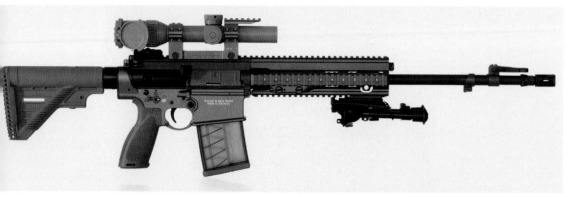

The big brother to the HK416A5, the 7.62 × 51mm HK417A5 with 20-inch barrel and RAL 800 finish mounting a Schmidt and Bender Short Dot, also in RAL 800. (*Heckler & Koch*)

The 7.62 × 51mm battle rifle will continue to soldier on in increasingly limited roles for the foreseeable future. The Mk14 EBR, Mk17 SCAR and the shorter barrel variants of the HK417 have shown there is a requirement for such a platform although if a new intermediate calibre in the .270 to .300 range is eventually adopted by a major SOF organisation, the days of the 7.62 × 51mm battle rifle may indeed be numbered. The calibre itself of course won't go away any time soon and marksman and sniper rifles will continue to be chambered for the big 7.62 × 51mm.

An Army Special Forces operator provides security for a convoy in Afghanistan. His rifle at first glance looks like a modified 5.56 × 45mm Mk11, but upon inspection it looks more like a custom platform built by Barnes Precision Machine as a unit purchase. Special Forces units have some discretionary budgets to purchase weapons and equipment outside of normal military procurement channels. (*SPC Connor Mendez, US Army*)

Chapter Five

Combat Shotguns

Overview

The first modern use of the shotgun as a military weapon was documented during the Great War when combat on the Western Front had largely deteriorated into static trench warfare. Night raids would be conducted upon enemy trenches to capture prisoners. The soldiers conducting these trench raids needed a powerful yet compact weapon that would reliably incapacitate – the standard issue rifles of the day were certainly powerful enough but were very unwieldy and difficult to aim within the close confines of a trench or fighting position. Revolvers and pistols quickly became the preferred weapon with some raiders also carrying an archaic mix of hand-to-hand weapons: bayonets, trench knives, knuckledusters and even spiked maces.

As mentioned previously, these trench raids were largely responsible for the development for the first submachine guns, although American and

US Army Green Berets clearing a compound during an exercise in 2014. The closest operator carries a breaching shotgun, a pistol-grip Remington 870, secured under his right arm by a bungee cord sling. *(MC1 Elisandro T. Diaz, US Navy)*

British raiders fell back on a more traditional weapon, the shotgun. Initially double-barrel sporting models were employed with much success. Along with delivering a potent blast of pellets, the shotgun proved ideal for engaging fleeting targets as the shot spread out to catch the target. This benefit would see shotguns employed many years later by SOF units such as the British SAS in the jungles of Borneo, instinctively engaging fast moving targets, often in low light conditions with the spray of pellets.

Early pump-action shotguns made an appearance as the war wound down but the American Winchester M1917 was the first pump-action shotgun designed specifically for combat. The M1917, which featured a bayonet lug to mount a blade, was even called the Trench Gun and caused the Germans to unsuccessfully protest that the use of the weapon in warfare was a contravention of the Hague Conventions (the same Hague Conventions that have to this day hindered Western militaries from employing the most efficient bullet designs, as we have discussed earlier).

Shotguns saw some limited use in the Second World War, particularly with the Marine Corps in the Pacific Theatre, including by Marine Raiders, the descendants of today's MARSOC operators. After the war the British SAS in Borneo armed their forward scouts with the 12-gauge Browning A-5 semi-automatic shotgun. The US Navy SEALs deployed to Vietnam with the pump-action Ithaca Model 37 with a 'duckbill' muzzle device that spread the shot, increasing the chance of a hit. The SEALs also deployed the world's first fully automatic shotgun, the Remington 7188 Mark 1 that could empty its seven-round magazine in little more than a second (although with abhorrent recoil that would almost certainly guarantee missing the target!). The 7188 was apparently also very sensitive to mud which eventually limited its use amongst the SEALs.

Shotguns are another weapon whose SOF role is now widely misunderstood thanks to generations of Hollywood blockbusters. The situation has not been improved by the recent spate of console video games. These films and games commonly portray the shotgun as some kind of handheld cannon that blows apart its victims. The portrayal of the fully automatic shotgun is even more farcical. In fact, shotguns are rarely the weapon of choice for modern special operators. Although the impact of a double ought buckshot shell (commonly containing nine .33 calibre pellets) at close range against a human target will be devastating, the shotgun has too many inherent disadvantages to become a primary shoulder weapon of SOF teams. Shotguns are generally rather bulky due to the size of the shells, have a low ammunition capacity, again due to the size of the shot shell, cannot be suppressed and are normally slow to reload as most are not box magazine fed.

Additionally, shotguns have a very limited range with most types of buckshot, 50 metres at best in most cases. Beyond this range, a human target may still well be wounded by buckshot pellets but the chances of inflicting an

The venerable Knight's Master Key system mounted under an SR-16 carbine. The Master Key is a specially modified Remington 870 12-gauge carried underslung much like a grenade launcher. (*Knight's Armament Company*)

incapacitating wound reduces greatly as the pellet spread increases. This is conversely precisely what makes the shotgun the weapon of choice for duck hunters. Shotguns can be loaded with a type of ammunition known as a solid slug originally designed for large game although even these are only accurate out to 75 metres or so. These all-metal solid slugs have found their way into law enforcement use as a means of stopping an escaping car by firing into the engine block. This technique is one that has also been employed by SOF, including deploying an operator with a pump-action shotgun firing slugs from a helicopter to immobilise a target vehicle.

Shotguns have been gainfully employed by modern SOF units in two distinct areas: as a breaching tool and as a weapon for a point-man or lead breacher as they enter a hostile building. Shotguns have been used for many years as breaching tools but using standard buckshot loads. Today most units use specialist munitions such as the Hatton to destroy the locks or hinges on a door. The Hatton was developed as a safer alternative to standard buckshot as the round won't typically over-penetrate through the door to injure non-combatants on the other side. It's also safer for the breacher as it reduces the chance of splash back of pellets from a metal lock or hinge.

Shotguns also make sense for the lead man in the entry stack when he secures the entry point as he can engage a point blank target with a high degree of confidence of incapacitating his target. It also provides a less-than-lethal option to deploy beanbag or similar munitions to force compliance, although this is more in the realms of law enforcement than military special operations. In hostage rescue situations, at close ranges, a shotgun can be just as accurate and discriminatory as a submachine gun but with far less over-penetration concerns. Indeed in European tactical and counter terrorist units, the shotgun saw widespread adoption in the 1980s with Italian designs like the Franchi SPAS-12 and the magazine fed SPAS-15 dominating with units such as the French GIGN, Spanish GEO and the Italian NOCS.

Many police departments in the United States still deploy the 12-gauge shotgun as the assigned 'long gun' stored in an officer's police cruiser, however it is increasingly being replaced by 5.56 × 45mm semi-automatic carbines to give the officer greater stand-off distance when confronting an armed suspect. Many SWAT units still employ the shotgun, but largely for either ballistic breaching purposes or to deliver less-than-lethal ordnance like Ferret CS gas shells or beanbag rounds.

No SOF unit has deployed a fully automatic shotgun in combat since the SEALs with the Remington 7188 in Vietnam, despite some manufacturers' claims to the contrary. Several designs have been tested over the years, including the Pancor Jackhammer, the Daewoo USAS-12 and the Atchisson AA-12, but none have been adopted. Another type of shotgun that has failed to find SOF adoption is the South African designed Armscorp Striker or Protector. This shotgun uniquely feeds from a revolver like cylinder and can fire twelve rounds in rapid fire.

Fully automatic shotguns are appealing in theory for room clearance and CQB and indeed would be fearsome in a Stalingrad-style scenario where there are no non-combatant considerations, but these advantages also turn the weapon into something of a one-trick pony. Once the room clearing component of the operation is over, the operator may then need to engage targets out in the street or surrounding terrain, likely at distances beyond that which a shotgun can reach. This is the same kind of issue experienced by the SEALs with their MP7A1 submachine guns – great at room clearance but not much use beyond 100 metres. Add in the extra bulk and weight of shotgun ammunition and it's easy to see why a HK416 or M4A1 makes more sense in all but the narrowest of circumstances.

The US Marines have issued a 12-gauge semi-automatic shotgun, the Benelli M4 type classified as the M1014, primarily as a crowd control weapon as it can fire less-than-lethal munitions. Although as a semi-automatic design it's arguably not the best choice for such loads as many lack the necessary powder to reliably cycle the action. The M1014 is also used as a breaching tool and is an excellent choice for clearing the close confines of a ship. The M1014 uses the US issue M1030 breaching round comprised of powdered metal in a wax binding in a similar fashion to the better known Hatton.

The US Army adopted the pump-action Mossberg M590 for use in Iraq. Army Special Forces modified the weapon with an enhancement kit that added a breaching barrel, Picatinny rails and an M4-style collapsible stock. Stocks of older folding stock Remington M870 shotguns are still held by the Special Forces, SEALs and the Rangers and a pistol-grip version with a specialist breaching muzzle device has become their standard shotgun. The Army also purchased a number of Remington M870 MCS (Modular Combat Shotgun) shotguns in 2004 for the Special Forces. The MCS features a pistol-grip Pachmayr stock and comes with three barrels of 18-inch, 14-inch and a 10-inch length allowing the operator to switch out the barrel dependent on tasking.

A display of small arms used by US Naval Special Warfare units in 2008, including the SEALs. Of particular interest are the two Remington 870 shotguns shown, one with a light mount whilst the other features a stand-off breaching device on its muzzle and a Tango Down Stubby vertical foregrip. Note also the 9 × 19mm Mk25 (P226) with weapon light in the foreground and the 5.56 × 45mm Mk46 and 7.62 × 51mm Mk48 machine guns in the background. Also notable is the 40mm M79 launcher that continues to soldier on.

(MC3 Michael Russell, US Navy)

Based on their experiences in Afghanistan, the British Army has also issued a new semi-automatic shotgun called the L128A1. This weapon is also based on the Benelli M4 and incorporates several features, including a Picatinny rail mounted EO Tech sight, folding foregrip and collapsible stock. The L128A1 was procured to meet an urgent operational request from troops in Helmand province who felt they needed a weapon that could engage fleeting targets at very close ranges whilst they cleared Afghan compounds, precisely the same reasons the SAS had adopted the shotgun in Borneo some forty years earlier. The L128A1 went into the hands of the point man of an infantry section and has proven popular as it can also be used as a breaching shotgun.

Calibres and Ammunition

In terms of calibre there is only one in terms of combat shotguns, the 12-gauge, also known as the 12-bore in the UK. The 12-gauge has dominated both the military and law enforcement markets largely thanks to its heritage as a sporting weapon. The 12-gauge was seen as the best compromise of calibre – the formidable recoil of the heavier 10-gauge, along with the size of its shells further limiting magazine capacity ruled it out of the running, whilst the smaller 20-gauge was viewed as a duck-hunting weapon that did not have the requisite punch. American soldiers and police were also often comfortable with the 12-gauge from their own sporting activities.

The calibre's widespread use in civilian hands also meant that ammunition developments were more likely in 12-gauge than in any of the other calibres, beginning with plastic cased shells to counter moisture problems encountered with previously paper-based designs. The SEALs' use of the 12-gauge Ithaca and Remington 7188 also saw work on fletchette rounds begin to extend the range and lethality of the shotgun. Vietnam-era special operations heralded the first CS or tear gas rounds designed to be fired from a shotgun, a concept that was later built upon and perfected with the AAI Ferret.

The Ferret was designed to penetrate barriers such as windows and light doors to deliver CS (or later CN gas and OC or pepper spray) to targets within a building. They also proved useful in delivering irritant gas into motor vehicles. Obviously the amount of CS delivered in this manner was far less than that possible from the more traditional 37mm and 40mm gas grenades (versions of the Ferret in these calibres are also available giving a barrier penetration capability). SOF units often deploy the 12-gauge Ferret in hostage rescue operations.

The most common round used in breaching or entry shotguns, as we've seen, is the Hatton produced by Clucas MOE in the United Kingdom. The Hatton and similar breaching rounds are typically made of powdered metal held in a wax suspension and are designed to be used against door locks and hinges, although it has been increasingly deployed by SOF units to shoot into car tyres to deflate them. They will also penetrate doors that have been reinforced with metal sheeting, a common insurgent tactic in Iraq.

A Hatton round could also be used as a point-blank defensive round against a human target with likely devastating effect – such an occurrence has never been documented but the round might well operate like a massive Glaser Safety Slug or similar pre-fragmented round causing a relatively shallow but massive wound. SOF units like the US Army Rangers, that conduct thousands of opposed breaches every year, issue both the Hatton and the double ought buckshot, although the latter is rarely used.

Tactics and Techniques

In combat the shotgun is used in a similar fashion to a rifle, bringing the stock into the shoulder and aligning front and rear sights. In SOF use, instinctive shooting using only the front sight or a combat optic is common. The shotgun's role when carried by an SOF point-man is to engage and neutralise a close range threat to allow other assaulters to clear the target building. If

A Marine blows in a door whilst clearing an Afghan compound with the issue 12-gauge M1014 in Helmand 2009. The M1014 is based on the Benelli M4 design.
(Sgt Pete Thibodeau, US Marine Corps)

carried as a ballistic breaching device, the shotgun will be immediately slung and the operator will transition to his primary shoulder weapon.

In terms of ballistic breaching, there are several techniques taught in terms of how to employ a breaching shotgun against a locked door. For many years the SAS and the Navy SEALs, for instance, used their breaching shotguns against the hinges rather than directly against the lock, a technique conversely favoured by the Rangers and Delta. Breaching rounds offer no guarantee and experienced operators will keep a manual breaching tool like a Hooligan Bar or a handheld ram handy should the door resist the tender mercies of the shotgun. Former Delta operator Paul Howe, a veteran of the Battle of the Black Sea in Mogadishu, instructs his pupils to fire two rounds into the locking mechanism followed by a further two if the lock still will not open. If the lock remains intact, Howe teaches that another assaulter should step up with a manual breaching tool and take out the door.

The Rangers carry their shotguns with an empty chamber and the safety in the off position. When the Ranger approaches the targeted door, he simply racks the shotgun to chamber a Hatton round. Once he has successfully breached the door, he will step away to allow other assaulters through and let the shotgun hang from its D clip whilst transitioning to his M4A1. Many breaching shotguns now also feature specialist muzzle devices designed to

US Army Rangers conduct a raid on a targeted compound in Afghanistan hunting for a high value Taliban insurgent in Helmand Province 2012. Along with their Block 2 M4A1s mounting Elcan Specters, the breacher to the right readies his sawn-off Remington 870 to blow the lock on the gate. *(SPC Justin Young, Department of Defense)*

assist with the breach, for instance some have sawteeth that allow the operator to ram the shotgun muzzle into a wooden door and fire the breaching round at contact range. They also allow the shotgun muzzle to be placed against the lock or hinge, letting gases escape safely without risking dangerous overpressure within the shotgun itself.

Current Trends

In recent years the shotgun has accompanied many SOF units in Afghanistan and Iraq on their raiding missions. Units will typically carry a shortened pump-action model that can be worn in a holster or clipped to their load-bearing gear, thus easily kept out of the way until needed. The pump-action is the near unanimous choice as it will reliably cycle all types of specialist ammunition. It's also far simpler to clear most stoppages with a pump-action by working the pump to eject the offending shell. Pump-action models also tend to be more forgiving of rough treatment of the sort experienced in urban CQB.

Some units have experimented with semi-automatic models but few have adopted them outside of European police counter terrorist teams. DEVGRU

SOPMOD M4
Special Operations Peculiar Modification to the M4 Carbine

Accessory Kit

Reflex sight
NSN: 1240-01-453-1916

4X Day Optical scope
NSN: 1240-01-412-6608

Sound Suppressor kit
NSN: 1005-01-437-0324

Rail Interface System
NSN: 1005-01-416-1089

M4A1 Carbine w/Carrying Handle
NSN: 1005-01-382-0953

Forward Handgrip
NSN: 1005-01-416-1091

Grenade Launcher Leaf Sight
NSN: 1010-01-418-4588

Knight Armerment Master Key Shotgun
NSN: 1005-01-504-6335

M203 9" barrel Asembly
NSN: 1010-01-410-7422

A very early poster from the SOPMOD Block 1 issue showing the Knight's Master Key along with a compact version of the M203 designed for use with the M4A1. (US SOCOM)

had a number of custom semi-automatic shotguns built for them in the 1980s in the form of the Sage International Sidewinder, a pistol-grip modification of the Remington 1100. Some of these exotic folding stock Sidewinders were also purchased for the regular SEAL teams but they have since been replaced with 870 models.

In the 1990s Delta experimented with under-barrel mounting systems from Ciener called the Ultimate Under/Over and from Knight's Armament Company called the Master Key. These systems attached a shortened pump-action Remington 870 shotgun under the barrel of a Colt carbine in a similar fashion to the M203A1 grenade launcher. These systems were trialled operationally in Somalia but Delta soon reverted to a stand-alone 870 shotgun.

Former operator John McPhee's opinion of the Master Key and similar systems is that they were too heavy and unwieldy for practical use. McPhee himself used a shortened pistol-grip 870 in Iraq as a breaching shotgun carried in an arrow quiver that served as a field-expedient shoulder holster. In fact the same quiver also carried his stand-alone M203 grenade launcher in Afghanistan.

The Master Key in action showing how the weapon is employed against door locks and hinges, firing specialist Hatton rounds. Delta deployed with the Master Key to Somalia but reverted to standalone shotguns due to weight and balance issues. (*Knight's Armament Company*)

Individual Weapon Summaries

Remington M870

Although never formally adopted by the US military, the Remington 870 has been employed operationally by the majority of American, and indeed international, SOF for many years. It has largely eclipsed almost all other shotguns in SOF use and as such will be the only make detailed here. It is a straightforward and reliable weapon that continues to function in adverse conditions. The basic Police Magnum model that is used by SOF holds five rounds in a tubular magazine and features a full wood stock and an 18-inch barrel. Commonly SOF units replace the stock with a Pachmayr pistol-grip and an aftermarket forearm often featuring Picatinny rails to mount weapon lights. An extended eight-round magazine will also often be fitted.

UK Special Forces, including the SAS and the SFSG, use a folding stock Remington M870 with an extended magazine known as the L74A1. Some SAS examples seen in Iraq were equipped with Side Saddles keeping extra shells within easy reach. Later examples of the L74A1 seen in Afghanistan have been rather more extensively modified and modernized with extended eight-round magazines, collapsible SOPMOD style stocks, folding forward grips, AN/PEQ-2 infra-red illuminators (rather than the standard British Army

Former operator John 'Shrek' McPhee seen on the right in Baghdad. Notice the sawn off 12-gauge Remington 870 carried in a modified arrow quiver. McPhee used the same quiver to carry a standalone M203 on other occasions. Also of interest is the distinctive forward grip with red light switch mounted on the other operator's carbine – this was designed by a Unit armourer and later manufactured by Knight's. *(John 'Shrek' McPhee)*

issue LLM01), Picatinny rails and Aimpoint Micro optics. They are also often spray painted in desert camouflage colours.

The Rangers and Delta continue to rely on their simple but reliable pistol-grip 870s, with Delta totting theirs in custom shoulder rigs, whilst the Rangers tend to use a D-clip or bungee cord to attach the shotgun to their plate carriers. The Ranger model is a 10-inch barreled 870 with a four-round capacity, three in the tubular magazine and one in the chamber if necessary. The SEALs use the 870 too, often with a weapon light, vertical foregrip and breaching muzzle device fitted. The Special Forces also use the Remington 870 MCS alongside their various modified Mossberg 500 and 590 shotguns.

Future Trends

Considering the history of the under-barrel mounted shotgun, it's surprising to note that a new generation of under-barrel systems is one of the few innovations in shotguns that may be adopted by SOF in the future. The US Army has developed and issued the M26 Modular Accessory Shotgun System (MASS): an under-barrel system that harks back to the Ciener and KAC Master Key concepts. Uniquely, the MASS can be deployed as a stand-alone shotgun in much the same way as the M320 grenade launcher can be fitted with a stock and deployed sans the rifle. The M26 is intended to replace all Army issue Mossberg shotguns. Feedback from infantry units has been positive, although its size has precluded its adoption by the Rangers and other SOF units.

Intriguingly, Crye Precision, designers of the MultiCam camouflage pattern has recently developed a modular shotgun system that is attracting the attention of SOF users. Called the Six12 it can be mounted under the barrel of a carbine or deployed as a stand-alone bullpup shotgun. It is fed from a surprisingly compact six-round rotary cylinder that can be detached and reloaded individually or replaced with a fresh cylinder. The design of the shotgun when mounted under-barrel means that the support hand can take a natural grip on the carbine and still comfortably trigger the shotgun. It will be interesting to see in whose hands the Six12 ends up.

The 12-gauge M26 MASS (Modular Accessory Shotgun System) issued in limited numbers as a breaching shotgun to the US military. The M26 can be deployed either as a standalone system as seen here or mounted underslung the barrel of an M4. *(PEO Soldier)*

Chapter Six

Sniper and Anti-Materiel Rifles

Overview

The demarcation line between what exactly is termed a Special Purpose Rifle, a Designated Marksman Rifle or a Sniper Rifle is very, very blurred. Calibre is not a good indicator as weapons in all three categories are chambered in 7.62×51mm, or indeed in 5.56×45mm. Type of action is likewise a poor discriminator, as there are plenty of semi-automatic weapons in all three classes, although typically only sniper rifles are bolt action. Perhaps the only reliable indicator, however imprecise, is actual combat role.

Special Purpose Rifles and DMRs like the Mk11 and Mk12, discussed in Chapter Four, cloud the definition as, although they were originally developed not as a dedicated sniper rifle, they have since been deployed as such. Indeed one can find weapons like the SR-25 or the Mk12 used by assaulters,

A US Army Ranger sniper destroys an explosive target with his .50BMG M107A1 SASR (Special Application Scoped Rifle). The M107A1 is still employed for extended range shooting beyond 1,500 metres and for specialist duties such as destroying IEDs at distance. *(75th Ranger Regiment Public Affairs Office)*

marksmen and snipers – sometimes all in the same unit! Sniper rifles, however, are deployed only by actual school trained snipers for extended range shooting and it's this loose definition we will use here to decide where in the book a particular weapon system is placed. This will lead to some overlap, particularly in terms of the semi-automatic platforms like the Mk11 and Mk12. With anti-materiel rifles, no such uncertainty thankfully exists. These behemoths are the heavy calibre extended range platforms designed to hurl a .50BMG bullet at distant targets sometimes kilometres away from the sniper.

The development of SOF sniper rifles has largely mirrored the evolution of the sniper and his weapons in conventional military forces. It was not until the 1970s when a dedicated military response to terrorism was needed that the SOF sniper began to procure specialist weapons and techniques to deal with the new threat. In the Second World War for instance all special operations snipers typically carried the same rifles as their infantry counterparts. One SOF specific weapon they did carry was the .45ACP DeLisle Carbine.

Although officially termed a carbine, the DeLisle was more like a suppressed short range sniper rifle; indeed the concept is now reminiscent of recent Russian developments like the VSS Vintorez. Firing the relatively low powered, but importantly subsonic .45ACP ball round, the bolt-action DeLisle was integrally suppressed and fed from a standard seven-round M1911 pistol magazine. The weapon itself was something of a Frankenstein's Monster built from the barrel of a .45ACP Thompson submachine gun and the action and stock of a .303 Lee Enfield service rifle.

Through Vietnam, United States SOF units deployed the same core weapons systems as the regulars, apart from perhaps an increased use and availability of Starlight night vision devices and sound suppressors. In the 1980s units began to look at sniper rifles that offered reduced weight, compactness or an extension in range, or ideally all three in the one package. For the largely urban counter terrorist role, teams needed rifles that offered surgical accuracy out to several hundred metres, could be suppressed and that were handy enough to fire from helicopters.

Many of these units adopted a mix of bolt-action and semi-automatic designs. The bolt action has traditionally held the edge in terms of accuracy, however bolt-action rifles also tend to be slow to reload, are longer in length due to their design roots in hunting rifles, and obviously lack the firepower of a semi-automatic platform. The British SAS initially adopted a number of Tikka bolt-action designs, including an integrally suppressed model, but also had available scoped semi-automatic Heckler and Koch G3 variants. The British SBS actually approached a fledgling company known as Accuracy International to develop a folding stock, 7.62 × 51mm boltaction sniper rifle for them that could be easily suppressed. That rifle ended up forming the basis for the L96A1 that eventually won the contract for the new British Army sniper rifle in the mid-1980s.

In military SOF units, the bolt-action designs were seen as the most accurate platform for extended range shooting, whilst the semi-automatic became favoured for urban operations. The semi-automatic also offered fast follow-on shots that were important in any situations where the operator found himself facing numerous enemy. The semi-automatic could also be used for CQB if required offering even further versatility. There was also, of course, the semi-automatic anti-materiel rifle too.

The anti-materiel rifle class really owes its existence to the .50 calibre Barrett M82A1. Developed as a long-range rifle for SOF and EOD operators, the Barrett was intended to engage materiel rather than people. It was developed in 1982 with the aim of creating a weapon that could immobilise or destroy enemy light armour, communications masts, radars and similar high value targets. It was purchased in limited numbers by the Army Special Forces and SEALs before being adopted by both the Army and the Marine Corps during Operation Desert Storm as the M107 Special Application Scoped Rifle (SASR).

While we are discussing these monsters, it's worth shooting down yet another myth – that the .50BMG cannot be used against human targets. Where this one originated is uncertain but it's been around for almost as long as the calibre itself has been. To set matters straight, there is no prohibition on the use of the .50BMG in the Hague Conventions, the Geneva Conventions, or any other agreement or treaty, nor within the Laws of Land Warfare. People can be legally engaged with the .50BMG just as certainly as vehicles or aircraft can be.

To equip themselves for the counter terrorism mission during the late 1970s and into the 1980s, SOF adopted a range of bolt-action Tikka, SAKO and Remington designs, typically in 7.62 × 51mm NATO, although the SAS also had available a number of .22-250 Tikka M55s. The .22-250 variant was also adopted by the Australian SASR as their urban sniper rifle as they believed the smaller round reduced over-penetration and ricochet fears during hostage recoveries. The British and Australians also adopted the semi-automatic 7.62 × 51mm Heckler and Koch PSG1 during the same period.

By the late 1990s and into the outbreak of the War on Terror at the dawn of the new century, most SOF units had a range of optically equipped 5.56 × 45mm and 7.62 × 51mm semi-automatic rifles, bolt-action 7.62 × 51mm and increasingly .300 Winchester Magnum rifles, plus a number of both bolt-action and semi-automatic .50BMG anti-materiel rifles. As always, operators could select the most appropriate tool for the job at hand, whether that be aerial sniper support for a ground assault force or precision fire to eliminate an insurgent leader.

Calibres and Ammunition

In terms of range effects, many operators will consider under 400 metres to be 5.56 × 45mm territory, whilst the 7.62 × 51mm is the platform of choice out

US Army Ranger snipers zero their weapons in Afghanistan, 2013. The snipers in the foreground are firing the standard US Army issue M2010 in .300 Winchester Magnum. These will be replaced in SOCOM units with the Mk21 Precision Sniper Rifle that accommodates 7.62 × 51mm, .300 Winchester Magnum and .338 Lapua Magnum. In the background are several SCARs including an Mk20 SSR, a Mk46 light machine gun and an M110 SASS.
(1LT Tyler N. Ginter, US Army)

to around the 800 metre mark (although talented snipers with a good rifle, ammunition and optics can push the 7.62 × 51mm out to well beyond this range). The .300 Winchester Magnum is considered the best choice for the next range bracket out to around 1,200 metres. Beyond this it is the realm of the .338 Lapua Magnum or the big .50BMG.

The most common sniper rifle calibre remains, however, the 7.62 × 51mm or .308 Winchester in commercial terms. Most semi-automatic platforms like the SR-25, Mk11 and the Accuracy International variants are chambered for the 7.62 × 51mm. We have looked at the use of 5.56 × 45mm as a marksman or light sniper rifle in Chapter Four and thus we won't be examining it here in any detail, but to suffice it to say that SOF spotters and sniper security teams will often be equipped with scoped 5.56 × 45mm platforms like the Mk12 or HK416.

Thanks to its historical use as a sniper calibre, 7.62 × 51mm has become the standard for its relative stability and accuracy at range, and of course its lethal effects on human targets. The 7.62 × 51mm also makes a lot of sense in terms of logistical support, as an SOF unit can resupply from a conventional unit or a Coalition SOF unit from another nation. The gold standard in military long-range ammunition has long been the M118LR, a 175-grain Sierra Match King round designed for accuracy. It is now being replaced by a round developed for SOCOM called the Mk316 Mod0. The Mk316 was designed to address inconsistent accuracy issues with the M118LR and was developed to relieve reliability issues with gas-operated semi-automatic platforms.

Certainly 7.62 × 51mm offers the best general purpose sniper round out to 800 metres, although in Afghanistan ranges were sometimes much further than this. The US and UK militaries have seen that their snipers needed a larger calibre to engage more distant targets than the 7.62 × 51mm could comfortably service. The US looked to the .300 Winchester Magnum whilst the British adopted the .338 Lapua Magnum. The US Marines, apart from MARSOC, maintained their M40A5 and M40A6 bolt-action platforms in 7.62 × 51mm despite mounting evidence that a .300 Winchester Magnum or .338 Lapua Magnum platform was needed.

The .300 Winchester Magnum is largely favoured by American SOCOM snipers using the Mk13 platform. SEALs and MARSOC in particular seem to appreciate the calibre. DEVGRU snipers deployed with Task Force Ranger to Mogadishu in 1993 carried .300 Winchester Magnum bolt-action rifles manufactured by McMillan, earlier marks of what would later be marketed as the McMillan TAC-300. On the same operation, they also brought with them early examples of what would be termed the 'M4 Sniper' or 'Recce Rifle' in 5.56 × 45mm as discussed in an earlier chapter.

A new bullet was developed for the .300 Winchester Magnum Mk13 Mod5 that has seen significant combat use in the later years of the War on Terror. The Mk248 Mod1 features a heavier 220-grain projectile than the older 190-grain standard issue .300 Winchester Magnum. The Mk248 also adds some 250 metres to the effective range of the standard .300 Winchester Magnum load, allowing it to engage targets out to 1,370 metres. The heavier bullet also reduces the impact of wind deflection.

The .338 Lapua Magnum expands upon the capabilities of the .300 Winchester Magnum both in terms of increased range and terminal effects. The concept for what would become the .338 Lapua Magnum (8.58 × 70mm) was actually initially developed by Research Armament Industries (RAI) at the behest of the United States Marine Corps. The USMC was looking for an extended range sniper cartridge that could penetrate combat body armour at over 1,000 metres. The round was finally completed by a conglomerate of the Finnish ammunition producer Lapua, Britain's Accuracy International and Finland's SAKO.

The round began to realise its potential when the British Army adopted an Accuracy International rifle chambering the .338 Lapua Magnum in 2007. This rifle, based on the successful 7.62 × 51mm L96A1, was called the L115A3 and replaced the L96A1 for use by all snipers within the British military. A slightly modified .338 Accuracy International AWSM rifle was also adopted by British Special Forces and has been extensively employed in Afghanistan and Iraq. In one operation in Baghdad, three SAS snipers firing the .338 achieved near simultaneous head shots against multiple terrorist suicide bombers as they left a safe house

MARSOC Marines in Afghanistan display their suppressed .300 Winchester Magnum Mk13 Mod5 sniper rifles to Marine Corps General James Amos. MARSOC are the only Marines currently authorized the .300 Winchester Magnum. Marine Corps snipers rely upon the venerable 7.62 × 51mm M40A5. (*Sgt Mallory S. VanderSchans, US Marine Corps*)

Operationally, the .338 Lapua Magnum bridges the gap between the .300 Winchester Magnum and the .50BMG (12.7 × 99mm) and provides a round that will reliably hit targets with accuracy beyond 1,000 metres and out to 1,600 metres or more. Indeed British Army snipers in Afghanistan were recording kills at well beyond this range with their L115A3s, including some at over 2,000 metres such as the record breaking 2,475 metre kills made by a sniper in Afghanistan in 2009. The calibre has also seen extensive operational use by Australian Commandos who deploy the excellent German Blaser Tactical 2 sniper rifle.

SOCOM have also now released a tender for armour piercing ammunition for the .338 Lapua Magnum platform that would penetrate heavy body armour (Class IV proofed against 7.62 × 39mm) at ranges in excess of 400 metres. Body armour, particularly such heavy combat body armour, was and still is thankfully a rarity on the battlefields of Iraq and Afghanistan. Insurgents were reported wearing older US PASGT type armoured vests during the second battle for Fallujah in 2004 but this was an exception rather than the rule. With the advance of ISIL/ISIS in Iraq and Syria capturing Iraqi and Syrian Army stocks however, body armour will become far more prevalent and the SOCOM tender begins to look very prescient indeed.

The final round we need to consider is the .50BMG, a round that perhaps needs little introduction. Designed as a machine-gun calibre, it was first chambered in a sniper rifle by Ronnie Barrett in 1982. Before then it had been deployed as a sniper rifle by the legendary US Marine sniper Carlos Hathcock in Vietnam who used a scoped M2 Browning heavy-machine-gun to hit a Viet Cong at 2,090 metres. Scoped M2s had been used even earlier in Korea. The Barrett however really brought the .50BMG into the spotlight as a sniper calibre.

In more recent times, a Canadian sniper supporting Operation Anaconda made a record kill with a McMillan TAC-50 at 2,430 metres in 2002, whilst an Australian 2nd Commando sniper team made a record 2,815-meter kill with the Barrett M82A1 in 2012 in Helmand Province. The most common SOF .50BMG round is the green-tipped M1022 Long Range Sniper, however a number of light armour piercing incendiary rounds are also available.

Tactics and Techniques

Despite video games and movies like *American Sniper* propagating the idea of the sniper aiming only for the headshot, in reality this is often a difficult shot for even the most skilled or experienced sniper to make. There are a limited number of scenarios that may force a sniper to attempt the headshot, for instance if the enemy is holding a hostage or is wearing a suicide bomb vest. There are only two small zones on the human head that will guarantee immediate incapacitation – a small area centred on the nose and the top of the spine.

Most often shots will be taken for the centre of body mass as it generates the greatest chance of a hit, and is the largest target area, and most of the body's vital organs are contained there. Snipers are also typically shooting heavier calibre that retain their velocity over longer distances and will cause a larger permanent and temporary wound track in the target. When using bolt-action platforms, snipers rely upon the calibre of the round to do the damage, with lighter calibre semi-automatics, faster follow-on shots are possible.

The urban environment of Iraq impacted tremendously on sniper tactics and techniques; engagement ranges shrank as lines of sight were broken by buildings. The environment allowed insurgents to attempt to encircle and swarm sniper teams who often had to fight their way out of compromised hide sites. The rise in the use of semi-automatics was also triggered by the Iraq experience as snipers needed the firepower of the Mk11 or SR-25 to engage multiple hostiles, often at ranges under 100 metres.

Despite that, there were exceptions. *Shooting Times* reported that the late Chris Kyle made his longest shot in Iraq at 2,100 yards (1,920 metres). Kyle explained in the interview:

> It took place outside of Sadr City while providing overwatch. We saw movement against a friendly convoy – a guy trying to hide on top of a roof. I noticed he had RPG and was raising it to attack the convoy, so I took the shot. I was using a .338 Lapua Mag rifle that day.

In Iraq, few sniper teams left the wire alone. Instead they brought with them a security element that would cover their backs whilst they were on the scope. Even the protection of sniper security teams did not guarantee safety. A US Marine sniper element of four Marines, all armed with M16A4s along with two M40A3 sniper rifles were killed in a rooftop hide in 2004, whilst three Marine sniper pairs working together were ambushed and killed near Haditha in 2005. The Army Rangers soon bolstered the security elements around their snipers after several close calls. The French in Afghanistan would routinely attach a machine-gunner and several riflemen to provide close protection for their snipers and marksmen.

If the engagement range mainly decreased in much of urban Iraq, ranges increased in Afghanistan where, as we have seen, insurgents tended to initiate contact at much greater ranges. High angle shooting, that rapidly reduces velocity and consequently effective range, was also common to the north and east of the country. Insurgent snipers, or better termed as marksmen, would often try to engage sniper teams as they knew their capabilities. Thankfully the abilities of these insurgents, often nothing more than a local with a Dragunov SVD or a bolt-action Lee Enfield or Mauser, were no match for the Coalition snipers.

The war in Iraq and Afghanistan also saw a number of new sniper tactics developed or refined for these asymmetric conflicts. One was aerial sniping from helicopters. The British SAS and SBS perfected the skill of firing from Lynx helicopters with one sniper and a spotter perched in the cargo area. The sniper would be typically armed with a .338 Lapua Magnum secured on a tether, whilst his spotter would carry a semi-automatic HK417. UK Special Forces have also adopted a technique of using twin-rotor Chinook helicopters as an aerial sniper platform with multiple snipers armed with .338 and .50BMG weapons firing from the side windows, whilst the door gunners add their firepower with their fearsome 7.62×51mm M134 miniguns.

Current Trends

The greatest trends during the War on Terror have centred upon the increasing use of heavier calibre sniper rifles, particularly in .338 Lapua Magnum, and the greater acceptance and use of both semi-automatic sniper platforms and the sound suppressor.

As detailed in Chapter Four, the advent of Designated Marksman Rifles and SOF Special Purpose Rifles to close the capability gap between 5.56×45mm carbines and dedicated sniper rifles has seen a huge growth in precision semi-automatic rifles. This has been led, of course, by the SR-25, the Mk11 and the HK417; most armies and military SOF units have adopted these within their sniper cells. Dependent on operational circumstance, the semi-automatic is often preferred to the bolt action.

A MARSOC sniper trains with the older M40A3 in 7.62×51mm in 2008. MARSOC later received the Mk13 and the M2010 and will be equipped with the Mk21 PSR. *(US Marine Corps)*

Bolt actions are still, however, very much in evidence. In Iraq and for much of the war in Afghanistan for example, Army Special Forces carried the dependable 7.62 × 51mm M24A2 Sniper Weapon System (SWS), a bolt-action design built from the chassis of a commercial Remington 700. The M24A2 is currently being replaced by another bolt-action design, the .300 Winchester Magnum M2010, to offer greater range and lethality. Conversely however, the Green Beret ODAs did also deploy the 7.62 × 51mm SR-25 and the Mk11 as a sniper platform, particularly during urban operations where long-range precision was less of a requirement and the operator may encounter a large number of hostiles at relatively close range.

Suppressors are the other big trend with current sniper rifle platforms. Suppressed .22LR rifles such as the Ruger 10/22 have been used to kill guard dogs by SEALs for many years and suppressed 7.62 × 51mm M21 sniper rifles were used in Vietnam, but it has only been relatively recently that the suppressor has become a common addition to the sniper rifles of both SOF and conventional forces. At close range you will hear both the bang of the muzzle report and the crack of the bullet passing by at supersonic speeds. At combat distances, you will hear the crack of the bullet before you hear the bang of the weapon that fired it. This is one reason why suppressors have become so popular with SOF teams and particularly designated marksmen and snipers. The suppressor effectively masks where exactly the incoming round came from even though the targets will know they are under fire.

In Afghanistan, concealed sniper teams have managed to engage and kill numerous insurgents with the Taliban never realizing where the fire was coming from. The Australian SASR conducted two successful ambushes at the same site in northwest Uruzgan Province in September 2008 by using suppressed SR-25 rifles. After ambushing and killing all members of the first insurgent group, a second group, sent to investigate the fate of the first, were also successfully engaged and killed.

Individual Weapon Summaries

SOCOM Sniper Rifles

SOCOM have issued a range of sniper and marksman platforms across the various units under their command. These range from the 7.62 × 51mm Mk11, the 5.56 × 45mm Mk12, the .300 Winchester Magnum Mk13, the 7.62 × 51mm Mk14, the .50BMG Mk15, the 7.62 × 51mm Mk20 and the recently adopted Mk21 PSR available in a range of calibres to include 7.62 × 51mm, .300 Winchester Magnum and .338 Lapua Magnum.

Mk13 Mod0 to 7

The Mk13 Mod0 was a 26.5-inch barrelled Remington 700 action embedded in a custom McMillan stock, featuring multiple Picatinny rails and equipped with the same suppressor that was designed by Knights Armament Company

A US Army Ranger sniper in Afghanistan firing his .300 Winchester Magnum Mk13 Mod5 bolt action sniper rifle. Note the weapon is, like the Rangers' carbines, also fitted with an AN/PEQ-15 infra-red illuminator allowing the sniper to mark targets with the invisible to the naked eye beam. *(SPC Liam Mulrooney, US Army)*

for the 7.62 × 51mm Mk11. The SEALs and many others within JSOC and SOCOM favour Nightforce Mil-Dot scopes and this is the scope that is still most often deployed with the Mk13 platform. The total package weighs in at over 9kg loaded and equipped with a Harris bipod, still considerably lighter than the SR-25 or Mk11.

A superbly accurate rifle and shooting the highly capable and flat-shooting .300 Winchester Magnum, the Mk13 was upgraded many times, including changes to the stock, barrel and optics. One of the most widely deployed was the Mk13 Mod 5 which was built using an Accuracy International stock and thus visually looks similar to an AI platform including the excellent folding stock. The US Navy SEALs are currently using the Mk13 Mod 7 in .300 Winchester Magnum, as are MARSOC and Army Special Forces.

Mk15 Mod0 SASR

McMillan Firearms have had a long and close relationship with the SEALs. They built the first versions of what would become the Mk13 and later the first of what is now classed as the Mk15, based on the commercial McMillan TAC-50. SEAL snipers were deployed in the late 1980s to the Persian Gulf to protect shipping and oil platforms. They took with them some of the earliest McMillan .50BMG platforms, the M88.

US Navy SEAL snipers engage targets on the range with the .50BMG Mk15 Mod0 SASR (Special Application Scoped Rifle) built by McMillan. Notice the amount of dust kicked up by the 'big .50'. Snipers will often use a shooting mat or wet the ground to reduce this telltale sign. (*United States Naval Special Warfare*)

The Mk15 is a huge, bolt-action rifle built around a fibreglass McMillan stock chassis to maximise strength and reduce weight. The Mk15 weighs in at a hefty 12kg complete with bipod and impressive muzzle brake (it can also be fitted with a surprisingly effective suppressor). Like the better known Barrett M82A1, it can engage targets well beyond the 2,000 metre mark, firing massive 750-grain bullets.

Mk20 Mod0 SSR
The 7.62 × 51mm Mk20 is the Sniper Support Rifle variant of the SCAR family. The Mk20 features a 20-inch barrel and is designed to act as either a sniper spotter weapon or as a marksman rifle. It is used extensively in the latter role amongst the SEALs and MARSOC Raiders.

Mk21 PSR
The recently adopted Mk21 Precision Sniper Rifle is based on the commercial Remington Modular Sniper Rifle (MSR) offering and is designed to allow any of three calibres to be fired – 7.62 × 51mm NATO, .300 Winchester Magnum and .338 Lapua Magnum. The bolt heads can be quickly changed by the shooter and the free-floating barrel swapped out to change calibre. It is unlikely this would be conducted in the field, however it allows an SOF sniper to deploy with just the one rifle. It also brings the significant capabilities of the .338 Lapua Magnum into the hands of non JSOC units, indeed apparently DEVGRU were involved in combat trials of the .338 Lapua Magnum MSR.

The Precision Sniper Rifle programme aimed to provide a single, suppressor-equipped bolt-action sniper rifle for adoption across all Special Operations Command units for an initial total of 5,150 rifles. The programme began in 2009 with a requirement for a weapon that could reliably hold 1 Minute of Angle (MOA – keeping a grouping within 1 inch on the target) up to a range of 1,500 metres. It also required the rifle to weigh a maximum of 18lbs loaded with a five-round magazine (8kg), be no longer than 52 inches (excluding the suppressor) and be equipped with at least one Picatinny rail at the twelve o'clock position.

A large number of contenders entered the programme, including Remington, Accuracy International, Barrett, Blaser, Fabrique Nationale and SAKO. It was eventually won by the Remington design. The wider US Army adopted an upgraded M24A3 known as the M2010 in .300 Winchester Magnum with a 24-inch barrel with a five-round magazine. Designed to accept an AAC suppressor, the M2010 features the standard Leupold Mk4 with clip-on night sight optic along with the requisite Picatinny rails.

Accuracy International

Rather uniquely, the first Accuracy International sniper rifles ever built were purchased by the British Special Boat Squadron (now Service). Eight AI PM (Precision Match) rifles in 7.62 × 51mm were procured by the SBS in 1985 with

A sniper pair from the 10th Special Forces Group engage targets with their sound suppressed .300 Winchester Magnum M2010. *(LCpl Charles Santamaria, Department of Defense)*

US Army Special Forces and French SOF snipers training together in Djibouti in 2013. The rifles are a mixture – at the top of the photo is what appears to be a .338 Lapua Magnum Sako TRG-42, while closer to the camera are a pair of .338 Lapua Magnum Accuracy International Artic Warfare Super Magnum platforms.

(MAJ Duncan Smith, US Army, Special Operations Detachment – Africa)

thirty-two more going to the Hereford headquarters of the SAS to replace their aging Parker Hale and Tikka rifles. Ten years later, a modified version of that rifle became the new British Army sniper rifle, the 7.62 × 51mm L96A1.

Accuracy International sniper platforms have been adopted by numerous of SOF units internationally, most commonly the integrally suppressed 7.62 × 51mm Arctic Warfare Suppressed (AWS) and the Arctic Warfare Covert (AWC) folding stock, break-down version of the AWS. Both of these rifles have been deployed by UK Special Forces and JSOC units. The German KSK deploy the AWC as the G25.

The Arctic Warfare Super Magnum was one of the first purpose-built military sniper rifles chambered for the .338 Lapua Magnum and was adopted by the SAS and SBS. It also went into service with the British Army in 2007 as the L115A3. The Canadian PGW Timberwolf in .338 Lapua Magnum has been seen in recent combat use by the British SAS in Helmand Province, Afghanistan and may have replaced the AWSM platforms amongst UK Special

Dutch snipers firing the Accuracy International Artic Warfare model in 7.62 × 51mm. This rifle in various guises was adopted by many Western SOF and was used for many years by UKSF. A modified version serves in the British Army as the L96A1. *(MC1 Josh Kreim, NATO)*

Forces. AI also developed an upgraded version for the SOCOM PSR trials called the AX338 and also produce a number of .50BMG anti-materiel rifles including the bolt-action AW50 and the semi-automatic AS50.

Other Designs

As mentioned earlier, the SEALs have maintained a long relationship with McMillan Firearms and continue to do so. A number of unit purchased McMillan TAC-338s have been deployed by the SEALs in both Afghanistan and Iraq, topped with either a Nightforce or Leupold optic. The Australian Commandos use the 9kg German Blaser Tactical 2, a .338 Winchester Magnum design that features a straight-pull bolt more commonly seen on competition rifles, that both minimises movement from the action of chambering a new round and increases the speed with which that new round can be fired. Officially the Australian Blasers are rated as able to engage precision targets out to 1,500 metres and provide harassing fire out to 2,000 metres. Like most modern designs, the Blaser is equipped with an effective suppressor. The Australians also deploy the .50BMG Barrett M82A1 and the AI AW50F.

French SOF units have used the domestically designed 7.62 × 51mm PGM Ultima Ratio as their principal sniper platform, along with the .50BMG PGM

An Australian Commando sniper searches for targets in Afghanistan 2011. He is armed with the .338 Lapua Magnum Blaser Tactical 2. (SOCOMD)

Hecate II. Some elements also have access to the Barrett M82A1. Along with the German KSK, the French also deploy the venerable 7.62 × 51mm Heckler and Koch MSG90 and G3/SG1 along with the more recent HK417.

Future Trends

Modularity and optics will be the bywords of future sniper developments. For SOF use, compactness can be added to that list. In terms of modularity, the SOCOM Mk21 has shown what can be done with a weapon system that is being produced in significant numbers. Many commentators have questioned why the broader US Army requirement for the M2010 was not rolled into the SOCOM requirement, particularly with Marine and Army snipers crying out for more access to .300 Winchester Magnum and .338 Lapua Magnum platforms. The Mk21 is a true example of successful, practical modularity in small arms design. Barrett recently developed their own contender for the SOCOM PSR trial, the Barrett MRAD which can fire the 7.62 × 51mm, the .300 Winchester Magnum and the .338 Lapua Magnum. All future SOF sniper rifles, apart from those with niche applications like the AMRs and covert Break-Down Rifles, will likely feature calibre interchangeability.

Optics will continue to improve as developments like the RAZAR (Rapid Adaptive Zoom for Assault Rifles) are fielded. The RAZAR allows magnification changes to be made literally at the touch of a button without the sniper having to take their eye off the scope. The other big development is in smart optics systems like the now defunct Tracking Point. This system allowed the shooter to mark a target through the optic, much as one would using a laser designator. The system then takes over calculating the range, drop and literally tracks the target until you are ready to engage. At that place, the shooter merely lines up the reticle on the red target marker and fires. The system electronically zeroes the rifle, eliminates the effects of shooter trigger jerk, movement and breathing, and tracks the moving target until you are ready to engage. These types of Precision Guided rifles will become the new standard.

SOF sniper rifles will also continue to get smaller, at least for some applications. In 2010, Joint Special Operations Command was soliciting for a new style of sniper rifle with more similarities to something seen in a Jason Bourne thriller than anything normally seen on the battlefield – a Clandestine Break Down Rifle, that was more commonly referred to as the Clandestine Sniper Rifle (CSR). The JSOC requirements called for a 16-inch match barrel carbine in 5.56×45mm that could be easily and quickly broken down and stored in a

A US Navy SEAL from SEAL Team 1 explains a range of sniper platforms deployed by the SEALs in 2010. Visible are a 7.62×51mm Mk17 SCAR Heavy with folded stock, a .300 Winchester Magnum Mk13 Mod5 and, closest to the camera, a .50BMG Mk15 Mod0. *(MC2 Shauntae Hinkle-Lymas, US Navy)*

A 7th Special Forces Group sniper competes with his recently issued .300 Winchester Magnum M2010. The M2010 has replaced the 7.62 × 51mm M24 that was the standard sniper rifle for the Special Forces and Rangers for much of the War on Terror.
(*MSG Alex Licea, SOCOM South*)

compact case. A US company called DRD Tactical developed a folding stock rifle called the Paratus in response to the JSOC tender that could break down into two major components and fit within a small case. As the results of the trial were classified, it is unknown what CSR platform was adopted. The CSR harks back to an earlier Delta driven development in the 1990s – the Knight's Silenced Survival Rifle or SSR. This .30 platform was based on a heavily modified Ruger Redhawk revolver and used sheathed rounds and a highly effective suppressor to virtually silence the weapon. It was deadly accurate within 100 meters and could be broken down into its component parts – stock, action, suppressor and bipod for portability.

Finally, it's unlikely any new calibre will join the fray in the immediate future, but with the widespread popularity amongst snipers of the .338 Lapua Magnum, it is perhaps surprising that a semi-automatic platform firing that round has not been introduced by any of the major manufacturers. The situation is changing with the SWORD Mk-18 in .338 Lapua Magnum seen by many as having great potential amongst SOF snipers. The weapon was developed by a former Army Ranger and a former Green Beret and is marketed by a former DEVGRU sniper. It is broadly based around the AR-10 design and looks set to be a very strong contender.

Chapter Seven

Squad Automatic Weapons and Machine Guns

Overview

In many ways, the role of the machine gun in special operations is no different to its role in more conventional military operations: to provide suppressive fire against point or area targets to facilitate manoeuvre, be that breaking contact, recovering a wounded operator or enabling a fire team to close with and assault an enemy position. With the changing nature of asymmetric warfare and particularly in urban environments like Iraq the machine gun is now also often pressed into service during room and building clearances with the machine gunner acting as an additional assaulter, firing his weapon from the shoulder.

A Ranger SAW gunner maintains his arcs whilst an assault element searches a suspect compound. His weapon is the 5.56 × 45mm Mk46 equipped with an AN/PEQ-15 infra-red illuminator and an EOTech 553 optic. (*SPC Walter Reeves, US Army*)

For special operations use, the machine gun must be compact and light-weight enough to enable it to be carried during any number of insertion methods, from HALO and HAHO parachuting, to waterborne infiltration by Zodiac small boats or SCUBA. For these reasons many of the models of machine guns deployed by SOF units during the War on Terror are variations on tried and true designs carried by their infantry colleagues. Reliability is the key requirement for such weapons, whether in the hands of infantry soldiers or special operators. The guns need to be able to continue to operate at high rates of fire in the most demanding of conditions. For this reason, it is usually already combat tested designs like the Fabrique Nationale MAG58 or Minimi which are modified and adapted for SOF use.

During the Second World War, British Special Forces used the standard issue .303 Bren light machine gun as their principal support weapon. Although limited by its thirty-round magazine, the Bren was handy, reliable and supremely accurate, in fact, some would argue too accurate for its intended role. The Bren was supplemented by a number of vehicle mounted machine guns used by both the LRDG and the SAS such as the .303 Vickers K, which was originally an aircraft mounted weapon that was 'liberated' by the SAS from Royal Air Force stocks, and the venerable .50BMG Browning M2. Even some Great War vintage .303 Lewis medium machine guns were pressed into service mounted upon the LRDG's trucks. The SBS also employed a range of captured machine guns in the Mediterranean including the German MG15 and the Italian Breda.

German wartime SOF used the standard issue MG34 and MG42 along with the paratrooper FG42, which was officially more a battle rifle but also fulfilled the light machine gun role. The 7.92 × 57mm FG42 and the American .30-06 Browning-Automatic-Rifle or BAR were two precursors to the development of the modern light machine gun and squad automatic weapon that could be carried and fired by a single operator. Post war the Americans produced a fully automatic M14 variant that served as a replacement for the BAR. Its operational life was short-lived, however, as the USMC and US Army transitioned to the selective-fire M16. Although some M16s were issued with bipods, the squad automatic rifle role was left vacant with the platoon level 7.62 × 51mm M60 medium machine gun, itself based on the German MG42, providing suppressive fire.

In Vietnam, SOF units relied principally upon modified versions of the standard-issue M60 or upon exotics like captured Soviet 7.62 × 39mm RPDs or fully automatic heavy barrel FALs. The SEALs in Vietnam carried perhaps the world's first modern SAW in the form of the 5.56 × 45mm Stoner 63A or the Mk23 in US Navy service. The Stoner was also something of a nod toward today's increasingly modular approach, being able to swap out barrels and feed systems for specific tasks, there was even a folding stock carbine version.

With different barrel lengths and feed mechanisms, four primary weapons could actually be constructed from the base 63A.

The Stoner design was a well-liked but temperamental weapon that would perform as long as it was maintained correctly. Cadillac Gage who manufactured the Stoner tried to interest the US Army Special Forces in the machine gun to no avail and the weapon remained a SEAL oddity. Sadly, it was eventually withdrawn from service in 1983, with some claiming a number of SEALs deployed to Grenada with the weapon one last time, as spare parts had become impossible to obtain.

The US Army Special Forces adopted the general-issue 5.56 × 45mm M249 Squad Automatic Weapon (SAW), a variant of Fabrique Nationale's Minimi that was fed from a two hundred-round drum (in emergencies it could also accept STANAG M16 magazines although this often caused stoppages). In its standard version, the M249 was considered by many to be excessively long and heavy for SOF purposes, weighing in at over 10kg loaded and measuring over 40 inches with the issue 21-inch barrel. Fabrique Nationale and SOCOM soon began looking at ways to shave both weight and length from the SAW.

Before the advent of the M249, Delta Force had needed a reliable and accurate general purpose machine gun. They found it in the 7.62 × 51mm HK21. Delta's founder Colonel Charlie Beckwith described the HK21 as:

> ... a Rolls Royce. It fires full automatic or single shot, has an effective range of 1,200 meters, a cyclic rate of 900 rounds per minute and can fire drums, link belts, or box magazines. And unlike the M60, which is a two-man gun, the HK21 requires only one operator. Light, flexible, and accurate, for the tasks we had to perform, its one hell of a good weapon.

The HK21 accompanied Delta operators on their first operation into Iran to rescue the hostages held at the American Embassy in 1980. The Rangers who provided the force protection element for the operation carried the standard M60 in the light role.

In the mid-1980s, the SEALs' stocks of worn and ageing Vietnam-era M60s were replaced by the new Navy issue M60E3, a lighter and more reliable refinement that featured a shorter barrel and a vertical forward pistol-grip. The M60E3 proved popular with the SEALs who had lacked a truly man-portable machine gun since the retirement of the Stoner 63. The SEALs eventually replaced their M60E3s with an enhanced product-improved version designed by Saco Defense and type classified as the Mk43 Mod0 that came into Naval Special Warfare service in the mid-1990s.

The SEALs had also trialled the M249 SAW adopted by other SOCOM units, but found it to be unreliable in maritime conditions. Instead they evaluated a number of other platforms including the Singaporean Ultimax and an updated Stoner design, although neither were subsequently adopted. SEAL Team Six had followed Delta's lead and adopted a handful of the 7.62 × 51mm

A SEAL from SEAL Team 8 carries the 7.62 × 51mm M60E4 in Kuwait in 1998. The M60E4 would be largely replaced by the Mk48 but several examples would soldier on in Afghanistan and Iraq up until 2004. *(JO2 Charles Neff, US Navy)*

HK21, impressed by its closed bolt accuracy. In common with the regular SEAL Teams however, DEVGRU still needed a lighter weight 5.56 × 45mm machine gun.

Delta had adopted the M249 and during Operation Just Cause in Panama in 1989, a Delta operator assigned to a rooftop overwatch team famously fired some 900 rounds from his SAW (and used two fragmentation grenades) to kill some fifty-five enemy combatants during the rescue of an American civilian from a Panamanian jail. The M249 was also carried by operators into the Iraqi desert in 1991 alongside several 7.62 × 51mm Fabrique Nationale MAG58s, the design that would several years later equip all US forces as the M240. Delta preferred the reliability of the MAG58 over the often temperamental M60, particularly in Middle Eastern climes, and had the discretionary budgets to purchase whatever they needed.

The British SAS had also been looking for a lighter weight, magazine-fed machine gun to complement their beloved L7A2 GPMG or Gimpy which was the British version of the Belgian MAG58. Lacking a suitable LMG, the veteran L4A1 Bren since rechambered for 7.62 × 51mm soldiered on during the Falklands campaign with UK Special Forces and the Royal Marines Mountain and Arctic Warfare Cadre. In the late 1980s, the British SAS followed the

An Australian Commando from the Special Operations Task Group (SOTG) in Afghanistan 2013 provides top cover with his 7.62 × 51mm MAG58 general purpose machine gun mounted on a Bushmaster Protected Mobility Vehicle. Note the weapon is fitted with a four-power magnification Trijicon ACOG optic. (*SGT Jessi Ann McCormick, US Army*)

American lead and adopted the 5.56 × 45mm Minimi in the form of the L108A1 with fixed stock and full-length barrel.

The L108A1 made its public debut with the regiment in 1991 in the deserts of western Iraq during the famous Scud hunt. The Minimi was issued to four members of the infamous Bravo Two Zero patrol (with the other four patrol members all carrying M16/M203 rifle grenade launcher combinations). It performed well in Iraq and was liked within British Special Forces. When the shorter 18-inch Para barrel was produced some years later, the SAS made both versions available to its operators depending on tasking and mission. Other nations' SOF, such as the Canadians and Australians, followed suit, adopting the Minimi in various guises along with the MAG58 to replace the M60.

Calibres and Ammunition

Two calibres dominate in the field of squad automatic weapons and machine guns: the 5.56 × 45mm and the 7.62 × 51mm. The .50 or 12.7 × 99mm is, of course, also used with vehicle mounted Browning M2s. The lighter and handier SAWs and LMGs, like the Minimi and the Mk46, tend to be chambered for the 5.56 × 45mm round, ensuring ammunition compatibility with the likes of the M4A1. The SAW or LMG has traditionally been expected to

A US Navy SEAL prepares for operations in Fallujah, Iraq in 2007. The weapon is a 5.56 × 45mm Mk46 with 200 round assault drum, older AN/PEQ-2 illuminator and Aimpoint red dot optic. (*MC2 Eli J. Medellin, US Navy*)

provide suppressive fire support to SOF assault teams on, or close to, the objective and thus the relatively short range of the 5.56 × 45mm has never caused significant problems.

As we've seen in earlier chapters, the situation has changed with deployments to Afghanistan with a majority of engagements occurring at ranges in excess of 300 metres. The Para barrel configuration on the Minimi and Mk46 variant, favoured by most SOF units, really limits the weapon to an effective range of between 200 and 300 metres. Beyond that the Minimi Para loses most of its accuracy and becomes more of a hindrance than a threat to insurgents.

According to an exhaustive 2008 British Army report, effective suppressive fire is made up of three parts: proximity, in that the suppressing rounds are striking within a relatively close distance to the intended target; kinetic energy from the physical mass and velocity, meaning that larger calibres at higher velocities are more effective than smaller ones at lower velocities and finally the volume or weight of the fire that is directed toward the enemy. No real surprises there, although for British Army infantry who relied upon the short barrelled Minimi, it was a cause for considerable alarm and the eventual reintroduction of the 7.62 × 51mm L7A2 GPMG to the section level.

The 7.62 × 51mm platform solves the range challenge with the engagement window opening up to some 800 metres when the machine gun is

A US Army Green Beret firing a 7.62 × 51mm M240B medium machine gun from the rear swing mount of a GMV (ground Mobility Vehicle). Note the Elcan M145 optic and the barrel of the .50BMG M2 just visible above his head. *(A1C Jeff Parkinson, US Air Force)*

supported on its bipod. Terminal effects also improve with the 7.62 × 51mm as the round maintains its velocity over greater distances. The greater size of the round itself helps contribute to effective suppression. Again though, like the on-going rifle calibre debate, the 7.62 × 51mm has its drawbacks in increased weight and size. Ammunition weight is also a factor, but belts and drums of linked ammunition are distributed to all members of the patrol or assault team to reduce the load on the machine gunner himself.

The other key calibre used by SOF is, of course, the .50BMG or 12.7 × 99mm heavy machine-gun round. The most common .50 ball round weighs an impressive 709 grains. Compare this to the 7.62 × 51mm M80 at 147 grains or the 5.56 × 45mm M885 at 62 grains. It also offers far greater range than even the 7.62 × 51mm, with point targets able to be engaged out to 1,500 metres and area targets out to at least 2,000 metres. As we have seen, SOF of course also deploy the .50BMG in a range of anti-materiel sniper rifles. From the British Army study mentioned earlier, there is a useful comment on the effectiveness of the different machine-gun calibres in inflicting suppression, '*5.56mm Taliban ignore, 7.62mm worries them and .05-inch scares them.*'

Some other calibres are seeing significant experimentation, including rounds such as the .300 Blackout and the .338 Norma Magnum, specifically the Mk46 in .300BLK and the outstanding General Dynamics manufactured LWMMG (Lightweight Medium Machine Gun) in .338 Norma Magnum. The .300BLK MK46 was a prototype developed by AAC and came complete with suppressor firing subsonic .300BLK ammunition. Such a platform could easily be seen as an intimate support weapon for SOF assaulters armed with .300 BLK carbines, for instance. The LWMMG on the other hand is a serious contender to the throne and poses a real threat to the otherwise excellent M240 platform. The .338NM is ballistically similar to the better known sniper round, the .338 Lapua Magnum, and features an impressive 300-grain projectile, but in a shorter casing than the Lapua. The round is rated at an effective range out to some 1,700 metres, which is impressive in anyone's books.

Tactics and Techniques

Machine guns in SOF use tend to be deployed in two more or less common ways. One is as the traditional base-of-fire element, suppressing an enemy position to allow other friendly forces to manoeuvre against that enemy. This was practised daily on operations in Afghanistan where machine guns were used to suppress suspected or identified enemy firing points during the extraction of casualties, or to facilitate the landing of an aeromedical evacuation helicopter.

Light machine guns and SAWs were also used in deliberate attacks on enemy locations with several members of the assault team carrying them to provide instant and withering firepower at close range. The short barrelled Mk46 and Para Minimi excelled in this role, as does the recently adopted M27

Marine Recon Battalion operators engage insurgents in a firefight in Afghanistan 2010. The 5.56 × 45mm M249 Para SAW has been equipped with a Trijicon ACOG sight. Note the Marine closer to the camera carries a suppressed M4A1 carbine with M203 grenade launcher. (*Sgt Ezekiel Kitandwe, US Marine Corps*)

Infantry Automatic Rifle. Light role machine guns (i.e. those deployed on bipods rather than tripods) like the Mk48 were also deployed by overwatch elements during raids on insurgent compounds, providing intimate over-watch as the assaulters conducted the breach and clearance.

In terms of actual techniques, like all automatic weapons, short bursts are recommended. Short bursts maintain accuracy and reduce the requirement to swap out a hot barrel. After several hundred rounds fired in rapid succession, machine-gun barrels can become white hot and, if the weapon is not rested or the barrel changed, the weapon may experience a catastrophic stoppage or the barrel may even droop or deform. In the US Army Rangers in every platoon there is a fourth squad known as the Weapons Squad that are specially trained and equipped with three M240L or Mk48 general purpose machine guns. They deploy either attached to the rifle squads organically or as a support-by-fire grouping of the three guns. Along with the gun itself and more than 800 rounds of linked 7.62 × 51mm ammunition, the team typically carries a sustained fire tripod and at least one spare barrel for the weapon. This allows them to swap out overheated barrels during combat.

Rangers from the 2/75th practise close range shooting with their 5.56 × 45mm M249 SAWs. The Rangers use a variety of Mk46s and modified standard issue M249s.
(75th Ranger Regiment Public Affairs Office)

Current Trends

As with all SOF weapons, units are attempting to get the biggest bang from the lightest and shortest weapon system and it's no different with machine guns. As Operation Enduring Freedom wore on, the need for 7.62 × 51mm platforms became evident and Direct Action units began to look to the Mk48 and the Maximi to supplement or replace their Minimis and Mk46s. Elite infantry units such as the Rangers and SFSG likewise aimed to lighten their load with reduced weight versions of the GPMG and M240.

Most units tended toward 7.62 × 51mm versions of their existing LMGs or SAWs to minimise training and logistics. From Afghan experience units were seeing the advantage of the heavier round, but still in a relatively compact package. Some teams were carrying a spare longer barrel for their Maximis or Minimis to allow: (a) barrel changes should they be involved in a protracted contact with the enemy, and (b) to swap out to increase the range of the machine gun. The longer barrels can literally add several hundred metres to the effective range of the weapons.

Often units would land at an off-set LZ and walk into the objective in order to maintain the element of surprise. This was difficult work carrying a 12.5kg machine gun along, with perhaps 800 rounds of linked 7.62 × 51mm, plus body armour and helmet, water, pistol, night vision and intra-team radio, particularly at night in the rugged Afghan terrain. Any weight savings were appreciated by the operator on the ground.

Using different materials in a weapon's construction has paid dividends. The 7.62 × 51mm M240L, for instance, is built largely from titanium. It too has taken a proven design and adapted it for current operational conditions. The Rangers even apparently prefer the M240L over their Mk48s, although some of this may come down to budgetary pressures, as the Army pays for the M240L whilst SOCOM pays for the Mk48s.

Machine guns have seen more combat use by SOF units in the War on Terror than at any other time in their post war history and a lot of that use has been vehicle mounted. Special Forces and MARSOC Raiders will often patrol in a mix of MRAPs and Ground Mobility Vehicle versions of the HMMWV. Often these GMVs will be festooned with three machine guns: a .50BMG M2 in the gunner's station (sometimes backed up by an M249 or Mk46 for closer range fire), an M240L or Mk48 on a swing-arm mount and a second M240L or MK48 mounted in the rear bed. Even the otherwise low profile British SAS have been seen in their up-armoured Toyota Hilux trucks with an L7A2 GPMG mounted on the rollbar.

The ultimate in suppressive fire – the 7.62 × 51mm M134 minigun. This example is mounted on a Green Beret GMV truck in Afghanistan. The minigun, more typically mounted as a helicopter door gun, has seen some use by American SOF. (*Sgt Pete Thibodeau; US Marine Corps*)

Individual Weapon Summaries

Fabrique Nationale Minimi, M249, SPW and Mk46 Mod0/1

The ubiquitous Minimi was first designed in the 1970s chambered for the NATO standard 7.62×51mm. It was modified to 5.56×45mm when the weapon was entered into the trials for the American Squad Automatic Weapon in the early 1980s, where it proved the successful design (beating out the HK23 amongst others). It was adopted by the US military as the M249 SAW, a role that harked back to the Second World War and the legendary BAR. The tactical concept was for the standard four-man fire team to be able to provide its own base of fire through the use of the M249 and the M203, whilst the M16A2 was used to engage individual enemy.

The M249 was liked by Army Special Forces but, as we have seen earlier, it failed to meet the maritime requirements of the SEALs. The Special Forces also wanted a shorter and lighter version than the issue weapon, more akin to their unique requirements. A version of the weapon taking into account the feedback from the SEALs, called the SPW or Special Purpose Weapon, was developed for SOCOM testing.

The SPW was formally adopted in 1998 by all SOCOM command units, officially designated as the Mk46 Mod0. The Mk46 had been lightened by

An Australian Commando poses with his 5.56×45mm Minimi Para. The Australian Army use the full-length Minimi as the F89 whilst SOCOMD units use both the Minimi Para and the 7.62×51mm Maximi. *(CPL Chris Moore; Australian Defence Force)*

An Army Ranger firing his 5.56 × 45mm M249 SAW in 2013. The weapon is fitted with a collapsible stock, Para length barrel, Elcan Specter DR optic, vertical foregrip and AN/PEQ-15 illuminator. (SGT Mikki Sprenkle, US Army)

the exclusion of the back-up magazine feed option and a lighter, shorter barrel was added. It was also fully compatible with the then recently issued SOPMOD Block I Kit allowing a range of sights and illuminators to be mounted to the Mk46. Firing from the M249's standard 200-round box, or a 100-round cloth bag first designed by the Australians for their F89 version, the Mk46 deployed with all SOCOM units to Afghanistan where it soon saw extensive combat.

The M249 gained a somewhat unwarranted reputation for poor reliability in Iraq and later Afghanistan with stoppages reported to be increasingly common during prolonged firing. The problem was not necessarily a fault in the design. The M249s carried by the majority of US forces were simply worn out after more than a decade's hard service in dirty, dusty climes. Its SOF version, the Mk46, regularly requires replacement barrels at roughly half the rate of the M249. The Mk46 weighs only 7kg unloaded, however, almost a kilogram lighter than the M249.

The fallen Red Squadron DEVGRU operator Neil Roberts carried an Mk46 Mod0 SAW when he fell from the ramp of an ambushed Chinook onto Takur Ghar Mountain in March 2002. The SEAL was immediately surrounded by Uzbek insurgents whom he valiantly engaged with his SAW until the weapon suffered a stoppage (accounts vary to the nature of the stoppage, but it may have been caused by an enemy round striking the SAW's receiver, putting it out of commission). Roberts had been struck by a round in the thigh that was causing heavy blood loss and he lost consciousness before he could draw his SIG-Sauer P226 to continue the fight. Tragically he was executed soon after by the insurgents.

All SOCOM units are now using the Mk46 although, as noted earlier, the Rangers are now reportedly using a modified M249 as their Mk46s come up for service-life replacement. The Minimi Para has been widely adopted across Coalition SOF including the Canadians, Australians, the French and the British. Many of these have been modified to near Mk46 standards with the addition of rails and heat guards.

Mk48 Mod0/1 and Maximi

After the successful adoption of the Mk46 Mod0 in 1998, SOCOM raised a requirement through Crane for a 7.62×51mm version. The result was adopted in 2000 as the Mk48 Mod0. The weapon took the Minimi concept back to its origins as a 7.62×51mm platform, but upgraded the Mk46 to handle the heavier calibre. Around 70 per cent of parts are common across the two platforms.

Two US Navy SEALs, the closer equipped with a 5.56×45mm Mk46 Mod0 and the operator in the background with the larger 7.62×51mm Mk48 Mod0. Note the unusually forward mounting of the EOTech 553 close combat optic. Note also that the Mk46 retains its original fixed plastic stock. (*US Naval Special Warfare*)

A US Navy SEAL scans for insurgents on operations in Afghanistan in 2012. Note the standard plastic fixed stock on his 7.62 × 51mm Mk48 Mod0 has been replaced by a SOPMOD collapsible stock and the weapon is fitted with an Elcan Specter optic.
(MCI Martin Cuaron, US Navy)

The Mk48 was even issued to a number of conventional units in Afghanistan, swapping out their M240Bs that proved too heavy and cumbersome in mountainous terrain. The weapon found much favour with these infantry units who appreciated the weight reduction along with its more compact size. The Mk48 was intended to replace the M240B in SOCOM service, however with the advent of the M240L, the two weapons systems serve currently side by side. The Mod1 variant was introduced in 2007 which added a heat shield over the barrel to assist with reducing heat build-up after prolonged firing.

The Mk48 is often deployed during special operations as part of an overwatch element to include marksmen and machine gunners positioned together. A former DEVGRU SEAL related that the Mk48 was *'very effective providing covering fire into thick tree lines and foliage'* in Afghanistan. Versions of the Mk48 known as the Maximi are in service with UK, Australian, Polish and New Zealand Special Forces.

Mk43 Mod0/1
The 7.62 × 51mm Mk43 Mod0 was first adopted by the SEALs in 1995 and was deployed by both regular SEAL Teams and DEVGRU. The Mk43 was a product-improved M60E3/E4 that had been made stronger with a heavier

barrel and newly designed flash suppressor. It filled the gap in the SEAL Teams for a lightweight machine gun that could be operated by one man. The Mk43 was finally replaced by the Mk48 as SOCOM pursued a 7.62 × 51mm version of the Mk46.

The Mk43 was deployed during early operations in Afghanistan, including ACOG equipped versions carried by DEVGRU operators, and in Iraq as late as 2004 where it was deployed with SEAL Platoons rotating through the country as part of the combined joint special operations task force. The Mk43 was also mounted on SEAL DPVs (Desert Patrol Vehicles), the armed dune buggies that the SEALS used up until the early 2000s.

Heckler and Koch HK21

As noted earlier in the chapter, the HK21 was a firm favourite with Delta and also saw limited use with DEVGRU. It remained Delta's preferred 7.62 × 51mm platform until the advent of the Mk48. Even with the Mk48 in service, a HK21 was seen on a vehicle mount on one of Delta's highly modified Pinzgauers during the invasion of Iraq and of course John 'Shrek' McPhee famously carried an ACOG equipped HK21E into the mountains of eastern Afghanistan as Delta hunted Osama bin Laden at Tora Bora in 2001.

The HK21E weighed just over 9kg empty and was a touch under 45 inches in overall length compared to the kilogram lighter and 5 inches shorter Mk48. The HK21E did offer the advantage of semi-automatic or burst fire and fired from a closed bolt using a free-floating barrel offering greater accuracy than the Mk48, or indeed virtually any competing design. It could also be field modified to fire from a box magazine or from a disintegrating link belt.

Fabrique Nationale MAG58

The 7.62 × 51mm MAG58 is better known in US service as the M240 series medium machine gun and in the United Kingdom as the L7A2 general purpose machine gun or the Gimpy (pronounced gym-pee). It is big and heavy at a touch over 12kg and just over 4 feet in length, but it spits out 147-grain 7.62 × 51mm projectiles at a cyclic rate of between 650 and 900 rounds per minute out to an effective range of over 800 metres. The MAG58 can be deployed in the so-called light role with a folding bipod for stability, vehicle mounted or deployed on a sustained fire tripod that increases its range out to 2,000 metres by using a high trajectory fire method.

In the US military the M240B or Bravo is issued to Army units, whilst the Marines deploy the M240G or Golf model. As mentioned above, since 2010 a titanium-based replacement specifically designed to lighten the weight of the weapon has been in combat trials and limited issue to Special Forces, Ranger and infantry units. This weapon is known as the M240L or Lightweight model. Drawing on feedback from SOCOM, it took 2kg off the weapon's weight and, using a 4-inch shorter barrel and collapsible stock, reduced the overall length by some 7 inches. The M240L is widely liked by users and is a

A US Army Ranger gun team fires their 7.62 × 51mm M240L medium machine gun equipped with Elcan M145 optic. The M240L is a lightened version of the standard M240B and features Picatinny rail, a shorter barrel and collapsible SOPMOD style stock. After proving successful in combat trials with the Rangers and Special Forces in Afghanistan, the M240L has now been adopted by the wider US Army. (SPC Justin English, US Army)

good example of product improvement to meet the needs of the SOF world. Along with SOCOM, the MAG58 design also serves with many Coalition SOF including the Australians, Canadians and UKSF.

Future Trends

In SOF use, machine guns need to be able to provide both surgically accurate and suppressive supporting fires as needed. Earlier platforms like the HK21 were exemplary in this regard as they offered exceptional accuracy in semi-automatic, along with being able to use bursts to suppress targets. Many of today's SOF machine guns are designed more with the latter function in mind. Future SOF machine guns may need to be able to seamlessly transition between the two, offering something of a hybrid between a marksman rifle and a light machine gun.

The Marines have adopted one option that may meet this requirement. The 5.56 × 45mm M27 IAR (Infantry Automatic Rifle) is designed to initially supplement rather than replace the M249 SAW. Developed from the HK416 and specifically modified for sustained fire use, the M27 feeds from a thirty-round magazine, a source of some scepticism, with observers noting comparisons to the British L86A2 LSW, widely considered a lame duck and now rarely seen operationally. Despite this, many see the M27 as a glimpse into the future of light support weapons.

A Marine officer commenting on the M27 IAR noted:

> In the current fight when there is a limited exposure and a fleeting target that blends in with the local populace, it is more important to have a more accurate rifle with a better optic. If you can get (positive identification) faster, you can kill the enemy rather than a weapon that provides audible suppression. Audible suppression being the bullets hitting everywhere but on target, and the enemy only hearing the sounds of gunfire.

Fabrique Nationale also developed a contender for the IAR requirement in the form of the Heat Adaptive Modular Rifle (HAMR) based on their 5.56 × 45mm Mk16 or SCAR-L platform. The HAMR is available in both 16 and 18-inch barrel lengths and uniquely is both an open bolt and a closed bolt design. The weapon is designed to switch from standard closed bolt firing (which enhances accuracy particularly in semi-automatic fire) to open bolt (which is safer in terms of heat build-up, particularly in sustained fully-automatic fire). A 'thermal actuator' measures the temperature in the

A Marine Force Recon automatic rifleman carrying the recently introduced 5.56 × 45mm M27 IAR (Infantry Automatic Rifle), a modified version of the HK416 designed to handle high rates of suppressive fire. The IAR is equipped with the Marine Corps standard Trijicon ACOG with newly issued RMR mini red dot. (*Cpl Austin Long, US Marine Corps*)

weapon's barrel and once it reaches the prescribed level, automatically switches from closed to open bolt.

The HAMR offers a practical solution to high rates of fire through what is essentially an assault rifle platform. The H&K IAR, based on the 416, fires from a closed bolt, although heat build-up is not as much of a concern thanks to the piston driven gas system. Along with such hybrid rifle/SAW designs, future SOF platforms will need to encompass significant modularity in barrel lengths, stocks, sighting systems and calibres.

A future SOF light machine gun system will need to be easily field configured for 5.56 × 45mm, 7.62 × 39mm and any newly adopted intermediate calibres on the horizon, whilst medium and general purpose designs will require both 7.62 × 51mm and .338 options, indeed perhaps including the exceptional .338 Norma Magnum. A design featuring all four options may well be on the drawing board. The Minimi redesigned for its original 7.62 × 51mm has shown that a strong basic design can be, within obvious limits, reconfigured to accept larger calibres. In fact the Mk46 and Mk48 programmes served as the perfect proof of concept to show how a core weapons system can be successfully modified with a range of stocks, barrel lengths and calibres.

The enemy's .50cal, the 12.7mm DShK heavy machine gun, here being test fired by Afghan Commandos under the watchful eye of Australian SOTG instructors.
(*CPL Christopher Dickson; Australian Defence Force*)

Chapter Eight

Grenades, Grenade Launchers and Rockets

Overview

Like their infantry counterparts, SOF units sometimes require a little more bang in the form of hand thrown or launched grenades, light anti-tank rockets or even a Javelin guided missile. For most SOF operations, a couple of fragmentation and smoke grenades (to screen movement or mark friendly positions), along with a couple of underslung 40mm grenade launchers will be more than enough extra insurance. But for deliberate offensive operations, targeting enemy base areas for instance, significantly heavier firepower may be required.

Historically SOF have carried the same hand grenades, 40mm launchers and disposable rockets as conventional forces. During the Vietnam War, the SEALs experimented with a number of grenade launcher designs including the infamous China Lake pump-action grenade launcher that held three 40mm rounds (and one in the chamber). Army Long Range Reconnaissance

Green Berets from ODA 0114 of the 10th Special Force Group train with the infamous RPG-7V, the weapon of choice of the insurgent and terrorist. (*SSgt Tyler Placie, US Air Force*)

US Army Special Forces and Polish GROM special operators fighting a street battle against insurgents in Iraq 2007. Of particular interest is the 40mm M79 standalone grenade launcher that, despite being Vietnam vintage, has remained in the armoury thanks to its reliability and accuracy. *(SGT Rob Summitt, US Army)*

Patrols also began the tradition of cutting down their 40mm M79 'Bloopers' to save weight, turning the launcher into essentially an overlarge 40mm pistol. This idea was recently resurrected by at least one JSOC unit.

The first major innovation for SOF purposes was in hand grenades in the late 1970s. We refer, of course, to the stun grenade or flashbang. The British SAS developed the first flashbangs during the late 1970s and supplied a number to GSG9 before they stormed the hijacked Lufthansa flight at Mogadishu. The SAS went on, famously and very effectively, to deploy the devices at the Iranian Embassy in London during Operation Nimrod.

Developed from British Army training munitions called Thunder Flashes which gave off a loud noise, the first flashbang known as the G60 was a fairly basic design. It was originally intended to be a noise maker only, but UK MOD scientists discovered that the effect of the sound could be increased by adding a magnesium based charge that would create a blinding flash. The G60 was effective, blinding and disorientating any enemy in a room for up to five seconds, giving the assaulters the chance to enter and engage them.

The use of the G60s at Mogadishu illustrated the one drawback with early flashbangs – they could easily cause fires. Indeed the fire that gutted the Iranian Embassy was thought to have been caused by either SAS flashbangs or CS gas grenades, which at that time were also pyrotechnic. GSG9 did not deploy the flashbangs inside the aircraft as they breached as the terrorists had poured lighter fluid over the inside of the cabin. The G60s were used instead to create a diversion outside the aircraft, drawing the terrorists forward as the GSG9 assaulters breached.

Several designs have improved upon the G60, including the US standard issue M84 and the SOCOM issue Mk141 Mod0 that was withdrawn from service in 2004 due to incidents involving injuries to operators when the device prematurely detonated. The European NICO BTV-1, widely used by Coalition SOF, was adopted as an interim measure by SOCOM units. The Rheinmetall Mk13 BTV-EL has been adopted by JSOC and a number of Coalition units like the British SAS.

In the arena of light anti-tank weapons, SOF have also traditionally used largely the same platforms as conventional units. The 66mm M72 LAW has proven popular with many SOF units since Vietnam as it provides a handy bunker-busting or anti-armour capability for patrols. During the War on Terror, SOF units have deployed these, and heavier systems such as the

A US Army Special Forces operator firing an AT4 (M136) 84mm rocket during training at Eglin Range. Note the impressive backblast. (*A1C Jeff Parkinson, US Air Force*)

An Army Green Beret training with the M203 replacement, the 40mm M320 equipped as a standalone launcher. Note the grenade in the air. (*A1C Jeff Parkinson, US Air Force*)

Javelin, to destroy enemy armour or technicals on occasion, or to engage insurgents who have taken refuge in buildings or prepared positions.

Calibres and Ammunition

In terms of rockets, missiles and recoilless rifles like the Carl Gustav, each are almost unique in their calibre and weapon types so they will be covered in a summary toward the end of the chapter. One area which does require some explanation is in the field of 40mm grenades.

The 40mm grenade comes in two main calibres – the 40 × 46mm low velocity standard used by most underslung launchers like the M320 or M203, and the high velocity 40 × 53mm round that automatic grenade launchers, like the venerable Mk19 or the Heckler and Koch GMG, are chambered for. The 40 × 53mm cannot be used in handheld or underslung launchers as the round will simply not fit and the weapons were not rated for the high impulse rounds.

There are now a bewildering array of 40mm grenade types available, however the commonest in SOF hands are the standard High Explosive Dual Purpose that provides both fragmentation and a light armour piercing ability

US Army Rangers firing at a heavy weapons range. The Ranger in the foreground is firing the 40mm Mk47 Mod0 fully automatic grenade launcher – a fearsome weapon that can be vehicle or ground mounted in a defensive or support by fire position. In the background can be seen other Rangers launching 40mm grenades from their M320 launchers.
(*SSG Teddy Wade, US Army*)

A US Army Ranger firing his M320 equipped SOPMOD Block 2 M4A1 on a range in Afghanistan. He has deployed the fold down forward grip on the launcher, normally used when the weapon is detached and is being used as a standalone launcher.
(Pfc. Rashene Mincy, US Army)

and coloured smoke that is used to mark targets or friendly positions. Flash-bang rounds exist for both 38mm (still sometimes used by European counter terrorist teams) and 40mm launchers and even thermobaric rounds like the M1060 have been developed that are designed to be used against enemy in buildings or prepared positions. There is even a recently developed anti-diver round that is designed to be fired into the water to create lethal shockwaves against an enemy frogman!

Tactics and Techniques
Flashbang grenades were a revolution and continue to save life and limb to this day. The three to five seconds of diversion they provide is often essential in allowing assaulters to clear a room of hostiles before the enemy can engage them or kill any hostages. SOF teams train so much with flashbangs that most are conditioned to ignore the effects of the flashbang detonating and enter the target location as the device is going off, again adding vital seconds.

Whilst we mention flashbangs we should take a moment to discuss their operations. Most flashbangs operate as per fragmentation grenades – the operator pulls the pin and once he or she releases the spoon that holds down the firing pin, the grenade will detonate after a predetermined period

The AG36, also known as the GLM (Grenade Launcher Module) A1, mounted under the forearm of a 5.56 × 45mm G36K. This arrangement is popular with Germany's GSG9 and French COS special operators. *(Heckler & Koch)*

(although the US M84 has two separate safety pins). With flashbangs this is often one and a half to two seconds of delay to counter an enemy kicking or throwing back the device.

Many designs of flashbangs have holes cut into the sides of the grenade. This is a safety measure to allow the explosive force to safely exit the device as it detonates, without causing potentially lethal shrapnel. A SOCOM issue flashbang called the Mk141 caused some injuries as it was not designed to vent the explosive pressure out of the grenade and was subsequently replaced. Most recent designs feature these safety cut-outs.

SOF units still use a range of fragmentation grenades, although the presence of non-combatants on today's battlefields often precludes their use. They will be deployed when assaulters are breaching into a known terrorist or insurgent safe house and clearance has been given for their use. A British hostage was tragically killed in Afghanistan when a DEVGRU operator deployed a fragmentation grenade. Many operators carry a couple of M67 fragmentation grenades in case they need to clear a bunker or building.

One newly developed type of hand grenade is the Mk14 Anti Structure Munition or ASM. Very little is known of this device but it has been deployed by both JSOC units and the Australian SASR in Afghanistan. The ASM is believed to be a thermobaric device meaning that it creates intense heat and pressure in confined spaces, literally burning the oxygen available. During one operation, an ASM was dropped into a stone hut being used by a Taliban machine gunner. The explosion completely demolished the building.

In terms of launched grenades, these will be employed by SOF operators to suppress enemy firing points. They can also be used to blow in doors or compound gates as a stand-off breaching method. LAW rockets and more modern designs like the 84mm AT4 or M136 can also be used explosively to create entry points. They are also very effective in suppressing enemy prepared positions. Many SOF patrols carry a few rockets with them just in case they run into a bunker or similar fortified position.

Weapon Summaries

Grenade Launchers

There are only a handful of 40mm launchers used by special operators. Chief amongst them is the M203 and its replacement the M320. Both are single shot, breech loading designs that are normally mounted underslung the barrel of an assault rifle. Both can also be deployed as stand-alone systems with their own stock and pistol grip.

The M203, a forty-year-old design, was officially replaced by the M320 in 2009, however the M320 had been in combat trials with SOF units for some time. The M320 is a development of the Heckler and Koch AG36 underslung launcher that is deployed with the G36 and HK416 families. It has been designed with the M4A1 in mind (the M203 required a specially shortened version, the M203A1 to work with the carbine) and features a side opening breech, allowing for all sizes of 40mm grenade to be used.

All SOCOM units are transitioning to the M320. The Rangers currently deploy the M320 both as a stand-alone system carried along with the Ranger's Block II M4A1 and as an integrated underslung grenade launcher (UGL).

An Australian Commando on patrol in Afghanistan. His 5.56 × 45mm M4A5 carbine mounts the older 40mm M203 still used by many SOF units. *(CPL Chris Moore, Australian Defence Force)*

US Army Green Berets in contact with the enemy in Afghanistan in 2014. The operator to the right is firing the standalone 40mm M320, whilst his colleague passes rounds to him. Of interest is both the custom holster the grenadier wears to carry the M320 on his belt and the .40S&W Glock 22 his partner carries. (*SPC Connor Mendez, US Army*)

Delta and DEVGRU had both been using the AG36 with their HK416s for a number of years prior to the adoption. Indeed the German KSK and French COS all use the AG36 on their 416s and G36KVs, as do the British on their L119A1/A2s where it is known as the L17A1. The SEALs and Special Forces have deployed the Mk13 Enhanced Grenade Launcher Module (EGLM) of the SCAR family as a stand-alone and underslung weapon mated to the Mk16 and Mk17.

The M203 is not dead yet, however, as it is still extensively used by international SOF units like the Canadians and Australians and many South East Asian units. The weapon is also deployed by both Afghan and Iraqi SOF units. LMT also produce an iteration of the M203 that features a SOPMOD style collapsible stock and pistol grip, allowing it to be carried as a stand-alone weapon system in a similar manner to the M79 or M320. The LMT M203 also features a full-length Picatinny rail allowing all manner of sights to be attached.

The Heckler and Koch 40mm AG36 launcher with mounting bracket for the G36 series of rifles. This launcher is the basis of both the M320 and UK L123A1/2 and L17A1. *(Heckler & Koch)*

Some units still use older designs including Canada's JTF-2 who have been seen carrying the H&K 69A1 stand-alone launcher. The M79 that was the first break-open grenade launcher to be adopted by the US military also still soldiers on. The M79 remains in Special Forces and SEAL armouries and has been seen in action in Iraq. As mentioned earlier, a customised sawn-off M79 known as the 'Pirate Gun' is even carried by DEVGRU operators in a custom S&S Precision holster that operators wear attached to their plate carriers or their daypacks. The 'Pirate Gun' has had the barrel cut back and the stock completely removed, instead cut down into a pistol grip with a mini red dot optic welded on. DEVGRU operators armed primarily with the MP7A1 routinely carry the 'Pirate Gun' as back-up whilst at least some of their recce/ sniper operators have been known to carry one as added insurance.

The other major type of grenade launcher in SOF use has been the Milkor multi-shot design. This is a six shot cylinder fed launcher than can fire the six rounds semi-automatically – the prefect counter ambush tool. The original South African Milkor design known as the MGL has been adopted by the German KSK amongst others. The US Marines adopted the platform as the M32. In SOCOM service, it has been termed the Mk14 Mod0 grenade launcher and is a shortened version of the standard M32. SEALs have been using the

The working parts of the 40mm M32 multi-shot grenade launcher procured by the US Marines and SOCOM. The M32 and the shortened SOCOM version, the M32A1 or Mk14 Mod0, is essentially a giant break-open revolver firing 40mm rounds. (*GySgt Mark Oliva, US Marines*)

The M32A1, or Mk14 Mod0 in SOCOM service, here being fired by a Marine. The M32A1 is fitted with a SOPMOD style positional stock and a railed sight that allows optics to be mounted. *(LCpl M. Kresse, US Marines)*

platform in Afghanistan since 2011. The Marines have apparently now adopted the shortened SOCOM version as the M32A1.

Rockets and Recoilless Rifles

As noted, disposable single-shot rockets are still widely deployed by SOF operators to engage enemy prepared positions. They have also proven effective against Taliban firing positions as the insurgents are frightened of the explosive charge. The most widely used are the M72 series (including by UK Special Forces where the weapon is known as the L72A9 Light Anti-Structure Missile) and the AT-4 or M136. All operate along similar principles, launching a 66mm in the case of the M72, or an 84mm in the case of the M136/AT4, from a lightweight plastic tube. The LAW is still more popular as two can be carried for every one AT4, although the effects on the target of the AT4 are far more pronounced.

The AT4 is somewhat more sophisticated as versions are now in service with the Rangers that are designed with a tandem warhead to first penetrate a structure before detonating. This AST model has been particularly successful in Afghanistan. A recently adopted version called the AT4-CS for Confined Spaces was developed to SOCOM requirements and allows the rocket to be launched safely from inside a building   a capability which traditionally

The trusted M72A5 Light Anti-tank Weapon (LAW), versions of which date back to Vietnam, here being fired by a US Army Green Beret. The 66mm single shot, throwaway, weapon is still valued for use against insurgent bunkers and firing positions and is still used by most Coalition SOF in Afghanistan. (*A1C Jeff Parkinson, US Air Force*)

the explosive backblast of such weapons has negated (incredibly using sea-water to absorb the blast). Thermobaric versions of the AT4 are also used by American SOF.

Thermobaric rounds are particularly important when dealing with insurgents or terrorists holed up in a fortified building such as occurred in Fallujah in 2004. In fact three Delta operators, supporting a platoon of young Marines, fought a pitched battle against upwards of 300 insurgents in April 2004 during Operation Vigilant Resolve. The operators were instructing the Marines in a range of thermobaric weapons they had brought along, including a thermobaric warhead variant of the AT4, and used these to help hold back the insurgent hordes. The thermobaric rounds are equally useful when faced by an enemy with chemical munitions at his disposal. They can also incinerate the chemical agent rendering the area safe. A thermobaric Hellfire anti-tank missile has also been recently developed to provide a similar capacity from supporting attack helicopters.

The other key support platform used by special operators is the 84mm Carl Gustav M3 recoilless rifle. The weapon is a favourite with the US Army Rangers where it is known as the Ranger Antitank Weapons System (RAWS), or more colloquially as the Goose.

Marty Skovlund Jr. interviewed a Ranger who engaged a Taliban machine-gun position using the recently issued programmable ammunition that can be set to explode at a specified range or airburst over the target: '*I grabbed the HE*

A US Army Green Beret returns insurgent fire in Afghanistan 2014 with an 84mm Carl Gustav M3. Note the tremendous backblast from firing. The operator is also armed with a standalone 40mm M320 in a holster on his belt. (SPC Sara Wakai, US Army)

round from my assistant gunner. I set the round to 400 meters. I set the range drum. I wanted to make sure this round explodes in their faces and not behind them.' The Ranger scored a direct hit and silenced the insurgent firing point, killing three enemy.

Along with the HE round, a HEDP or High Explosive Dual Purpose round is also issued which has an armour piercing capability. This is the preferred option for use against buildings and against vehicles. A recently introduced CS (Confined Spaces) variant allows the Carl Gustav to be fired from within buildings for the first time following on from the success with the AT4-CS variant. The downside to the M3 is its frankly impressive muzzle blast and report; when it is fired everyone can hear and see where it was fired from.

The Rangers deploy the M3 in two-man teams, both of whom are routinely armed with M4A1s and function as riflemen until the Carl Gustav is required. The Rangers task organise their M3 teams as an anti-tank squad attached to a company headquarters platoon. The M3s can then be attached as necessary to the assault or blocking force. The Ranger anti-tank squads are also equipped with M136 (AT4) rockets and the mighty Javelin anti-tank guided missile system which, although used by some SOF units, are really out of the scope of this book.

The Australian SASR commonly carry a Carl Gustav on their six-wheel Long Range Patrol Vehicles and their newer Nary Special Operations Vehicles.

During a September 2008 contact in Afghanistan, an SASR operator, Trooper (now Corporal) Mark Donaldson, used an M3 (and a handful of 66mm LAW rockets) to suppress a number of insurgent firing positions during a 4-km long rolling ambush. He was later awarded the Victoria Cross for his actions in rescuing an Afghan interpreter wounded in the ambush.

One final type of SOF support weapon should be briefly mentioned and that is the humble mortar. Various models of the 60mm light or Commando mortar are popular amongst the US Army Rangers and Britain's Special Forces Support Group who appreciate its organic indirect fire capability. The 60mm mortar is lightweight enough to carry in on foot if necessary, with the bombs distributed amongst the unit, and can provide indirect fire up to four to five times as far as 40mm underslung grenade launchers.

Future Trends

The future will include an enhanced range of 40mm grenades that can reach 600 metres from a hand-held launching platform such as the M320, easily adding a third to existing effective ranges from most launchers.

Rangers train in Afghanistan with the 60mm M224 infantry mortar, being fired here in handheld mode. It can also be fitted with a bipod for longer range and increased accuracy. Every army that has deployed the light mortar (often known as a Commando mortar because of their light weight) to Afghanistan has greatly appreciated the indirect fire capability they bring to the table. (*SPC Connor Mendez, US Army*)

The 5.56 × 45mm Heckler and Koch HK416A5 mounting an AG36 or GLM, also finished in RAL 800. Note the folding grenade launcher sight raised on the right hand side of the forearm. (*Heckler & Koch*)

Programmable ammunition is also a key requirement, mirroring the programmable 25mm rounds from the XM25 Punisher.

The Punisher, or officially the Counter Defilade Target Engagement (CDTE) System, is due to enter service in 2017 as the M25. The platform is a stand-alone 25mm semi-automatic grenade launcher with an integrated laser range

The 25mm XM25 Punisher semi-automatic grenade launcher. It has been criticized for both being too heavy and for not packing the punch of a 40mm round (apparently the 25mm round tends to only wound insurgents). (*Department of Defense*)

finder that allows the operator to manually set the detonation distance of the grenade allowing airbursts over enemy trenches for example.

The weapon has been trialed by several SOF units and was apparently not well liked by the Rangers who refused to carry the 6.5kg weapon with them on an operation to raid a Taliban compound in 2013. According to reports, the Rangers found the weapon too heavy and unwieldy and questioned the advisability of the limited amount of 25mm ammunition that could be carried by an operator (and that carrying the XM25 resulted in the loss of a rifleman, as the only other weapon an XM25 gunner could carry was his pistol). It has also been reported that the 25mm round does not produce large enough fragments to reliably incapacitate insurgents.

Whether the Punisher is adopted or not, the concept of programmable munitions will be seen in both 40mm grenades and in light anti-tank weapons, with the focus on tandem head warheads that can be fired from within buildings. Thermobaric options will also become wider spread in the future including launched and hand grenades.

Chapter Nine

Conclusion and the Future

Throughout this book we have considered each of the primary small arms types deployed by special operations forces in the first decade and a half of the War on Terror, or the somewhat less dramatic Overseas Contingency Operations as it is now referred to by the United States military. We have chronicled the developments based upon years of hard-won combat experience in Afghanistan and Iraq and shorter-term operations in Mali, Yemen and Somalia. We have seen how these experiences have shaped the nature of the weapons, and tactics, employed by special operators from Coalition nations.

We have also briefly considered the future trends for each type of small arms and how they may look in the future if current trends and experiences continue. We have not considered how these combat experiences will transform the weapons of the conventional infantryman, although the overlap with SOF will be significant in many areas. Principally, infantry small arms will follow many of the trends identified – they will become lighter, handier and more compact; they will fire rounds that are lighter in weight themselves yet offer greater range, intermediate barrier penetration and terminal effects on human targets; they will be modular allowing the soldier, or more likely his NCO, to nominate the type of barrel length, stock, sighting system or even calibre best suited for a particular mission. They will readily accept all accessories and come standard with the option of a suppressor. Many of these accessories may be powered by the rails systems themselves.

Many of these developments will be seen in the hands of elite light infantry units like the US Army Rangers or Britain's Special Forces Support Group before they trickle down to line infantry formations. This has been true for most of the worlds' special operations units since the Second World War. SOF, due to both increased budgets and operational necessity, tend to lead the way in infantry small arms development. Some SOF programmes, like suppressed, optically equipped pistols or ultra-compact carbines, will have no common requirement in the infantry world. Others, like lighter weight general purpose machine guns, or combat optics that automatically calculate the range to a target, or dial-able airburst 40mm grenades, will see significant commonalities in terms of operational need.

For the SOF soldier we can make a few general predictions about what his weapons, ammunition and optics will look like, and perform like, over the next few years.

Pistols will largely return to 9 × 19mm calibre. The .40S&W may well have had its day thanks to the increased wear and tear on the pistols themselves due to the pressures of the larger calibre, its significant felt recoil, and the recent evolutionary developments in 9 × 19mm bullet design. To paraphrase an old saying, today's 9 × 19mm is simply not your grand-daddy's 9 × 19mm, at least it isn't in terms of expanding projectiles. 9 × 19mm ball remains a poor choice, but thankfully most SOF can avoid its use.

The 9 × 19mm is comparatively easier to shoot accurately under stress and still holds more rounds in its magazine than its heavier calibre competitors. It is also easier to conceal and compact versions are nowhere near as punishing to the shooter than compacts in .40S&W or .45ACP; 9 × 19mm SIG-Sauers, H&Ks and Glocks are also amongst the most reliable of all pistols. For SOF operators permitted to carry expanding or hollowpoint type ammunition, any other choice in a defensive pistol simply makes little sense.

The .45ACP will soldier on, at least in American SOF hands, and potentially German with the KSK and Fernspaeher (Long Range Reconnaissance) use of the .45ACP Heckler and Koch P12, a modified version of the USP Tactical. Both Tier One American SOF and the German units still employ the .45ACP pistol for one very special function, suppressed close-range killing. When a subsonic round is required, the .45ACP still makes some sense over the 9 × 19mm. This harkens back to the .45ACP Mk23 Mod0 developed for SOCOM – an offensive pistol by any measure. These suppressed .45ACP platforms will continue in that narrow niche for a handful of units that require that capability.

Ruger and similar .22 Long Rifle pistols will still remain in operational use for shooting out street lights and putting holes in car tyres during urban raiding missions, while .380ACP and similar calibres will also remain in the inventory for deep concealment use. SOF pistols themselves will see an increased use of mini red dot and reflex sights as operators begin to appreciate the increased speed of acquiring a sight picture using such devices in CQB. Suppressors will become even more commonplace as will rail mounted white light and infra-red LAMs.

The use of submachine guns will virtually disappear, although many would argue that this has already occurred. The legendary MP5 in 9 × 19mm will remain, loaded with frangible ammunition, for a limited number of hostage rescue scenarios. The MP5K may also soldier on in the hands of SOF employed in the close protection role, although with the decreasing size of ultra-compact 5.56 × 45mm carbines, its days may also be numbered. The use of the MP7A1 as a suppressed CQB weapon will reduce as suppressed carbines like the SIG-Sauer MCX in either .300 Blackout or in 5.56 × 45mm are adopted for that specific assaulter role. Unfortunately the MP7A1's 4.6 × 30mm calibre is its own worst enemy. If a platform can be found in broadly the same dimensions that can fire a heavier round out to much further distances, (and in the .300 Blackout's case apparently subsonically) the days of the MP7A1 will also be marked.

This new generation of suppressed carbines like the MCX and the Honey Badger may also impact on the dominance of the M4A1 and the HK416 in the hands of SOF assaulters. Whether this challenge will come in the form of the .300 Blackout remains to be seen as we simply don't have any evidence one way or another about the actual terminal effects of the round in combat use. Tier One special operators know from hundreds if not thousands of dead terrorists and insurgents that the combination of the Barnes Optimized Brown Tip 5.56 × 45mm bullet and the 10-inch barrelled Heckler and Koch 416 will perform as advertised. The same cannot yet be said of the .300 Blackout, or indeed any of the newer intermediate calibres, like the 6.5mm Grendel or the .264 USA. If even some of the older designs like the 6.8mm SPC have been fired into real living and breathing enemy combatants in Afghanistan or some other third-world hellhole, we have yet to hear about the results.

A new intermediate calibre makes a lot of sense for the infantryman, however. He has been consistently out-gunned in the long-range fight in Afghanistan with Taliban insurgents initiating contact with 7.62 × 54mm platforms like the PKM medium machine gun and the Dragunov SVD sniper rifle, along with the ubiquitous rocket-propelled-grenade. The 7.62 × 54mm imposes a capability gap of several hundred metres on Coalition Forces, with the majority of soldiers armed with short barrelled 5.56 × 45mm carbines and SAWs.

As we've seen in our earlier discussions around 5.56 × 45mm, the round is hampered by abbreviated barrel lengths, particularly when firing the standard ball ammunition. Coalition Forces must instead rely upon their Designated Marksmen and any 7.62 × 51mm machine guns they are lucky enough to have. Truly lucky units have a 60mm mortar that far out distances the 40mm underslung grenade launcher more common in infantry fire teams. The infantry either need a new calibre somewhere in the .260 to .300 range to win back what one American officer termed '*the infantry half-kilometre*' or they need an improved M4A1 with a longer 16-inch barrel, variable magnification optics (like the excellent ECOS-O Enhanced Combat Optical Sight-Optimized that is being fielded by SOCOM featuring an Aimpoint Micro T-1 red dot slaved to a Leupold Mark 6 3-18 × 44mm magnified optic) and firing the Mk262 or Mk318 round. Despite the current solicitation for the M4A1+, whether they will get either in the near future is another story.

For our special operators, there will be an increase in modular rifle and carbine systems that will attempt to fulfil the ultra-compact, assaulter, general-purpose, marksman and sniper support requirements. The Fabrique Nationale SCAR system showed that user transformable modularity was possible. If a manufacturer can design a family of weapons built from the same common lower receiver, they may well win the next big SOF contract.

Such a family would need interchangeable calibres in at least 5.56 × 45mm, .300 Blackout, 7.62 × 39mm and 7.62 × 51mm including suppressors able to cope with this calibre range. It will need upper receivers that offer barrel lengths to accommodate anything from an 8 to 9-inch ultra-compact through to a 20-inch sniper support or spotter variant. Along with barrels, the stock should be easily swappable with a range of collapsible and side-folding options. It will also need optics that can cope with all these roles and are instantly switchable from CQB distances through to shots out to 800 metres. And it all needs to be light and dependable – tall order but certainly not unthinkable – indeed most of the components are already available commercially. They need to be put together in a similar fashion to the SOPMOD increments.

Shotguns will remain in their role as breaching tools and the simple dependability of the sawn-off Remington is hard to beat. The likes of the Crye Six12 may make inroads, particularly if sold as part of a SOPMOD style modular kit, but despite its innovation, it's difficult to see where it offers the operator much more than the older Knight's Master-Key and similar systems. Where we will see advances will be in SOF sniper platforms. These will continue to reduce in weight and increasingly offer folding stocks. Their optics will become more computerised and may incorporate guided rounds as the technology becomes more stable. SOF sniper rifles will be integrally suppressed as standard and .338 Lapua Magnum will increasingly dominate as the calibre of choice. A reliable semi-automatic .338 in a platform like the SWORD International Mk-18 Mjölnir (Thor) seems a logical choice.

In support weapons we will see increasingly smaller and lighter weight systems deployed by SOF units. SAWs and light machine guns will follow the Maximi model – shorter and lighter platforms in 7.62 × 51mm or in the .338 Norma Magnum for the assaulters. Certainly SOF general purpose and medium machine guns will be chambered for the .338 Norma Magnum and will be built largely from titanium like the current M240L. In fact an M240L firing the .338 Norma Magnum is a strong contender if the General Dynamics Light Weight Medium Machine Gun is not progressed.

Grenade launchers will remain largely the same. Multiple shot systems may eventually make sense in terms of the weight versus capability pay-off but until that time single-shot systems will dominate. Where grenade launchers will be enhanced is in the ammunition. Programmable ammunition than can airburst or use a tandem warhead to punch through cover will be the 40mm rounds of choice for the special operator and these are just around the corner.

The fifteen years since the beginning of the War on Terror has spurred small arms development at a greater pace and to greater depth than during any period since the Second World War. Although conventional forces have withdrawn from Iraq and are largely withdrawn from Afghanistan, the special operations war will continue with no end in sight. For instance Delta conducted a successful kill or capture raid into the heart of ISIL/ISIS territory in Syria just as this book was being completed, killing an insurgent financier, capturing his wife (herself a senior ISIS/ISIL figure), and rescuing a slave girl the couple had held prisoner. A dozen insurgent fighters were also engaged and killed by the operators. The only damage sustained was to several aircraft that were struck by insurgent gunfire as the assaulters inserted at the objective.

These kinds of operations will continue in Iraq, Syria, Afghanistan, Yemen, Somalia and any number of hotspots around the globe. To give these superbly trained and motivated operators the best possible chance of mission success, they must be supported by the finest weapons, ammunition and optics available. As we noted back in the Introduction, Admiral McRaven listed six mission critical components to a successful special operation – purpose, simplicity, speed, security, repetition and surprise. A seventh could and perhaps should be added and that is equipment – the right tools for some of the most difficult missions ever conceived.

Bibliography

Bartocci, Christopher R.; *Black Rifle II: The M16 into the 21st Century*, Collector Grade Publications, 2004.

Couch, Dick; *Sua Sponte: The Forging of a Modern American Ranger*, Berkley, 2013.

Dockery, Kevin; *Weapons of the Navy SEALs*, Berkley Publishing Group, 2005.

Fury, Dalton; *Kill Bin Laden: A Delta Force Commander's Account of the Hunt for the World's Most Wanted Man*, St Martin's Press, 2008.

Irving, Nicholas and Brozek, Gary; *The Reaper: Autobiography of One of the Deadliest Special Ops Snipers*, St Martin's Press, 2015.

Lamb, Kyle E.; *Green Eyes & Black Rifles: Warriors Guide to the Combat Carbine*, Trample and Hurdle, 2008.

Lamb, Kyle E.; *Stay in the Fight!! Warriors Guide to the Combat Pistol*, Trample and Hurdle, 2011.

Markham, George; *Guns of the Elite: Special Force Firearms 1940 to the Present*, Weidenfeld Military, 1989.

Martin, Chris and SOFREP; *Modern American Snipers: From The Legend to The Reaper – on the Battlefield with Special Operations Snipers*, St Martin's Press, 2014.

Naylor, Sean; *Not A Good Day to Die: The Untold Story of Operation Anaconda*, Berkley Books, 2005.

Neville, Leigh; *Special Operations Forces in the War on Terror*, Osprey, 2015.

Owen, Mark; *No Easy Day: The Autobiography of a Navy SEAL*, Dutton, 2012.

Owen, Mark; *No Hero: The Evolution of a Navy SEAL*, Dutton, 2014.

Popenker, Maxim and Williams, Anthony G,; *Assault Rifle: The Development of the Modern Military Rifle and Its Ammunition*, Crowood Press, 2004.

Popenker, Maxim and Williams, Anthony G.; *Machine Gun: The Development of the Machine Gun from the Nineteenth Century to the Present Day*, Crowood Press, 2008.

Popenker, Maxim and Williams, Anthony G.; *Sub-Machine Gun: The Development of Sub-machine Guns and Their Ammunition from World War 1 to the Present Day*, Crowood Press, 2011.

Rottman, Gordon L.; *The Book of Gun Trivia: Essential Firepower Facts*, Osprey, 2013.

Self, Nate; *Two Wars: One Hero's Fight on Two Fronts – Abroad and Within*, Tyndale House Publishers, 2008.

Skovlund Jr, Marty; *Violence of Action: The Untold Stories of the 75th Ranger Regiment in the War on Terror*, Blackside Concepts, 2014.

Tilstra, Russell C.; *Small Arms for Urban Combat: A Review*, McFarland, 2011.

Tilstra, Russell C.; *The Battle Rifle: Development and Use Since World War II*, McFarland, 2014.

Urban, Mark; *Task Force Black The explosive true story of the SAS and the secret war in Iraq*, St Martin's Press. 2011.

Index